ADVANCE

"COME

"The most important things we ever teach are these: you are a human being of incalculable value; you are, as well, a work-in-progress making your wobbly way through a living, cascading history in-the-making; you need no one's permission to interrogate your world. In this surprising collection the truth of those lessons is brought brilliantly to light in a wide range of settings and circumstances. Here artists and teachers and students together ask the fundamental questions: Who am I? How did I get here and where am I headed? What's my story and how shall I join with others to write the next chapter? The answers send all of them spinning off into projects of production and repair."

—William Ayers, Retired Distinguished Professor of Education and Senior University Scholar,
University of Illinois at Chicago;
Author of To Teach: The Journey, in Comics *and* Teaching Toward Freedom

"Against a world backdrop where people from Egypt to Wisconsin are once again re-asserting their ontological predisposition to be actors of history, [this book] could not be timelier. The contributors to this illuminating volume re-affirm, through their thoughtful and insightful narratives, Augusto Boal's conviction that, as humans, we are all born poets; institutions intervene from keeping us from continuing to be poets. The authors of 'Come Closer' not only provide readers with a language of critique to deconstruct the social drama of oppression, but they also meticulously and passionately challenge readers to embrace a language of hope that inspires and dares us to unleash our repressed poetry and imagine the potentiality of what it means to experience a fully liberating humanity."

—Donaldo Macedo, Distinguished Professor of Liberal Arts and Education,
University of Massachusetts, Boston

"'Come Closer' thoughtfully and usefully provides ongoing reflections, adaptations, and extensions of Augusto Boal's Theatre of the Oppressed. Well-structured around three endlessly dynamic topics—possibilities around forum theatre, the role of the joker, and the contexts in which TO takes place—the book provides accounts of practitioners across the world evaluating and renewing TO, at the same time honoring Boal and supporting what so many of us already know—that he was one of the great personages of theatre in the twentieth and early twenty-first centuries."

—Jan Cohen-Cruz, Director, Imagining America: Artists and Scholars in Public Life, Syracuse University;
Co-editor of A Boal Companion: Dialogues on Theatre and Cultural Politics

"This compelling text reveals the evolution of Theatre of the Oppressed initiatives over the last forty years. Grounded in Freire's ideas of praxis and Boal's belief that theatre can be a catalyst for transformational dialogue, these articulate authors illuminate how the work takes shape in a variety of contexts, from higher education to public education classrooms, to teacher education programs, to community based settings, to intercultural work. A compelling case is made for the flexibility of Boal's philosophical frame and strategies to create transformational dialogue across age groups, contexts, and formats, creating spaces where status quo is disrupted and oppression both external and internal is probed, challenged and acted upon. The roles of protagonist, of ally, and of joker, so familiar to us in TO, are considered from multiple lenses. This book is significant for those of us engaged in any transformational practices informed by Theatre of the Oppressed."

—Lisa Donovan, Director, Creative Arts in Learning, Lesley University

"COME CLOSER"

Studies in the Postmodern Theory of Education

Shirley R. Steinberg
General Editor

Vol. 416

The Counterpoints series is part of the Peter Lang Education list.
Every volume is peer reviewed and meets
the highest quality standards for content and production.

PETER LANG
New York • Washington, D.C./Baltimore • Bern
Frankfurt • Berlin • Brussels • Vienna • Oxford

"COME CLOSER"

CRITICAL PERSPECTIVES ON THEATRE OF THE OPPRESSED

EDITED BY *Toby Emert* AND *Ellie Friedland*

PETER LANG
New York • Washington, D.C./Baltimore • Bern
Frankfurt • Berlin • Brussels • Vienna • Oxford

Library of Congress Cataloging-in-Publication Data

Come closer: critical perspectives on theatre of the oppressed /
edited by Toby Emert, Ellie Friedland.
p. cm. — (Counterpoints: studies in the postmodern theory of education; v. 416)
Includes bibliographical references.
1. Participatory theater. 2. Drama in community development.
3. Drama in education. 4. Critical pedagogy. I. Friedland, Ellie. II. Title.
PN2049.E55   792.02'2—dc22   2011011358
ISBN 978-1-4331-1371-0 (hardcover)
ISBN 978-1-4331-1370-3 (paperback)
ISSN 1058-1634

Bibliographic information published by **Die Deutsche Nationalbibliothek**.
Die Deutsche Nationalbibliothek lists this publication in the "Deutsche
Nationalbibliografie"; detailed bibliographic data is available
on the Internet at http://dnb.d-nb.de/.

FSC
Mixed Sources
Product group from well-managed
forests, controlled sources and
recycled wood or fiber

Cert no. SCS-COC-002464
www.fsc.org
©1996 Forest Stewardship Council

The paper in this book meets the guidelines for permanence and durability
of the Committee on Production Guidelines for Book Longevity
of the Council of Library Resources.

© 2011 Peter Lang Publishing, Inc., New York
29 Broadway, 18th floor, New York, NY 10006
www.peterlang.com

Printed in the United States of America

CONTENTS

FOREWORD

Michael Rohd

IN 1988, I WAS an undergraduate at Northwestern University, and one of my teachers, Dwight Conquergood, told me I would benefit from reading Augusto Boal. He seemed convinced that my own interests in performance and community would find nourishment in Boal's work.

I respected Dwight greatly.

But my priorities leaned more toward graduating and having a career in acting, so I ignored his advice. I did not read Boal.

In the spring of 1994, after I had started the Hope Is Vital program (a theatre-based HIV/AIDS community dialogue resource), I visited San Francisco with my good friend Tom Kane (a theatre practitioner/educator who also had Dwight as a teacher). We were in the bookstore at the San Francisco Museum of Modern Art, and I was searching for books that would help me expand the body of work I was creating at the intersection of social change, structured performance, improvisation, and community building, and I saw a book called *Games for Actors and Non-Actors*. I didn't pay much attention to the author's name; I read the back cover, and thought there might be something useful inside. I bought it, immediately sat down on the grass in front of the museum, and began to read.

Five hours later, I had devoured almost the entire thing.

To Tom's amusement and perhaps irritation, I couldn't stop talking about the book, the author, and the feeling that what I was doing existed in a context of knowledge, practice, and experience. Different, but related. And with so much to offer me.

So, in this time before the Internet, before cell phones, I was determined to track down this Augusto Boal and meet him. Talk with him. Learn from him.

Through Dwight (who smiled as he reminded me of our previous Boal conversation five years before) I found out that Augusto had recently conducted workshops at a conference hosted by ATHE, the Association for Theatre in Higher Education. My friend Trish Suchy, who had been at the conference, told me that if I wanted to track down Boal, I needed to talk to Doug Paterson at the University of Nebraska, Omaha. And so I began a long period of unanswered phone calls to Doug, blurring the line between persistence and harassment, until I finally heard back from him in the fall of 1994. He told me that I was in luck—Boal was coming to Omaha in late winter 1995 for the first Pedagogy and Theatre of the Oppressed Conference. Doug and others felt that U.S. interest in Boal's work warranted an opportunity for people to study with him and talk about the work as it was being applied and re-conceived, in all sorts of settings vastly different from the context in which Boal initially developed and implemented it. Doug told me I could register and attend. Through a mixture of my own lack of resources and Doug's generosity, I ended up staying at his home while volunteering at the conference. My job—escorting Augusto Boal around the conference and Omaha.

So my good fortune was to travel within the span of a year from reading Augusto's words to having dinner with him. To go from reading about Forum Theatre to doing a workshop with him. To take questions I'd written in the margins of his books and ask them as we drove around a city neither of us knew. His generosity of spirit, his willingness to interrogate his own practice and mine, his delight in spirited conversation and debate—all moved me.

I didn't set out, in this foreword, to write so much about my journey with Boal (which continued for years after that time in Omaha), but I discovered that for me, as for many practitioners, there is "before him," and there is "after him." And our bodies of work are forever altered by that moment of contact. What I did before was not about Theatre of the Oppressed, and yet seemed to be leading me inevitably toward a learning that couldn't move forward without it. The work I've done since, the work I do now, seems often to have little to do with the body of work known as contemporary TO practice. But encountering TO has been a portal on the way to becoming the artist, educator, and community worker I am now—it was, and it remains, instrumental in my own journey.

This book is filled with practitioners detailing their experiences on both sides of their own moments of contact; and though the focus is on how we evolve a body of work developed for us and left to us by a master artist, thinker, and activist, the real question we are left with is how to honor what I believe is Boal's greatest legacy—the demand that we bring our best, most creative and compassionate selves to our work with people around the world in an effort to make beauty *and* shape spaces for change. I deeply believe that Boal wasn't interested in a slavish orthodoxy devoted to his every word and action, but rather a promise from anyone who works in the name of the tactics he forged to evolve the work, be true to ourselves, and be good to others.

I for one am as thrilled to read where these practitioners' journeys have taken them as I was to sit on the grass in San Francisco sixteen years ago and read Boal for the first time.

Michael Rohd, Founding Artistic Director of Sojourn Theatre
Assistant Professor, Department of Theatre, Northwestern University
Chicago, Illinois & Portland, Oregon
Fall 2010

ACKNOWLEDGMENTS

WE ARE GRATEFUL TO Donaldo Macedo for recognizing the need for a book that made the energy, critical analysis, and innovation we experience at the Pedagogy and Theatre of the Oppressed (PTO) Conference available to a wider audience, and for suggesting that we write it. His encouragement throughout the process and his willingness to assist us in connecting with Peter Lang Publishing were invaluable. We hope this book provides as much insight and motivation to act as his books have offered us.

INTRODUCTION

Toby Emert & Ellie Friedland

OMAHA, NEBRASKA. PEDAGOGY AND Theatre of the Oppressed Conference. May 2008. Augusto Boal sits forward in his chair; one hand rests on his knee, the other beckons to the roomful of participants seated on the floor around him, gathered for his Legislative Theatre workshop. "Come closer, come closer," he says, and no matter how close people are already sitting, they move toward him.

Boal began his workshops with this ritual invitation, which was an expression of his personality: he wanted engagement; he wanted to see people and feel their presence. But the ritual was also a metaphor for Theatre of the Oppressed (TO), the embodiment of his values, beliefs, and praxis. TO is about moving in close, questioning deeply, trying possible solutions, failing and sometimes succeeding, then examining actions even more carefully, always trying to get closer to what will create transformation in our flawed world.

For seventeen years, teachers, artists, activists, and scholars have gathered for the annual International Pedagogy and Theatre of the Oppressed conference (PTO), where Augusto Boal traditionally opened the conference by jokering Forum Theatre performances developed by participants who had attended his pre-conference workshops. These workshops served as a primary mode of initial training for many new to TO and ongoing training for established TO practitioners, a means by which Boal continued to create what he called "multipliers," those who translate his ideas into practice around the world. At the 2008 conference, Boal told PTO attendees that, regrettably, he was curtailing his travel schedule and that he would no longer be making a yearly trip to the U.S. What would the absence of Boal's presence mean for the spirit of the conference? For the furthering of his work generally? The answers to those questions were unclear, but it was clear that Boal's announcement marked an important shift, a transition in how TO would be promoted and understood.

Donaldo Macedo, a professor of linguistics at the University of Massachusetts, Boston, who was a translator and writing partner for Paulo Freire, attended the 2008 PTO conference as an invited speaker, and he was excited by the "special energy, critical dialogue, and tensions" he experienced (personal communication, April 17, 2009). It was he who first suggested that we consider editing a book that would bring the spirited dialogue that marks a

PTO conference to a wider audience. He spoke about the "urgency for this kind of alternative discourse among educators and activists" and suggested that we "make the book a re-articulation of Theatre of the Oppressed in multiple contexts, with hope" (personal communication, April 17, 2009). He also encouraged us to read *Mentoring the Mentor* (1997), a collection of writings that "talk back" to Freire about his ideas—in essence "teaching" him about his own work, demonstrating how it is generative and evolving. For that project, Freire wrote a response to the contributors, which became part of the conclusion of the book. Our original idea was to consider our book a companion text for *Mentoring the Mentor*, and Augusto Boal was planning to write a concluding chapter. His death in May 2009 means that we are not able to dialogue with him personally, but we want to honor the impulse of the "mentor" text and envision each chapter in the book as part of an extended conversation with Boal about how TO is transformative for those who practice it, but also how it is being transformed by their practice.

For many years Boal's son Julian collaborated closely with his father as a co-joker and co-teacher, and he continues to facilitate workshops and stage TO plays throughout the world. An interview with Julian, which took place in Boston in October 2009, serves as the final chapter for the book. Julian talks about his own work, how he and others are transforming the theory and practice his father developed, and what he imagines for the future of TO.

The other chapters in the book are written by TO practitioners living and working in a variety of settings: the United States, Israel, Palestine, Brazil, Great Britain, Bosnia, Afghanistan. We invited the authors to write about TO, especially how they are transforming the work, offering readers a collection of narratives that demonstrate Boal's influence on the worlds of theatre, arts, education, and activism. Many of the contributors have studied with Boal and all anchor their work, philosophically and practically, in the aesthetic structures he developed: Image Theatre, Forum Theatre, Newspaper Theatre, Invisible Theatre, Legislative Theatre, and the Rainbow of Desire. (See the illustration of "The Tree of Theatre of the Oppressed" on page 5 for a visual depiction of these structures.) Many of the authors also frame their chapters with Freire's ideas; it is impossible to speak and write about Theatre of the Oppressed without acknowledging Freire's profound influence. Though Boal and Freire presented together publicly only once—at the 1996 Pedagogy and Theatre of the Oppressed Conference—Boal often referred to Freire, when speaking of him, as "my last father."

We see the book as a tribute to Boal and his ideas, but also as a handbook of illustrative cases that demonstrate how jokers and practitioners are adapting TO's games and structures for new audiences and in new settings. We expect that readers who are just discovering Theatre of the Oppressed will be as interested in the ideas expressed here as are those who have been reading, studying, and practicing TO for many years. Structurally, the chapters in the book are divided into three integrated sections, each focusing on a theme that expresses how the primary components of Boal's philosophical framework for TO practice are evolving as jokers interpret the work: "Transforming the Forum Event," "Transforming the Context for TO," and "Transforming the Joker."

In the first section of the book, "Transforming the Forum Event," the contributors discuss Boal's conception of the roles of the protagonist and antagonist in a Forum Play, describe a series of theoretical shifts in TO that have taken place over the past four decades, and explore questions about the inclusion of modified versions of Forum work in educational settings and for pedagogical purposes.

In the section "Transforming the Context for TO," each author writes about using TO in a specific context—in the public speaking classroom, in an alternative high school, in diversity training workshops, with queer youth, as part of an international peace program, and in a gathering for Augustinian Catholics from around the globe. The final section, "Transforming the Joker," offers perspectives on how TO practitioners are re-imagining the role of Boal's joker for work in prisons, for reconciliation (in Israel and Palestine), as a guide toward communal healing after a one-man performance about torture, and for finding strategies to confront moments of physical violence through jokered re-enactments. The range of voices represented in the book is purposefully broad, allowing readers to experience the work of a variety of jokers—scholars, students, therapists, youth workers, teachers, activists, actors, playwrights, and directors. Each is one of Boal's "multipliers," building on his ideas, but also personalizing, revising, modifying, and adapting the work for the settings in which and the populations with whom they interact.

We titled this book *"Come Closer": Critical Perspectives on Theatre of the Oppressed* with the hope that it will spark continued dialogue, reflection, and action among organizers, activists, educators, and TO practitioners. We aim to make TO accessible to those who may not have investigated it before, perhaps because they do not see themselves as "theatre people," and we also seek to expand the discourse about Pedagogy of the Oppressed to include TO practitioners who are in ongoing "conversations" with Freire's ideas. Boal and Freire invited those who encountered their ideas to engage with them in a continuous critical dialogue, a "close reading" of their words and their worlds. At the time of Augusto Boal's death, his work had undergone a series of transformations—from the impulse to inform through Newspaper Theatre to the agitation stance of Invisible Theatre to the use of Legislative Theatre to educate and influence lawmakers, to the intra-psychic applications of Rainbow of Desire. We want this book to extend the conversation about Theatre of the Oppressed and its evolutions, to foster a continued critical stance toward TO practice, and to offer theatre artists, activists, educators, and scholars an opportunity to reflect on the revolutionary work of Boal and Freire, two extraordinary thinkers whose ideas continue to transform the world.

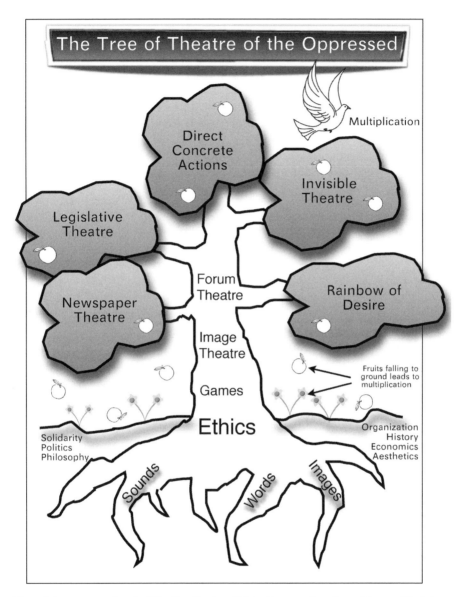

Adapted from notes taken by Ellie Friedland and Toby Emert at Legislative Theatre Workshop, conducted by Augusto and Julian Boal, Pedagogy and Theatre of the Oppressed Conference, Omaha, Nebraska, May 2008. Original sketch by Augusto Boal.

PART I

Transforming the Forum Event

CHAPTER ONE

Doug Paterson

Putting the "Pro" in Protagonist
Paulo Freire's Contribution to Our Understanding of Forum Theatre

IN A 1996 INTERVIEW in *High Performance*, Augusto Boal asked supporters and skeptics alike to offer a wide-ranging critique of his Theatre of the Oppressed (TO). He observed that, for the most part, he had received "the critique of silence" (Paterson & Weinberg, 1996, p. 18). As the second decade of the new century dawns, Boal has gotten some of what he wished for—critiques of, adjustments to, and digressions from the work he created. These include wonderful children's versions of Forum Theatre by Chris Vine, David Diamond's Image Theatre invention, "Your Wildest Dream," and bringing the officials at Legislative Theatre events more directly into the law-making process. Boal relished the many transformations TO inspired, yet held fast to several basic principles. In this chapter I address one of those principles—the role of the protagonist in Forum Theatre. The protagonic action, as Boal sometimes called it, not only lies at the heart of TO theory and practice, but also razor-focuses the action of the oppressed as described by Paulo Freire in his numerous texts. Key to the arguments I make in this chapter are Freire's insights on oppression and the oppressed, but especially his insistence that a dialogue among or with the oppressed must affirm, as a central principle, that oppression can be analyzed objectively. That is, bourgeois denial, reform, and liberal interpretations want to slip oppression into a subjective category—"Who is really oppressed?"; "Are they really oppressed?"; "Aren't others oppressed as well?" But Freire insists the practice of oppression and the experience of the oppressed *are objectively real* and thus clearly identifiable. In turn, the oppressed are able to resist and transform the oppression. In Boal's Forum Theatre, the protagonist must represent the oppressed in a way that is "clear, concrete, and urgent" (Boal, 2002, p. 230). The single protagonist is the only approach I have found that can bring this concreteness, clarity and even urgency. Therefore, I contend that Boal's vision of the single protagonist must be preserved and advocated as a fundamental principle of Forum Theatre. Moreover, Freire can help us in this advocacy.

The term *protagonist* derives from the Greek word *agon*, which meant, in the theatre, a struggle or debate. The *agon* of a Greek comedy was the intense exchange of views between two choruses or characters. Such a debate would sympathize with the "pro" side, making this sympathetic character the pro-*agon*-ist, or protagonist. The less sympathetic side, those who obstructed the understandable goals of the protagonist, were "anti-*agon*-ists," or antagonists. In the Greek tradition the protagonists, such as Clytemnestra, Oedipus, or Antigone, were not passive forces. Protagonists struggled valiantly in their pursuit of what they thought right. Thus the protagonist for Boal was a sympathetic person for the audience—capable, energetic, even likable—just like the members of the audience! Moreover, Boal's protagonist fought for what she or he believed needed to be done. No passive or quasi-protagonists for Boal. These are the general characteristics of the protagonist as the term is used in this chapter.

In 1993, Boal invited me to the Seventh International Festival of the Theatre of the Oppressed in Rio de Janeiro. While I had no theatrical production to bring, Boal wanted me to participate in a part of the festival that involved presentations and asked me to develop a talk on a topic of my choice. I put together a fairly wide-ranging analysis that tried to place TO in historical context. One of my primary conclusions was a warning: Given the bourgeois history of Western theatre, there was a real danger that Western practitioners would use TO in such a way as to appropriate it and infuse it, consciously or not, with bourgeois values. As a result, Western jokers, especially those in the United States, could empty TO of its intrinsic revolutionary character.

I am "pro" protagonist. I admire the idea of the protagonists in Boal's Forum Theatre being given the agency to anchor a scene, to struggle mightily for what they need, and thereby to invite audiences to conceive of new possibilities. The larger world stage offers all of us the role of protagonist, given the supremacy of racism, sexism, homophobia, and ultra-nationalism as antagonistic structures that continue to deny human freedom. The crushing weight and chaos of globalized capitalism and the slow but steady bourgeois process of making the planet unlivable demand that we assume this crucial role. Therefore, I want to outline thoughts that might help not only TO but ourselves as we organize a local/global struggle for more human and ecologically friendly structures.

Regarding the matter of multiple protagonists in TO's Forum Theatre, the following questions have been raised by theorists and practitioners.

1. What is oppression and what are its complexities?
2. In Forum Theatre, is only one protagonist to be focused on and replaced? Or should other characters in a Forum scene, or all the characters, be eligible for replacement?
3. What is the central purpose of Forum Theatre, and does an array of multiple protagonists support that purpose?

In this essay I use these questions as a frame for the argument I wish to make about the importance of maintaining Boal's original notion of the protagonist in a Forum Theatre scene.

What Is Oppression and What Are Its Complexities?

Each of the above questions emerges from the basic outlines Boal developed for Forum, which have been challenged by various theorists and practitioners. Marc Weinblatt, Founder of the Mandala Center for Change in Port Townsend, Washington summarizes some of the ideas behind such challenges on his organization's webpage:

> Although traditional Forum Theatre is used with great success in certain contexts, more and more there are significant adaptations. Rather than focusing on "oppression," many practitioners are finding it more useful to use words like "disrespected," "powerless," "silent." Even the definition of who is oppressor and who is oppressed in a Forum play is regularly in question.
>
> (http://www.mandalaforchange.com/articles.htm)

Oppressed, as a word and as a concept, does not fit well with bourgeois values. We prefer softer, euphemistic language that de-emphasizes the conditions of the oppressed. "Theatre for Living," "Theatre and Respect," my early use of "Omaha Public Theatre in Our Neighborhoods" (OPTIONS) or even "Theatre for Liberation" do not announce the uncomfortable implications of the terms oppressed and oppression–i.e., that oppression exists and can be identified and named. So why didn't Boal call his work Theatre for Liberation? Even more to the point, why didn't Paulo Freire, author of *Pedagogy of the Oppressed*, call his first text *Education for Liberation*? Why did they use the provocative word *oppressed*? After all, Freire did write *Education for Critical Consciousness* shortly after publishing his foundational text. What could he have been thinking?

I heard Boal answer this question several times. He said, in effect, that he, like Freire, called it oppression because that was the correct name. To soften the topic in order to mollify inevitable bourgeois outrage would, in itself, be an oppression. Even in his dedication in *Pedagogy of the Oppressed* (1993), Freire is adamant: "To the oppressed, and to those who suffer with them and fight at their side" (p. 5). The central audience was not the bourgeoisie, not the corporate world-killers. The audience was the oppressed and those who fight at their side.

Definitions

Perhaps surprisingly, Boal does not elaborate on definitions of oppression or on the character of the oppressor and oppressed. It is as if the articulation of terms had been sufficiently completed by Paulo Freire in his early texts and, therefore, the subject did not require a great deal of further development. But even Freire does not, as far as I can find, "define" oppression and seems to accept the meaning as prima facie. My computer dictionary gives me this definition: "the exercise of authority or power in a burdensome, cruel, or unjust manner." Merriam-Webster's online dictionary offers "a sense of being weighed down in body or mind." *The Shorter OED* suggests "harsh ... authoritarian ... cruel or unjust exercise of authority." But Freire's meticulous examination of oppression, oppressor, and oppressed is unsurpassed, not as definition but as revelation of the concrete specifics of oppression, and serves in this essay as the basic point of reference.

The best relationship of people and social structures, as described in *Pedagogy of the Oppressed* (1968), is dialogue: "Dialogue is the encounter between [humans], mediated by the world, in order to name the world" (p. 88). The oppressive actions of antagonists are described by the well-known Freire/Boal metaphor of monologue. As Freire says, "to substitute monologue ... for dialogue is to attempt to liberate the oppressed with the instruments of domestication" (1968, p. 65). Monologue is a violation at a fundamental level. "Hence, dialogue cannot occur between those who want to name the world and those who do not wish this naming–between those who deny others the right to speak their word and those whose right to speak has been denied them" (Freire, 1968, p. 88). As a metaphor, monologue–the denial of truthful expression—can be one-on-one or part of a large social force affecting whole groups. A college lecture is not necessarily a monologue, though not being able to comment or ask questions–a denial of naming–might be considered a monologue. Monologue and oppression imply substantial power differences that enforce a denial of naming, that is usually brutal, and, for the purposes of

TO and PO (Pedagogy of the Oppressed), the presence or at least the possibility of struggle on the part of the oppressed.

Freire on Oppression and Its Complexities

Freire articulated the cornerstones of liberatory pedagogy in 1968 in his landmark *Pedagogy of the Oppressed*. It is appropriate for us to examine that text. In the first chapter, Freire calls the problem "a culture of domination" (p. 36). Our subject is humanization, he says, which in a culture of domination also intrinsically implies de-humanization. The struggle to humanize "is thwarted by injustice, exploitation, oppression, and the violence of the oppressors; it is affirmed by the yearning of the oppressed for freedom and justice, and by their struggle to recover their lost humanity" (pp. 25-26). In his typically stirring language, Freire declares:

> This, then, is the great humanistic and historical task of the oppressed: to liberate themselves and their oppressors as well. The oppressors, who oppress, exploit, and rape by virtue of their power, cannot find in this power the strength to liberate either the oppressed or themselves. Only power that springs from the weakness of the oppressed will be sufficiently strong to free both. (p. 26)

Oppression is, first of all, oppression by class, as Freire makes clear. It is also primarily rooted in structures, not in individual human actions, though it is certainly present there. Moreover, Freire is adamant. Oppression exists. It is identifiable and can be looked at objectively. And it has two identifiable sides–oppressor and oppressed. Augusto Boal was so compelled by Freire's work that he titled his theatre, and his first book, *Theatre of the Oppressed*, and regularly acknowledged Freire's contribution.

One observation, that "the clear boundaries we like to think exist between oppressor and oppressed are very often not clear" (Diamond, 2007, p. 38), is perhaps too facile. I suggest neither Freire nor Boal thought the boundaries were clear. Few have problematized social and political struggle with more appreciation for "complexity" than did Paulo Freire and Augusto Boal. Boal often said that while we take the picture of an oppressive situation from one angle, that shows an oppressor-oppressed relationship (e.g., a policeman beating demonstrators), we can take the picture from another angle and the roles could reverse (e.g., policemen being first berated by their captain for not keeping order and second being hit by rocks).

Freire identifies the complexities; in *Pedagogy of the Oppressed*, he observes:

> In order for this struggle to have meaning, the oppressed must not, in seeking to regain their humanity (which is a way to create it), become, in turn, oppressors of the oppressors, but rather restorers of the humanity of both. But almost always, during

the initial stage of the struggle, the oppressed, instead of striving for liberation, tend themselves to become oppressors, or "sub-oppressors." (1968, p. 26)

Not only are the lines "not clear," but the "complex" transition out of oppression occupies much of Freire's early analysis. We in TO should be careful not to privilege our TO explorations by minimizing the foundations of liberatory theory or dismissing too easily the insights of our mentors. Paulo Freire wrote his initial text, and the next twenty, because he understood that oppression is complex.

If the subject is complex, then, why did Boal invent a Forum Theatre structure that asks scenarios to identify a single protagonist? Does a proposal to display several or many protagonists and oppressors serve people because it more closely reflects the complexity of oppression?

In Forum Theatre, Should Only One Protagonist Be Focused on and Replaced or Should All Characters in a Scene Be Eligible for Replacement?

This question has generated much discussion in the TO world. While I am not only "pro" protagonist, but also a proponent of the single protagonist, a number of practitioners have suggested a performance with poly-protagonists. As I understand the argument for multiple protagonists and replacements of them by spect-actors, the primary one seems to be this: To tell an audience that only an identified protagonist may be replaced is to limit the choices the audiences can make, and thus constrain the dialogue. That is, we should not coerce the audience by saying, "Only this person, who is the protagonist, can be replaced." The argument goes something like … let the audience members determine what they see and determine whom they believe is oppressed and oppressor. Audiences/communities know more than we do about their struggles. By unconstraining Boal's replacement guidelines, and by extension, unconstraining the representation itself, we all might learn more when the entire constellation of characters in a Forum scene can be replaced, when any and all might be seen as protagonists and oppressed, or as antagonists and oppressors.

This argument for multiple protagonists seems to ignore the fact that the Forum performance, in fact any theatre performance, already imposes many constraints. By the time the Forum begins, a Forum performance group has already established the following limitations:

Because we are involved in or are addressing a specific question, we already have determined the subject of the discussion. In a particular Forum we address undocumented workers, not ecology; or we address ecology and not violence against women; or we address violence against women and not undocumented workers. Setting the subject is a constraint.

Because we decide to present our Forum play in a specific location, we have determined the site of the exploration. This means that some people will be able to attend and not others. Choosing the site of a Forum performance is at least a condition, and likely a constraint.

Because we decide to work with this community and not others, we have yet further constraints. The group preparing a Forum piece also determines that certain actors will play certain characters. Different actors manifest different kinds of characters. Certainly the experience of the actors counts here. If the group determines that either someone new to the stage or an experienced person plays a role, the performance will be substantially different–and I acknowledge here the power of new actors in Forum. Their presence conditions audience reception significantly. What to represent and what not to represent; how a scene begins and ends; who is the joker; choosing to do Forum and not a straight scene–these choices channel the direction of a scene and can be said to be constraining factors.

Any attempt to create a drama without constraints or "bias" is impossible. Therefore, those of us working in TO need to admit our work is always tendentious; otherwise we risk compromising the highly-pedagogical process of community-based Forum Theatre by a "no constraint" concern that is both a poor criterion and minimizes the very real lines between oppressor and oppressed. It is, I fear, a monologue in Freire's description as quoted above: "Dialogue cannot occur between those who want to name the world and those who do not wish this naming" (1968, p. 88). That is, if our task is to make a scene with no real point of view, and certainly one with no vigorous stand with the oppressed (as we always saw with Augusto Boal), how can the oppressed involved in making the scene honestly "name the world" in which they live?

By Forum performance time, many predetermined choices have been "imposed." I am not only unconcerned with this reality, but also welcome it as part of human communication. Several TO theorists, however, have ignored the obvious constraints of the performance and, in turn, have generated a praxis that, because the joker and performance do not "constrain" the audience experience, claims the approach is more open, more democratic. But I suggest that this is simply not true, and it seems to be a bourgeois discomfort with the fierce demands of oppression. While we are clearly constraining, or shaping any dialogue, this approach makes it appear that we are not. In this interpretation of Forum we would have our own performance of non-partisanship accompanying our work with the oppressed. If we are criticized for being biased or political, we can say we were only asking questions, only making a theatre for investigating oppression, not fighting it. Therefore, both the Forum pieces and our position in them are comfortable. Nor does anything give away the class alliance more quickly than being sure there is a way to avoid responsibility.

Weak Protagonists

I submit that the multiple protagonists approach to Forum Theatre gives rise to another, and perhaps more serious difficulty, one also grounded in our bourgeois tendencies. Boal asks for the protagonists in Forum Theatre to be fighters, people who take vigorous action to overcome the oppressions presented in the scene. While the protagonist invariably loses, we identify with the courage and commitment demonstrated in a worthy cause. However, I have witnessed weak protagonists in single and multiple protagonist Forum. These were characters who were decidedly not fighters and seemed incapable of putting up any meaningful resistance. Often the word that came to my mind, in viewing such a scene, was "victim," a word Boal wanted us to avoid for the protagonist at all costs. The oppressed must not be represented as victims in Forum Theatre, but as capable of responding valiantly to oppression. Such characters are not victims.

While I have seen these weak protagonists on occasion in standard Forum, I have begun to see them more often in multiple protagonist scenes. I have been struck by how often an apparent protagonist, but one who is weak, is not replaced by spect-actors, but stronger, especially "witness" characters, are replaced instead. When this happens, discussions of oppression do not receive focus. I suggest that the decision not to foreground any one oppressed person as the protagonist leads to the virtual necessity of giving limited energy to all possible protagonists, or perhaps even all characters in the drama. This makes for perhaps the worst kind of Forum–dispirited and dull. But giving a single character the necessary vitality and ability to struggle as protagonist foregrounds that character and makes him or her into Boal's kind of protagonist, and enlivens the entire scene. Those who do not want to "condition the choice" avoid what is the basic structure of Boal's Forum Theatre.

The final option is to give all characters–witnesses, oppressed, oppressors–a somewhat equal political/moral stake in the action and the outcome. I have seen only one multiple protagonist Forum that achieved this, but again (1) the discussion was more about who was oppressed; and more importantly, (2) the joker was very involved (and I would say too involved) in the process of identifying characters to replace and in leading the discussion. Moreover, what we were watching was, in fact, a standard theatre scene with strong characters moderated by a joker, a person who sometimes mentioned the word oppression. But the central subject in this scene was not oppression. Rather we were watching "interactive theatre" that had little to do, in my opinion, with the legacy of Augusto Boal and Paulo Freire.

We must reclaim this essential ingredient. The issue is a struggle among TO practitioners, and I want to be as active an advocate for the single protagonist as possible because strong, single protagonists are central for TO. Why? Boal answers: It is essential to portray the oppressed as capable of fighting back. There must be a struggle during the original scene, he urges, in which we can see the vigor of resistance along with the possibility of the protagonist being able to succeed. In making weak, unclear, or compromised semi-protagonists, however, we make a decidedly less compelling scene, and we prevent the oppressed in the audience, and those sympathetic with the oppressed, from identifying with a protagonist.

Objectivism and Subjectivism

Paulo Freire wrote many times that for oppression to be analyzed, it must be viewed objectively. It is not enough to say a character is both oppressed and oppressor. Since it is a concrete situation in which the oppressor/oppressed contradiction is established, the resolution of this contradiction must be objectively verifiable. Hence, the radical requirement—both for the individual who discovers himself or herself to be an oppressor and for the oppressed— that the concrete situation which begets oppression must be transformed (1968, p. 32).

To be able to transform a situation, it stands to reason that an audience of potential spect-actors needs to know who could do the transforming. Freire is very clear: "This lesson and this apprenticeship must come ... from the oppressed themselves and from those who are truly [in solidarity] with them. Who are better prepared than the oppressed to understand the terrible significance of an oppressive society?" (p. 27).

This is why the single protagonist Forum is so important. It lends clarity to the question asked, it focuses the spect-actor's attention, it puts the focus on the oppressed and not on the maybe-oppressed. It shows the oppressed as capable of fighting back, it asks for action on behalf of the oppressed, and it recognizes that oppression exists objectively and can be analyzed, imagined differently, and as Freire says, acted upon. To dilute the protagonic role with many possibilities means that a character representing a truly oppressed people could be played with complete subjectivity (a little oppressed, a little oppressing, a little on the margins) so that the character is never replaced and the oppression revealed in the scene is never acted upon. In my experience that is what typically occurs in multiple protagonist efforts.

Freire realizes oppression is experienced and seen subjectively, but he argues that unless subjective experience is joined with reflection on objective reality, the inevitable trend will be toward supporting the analysis of the dominators, who themselves have concrete reasons to muddy the water and see their violence as justifiable, multi-faceted, and personal: "To achieve this goal, the oppressed must confront reality critically, simultaneously objectifying and acting upon that reality" (1968, p. 52). Here Freire nearly invents Forum Theatre before Boal did.

This is why I am "pro" protagonist. The presence of a clear protagonist invites action upon the "objective" reality presented. Without this clarity, the oppressor will "not precisely ... deny the fact [of oppression], but ... 'see it differently'" (1968, p. 52). In arguing for the subjectivist Forum, some are perhaps viewing TO and oppression as Freire referred to when he wrote "This rationalization as a defense mechanism coincides in the end with subjectivism. A fact which is not denied but whose truths are rationalized loses its objective base" (1968, p. 34).

Thus one of the initial problems with multiple protagonists is that it creates a subjectivist view of the world of oppression. Anyone can be anything, roles can reverse, and oppressors can be oppressed. It is almost as if a bourgeois intervention had happened in TO, with the shout, "It's not that simple!" To which Freire and Boal would likely reply: (1) of course not; and (2) at the foundational level, it is simple. In the immediate world of poverty, capitalism, abortion rights, ecological destruction, racial supremacy, and of violence and death, there is a clear divide. There are boots on necks—those with power, especially institutional/systemic power, versus those with limited or no power, who are denied their right to name the world and their oppression, and by being denied this right, are denied their right to transform the world. If they do attempt the transformation, the typical reply is violence wielded by those with power. This, Freire says, is the objective reality of oppression in the world, the place from which any analysis must begin. Oppression exists and it is describable. It has systemic permanence. The tendency in multiple protagonist Forum is to present a scene with no call for action, no clear point of view, and rather a scene with a diffuse, ambiguous, or even academic array of interesting possibilities. One more step and we perhaps have invited the community to an exercise in purely experimental theatre, jokered by those who magically understand the complexities of oppression.

Systems and Individuals

To conclude this discussion of single and multiple protagonist Forum, I suggest one final difficulty in Forum itself, and especially in the multiple protagonist Forum: they both put too much focus on the role of the individual and too little on structural oppression. While this subject is too broad for a thorough analysis here, I suggest that systems—such as slavery and capitalism— do create behavior, and that the dynamic of system/individual impact is not mono-directional, but dialectical. Freire, too, asks us to understand the important place of systems as primary sources of oppression. The individualist analysis implicit in Forum, on the other hand, seems to totalize the relation-ship by holding oppressed individuals entirely responsible for their circum-stances.

The individual/system dialectic is the reason many TO practitioners now create scenes, and urge others to create scenes, in which the characters and the audience are able, in the scenes of individual oppression, also to see the structures of larger oppression surrounding those scenes and are able to deal with them as well. Prior to his passing, Boal was deeply involved in attempts to broaden the practice of his Rainbow of Desire by inventing Rainbow methods that help link individual psychological oppression to larger social structures. I consider these explorations some of the most exciting developments of TO currently under way.

What Is the Central Purpose of Forum Theatre, and Does an Array of Multiple Protagonists Get in the Way?

Simply put, the objective of Forum Theatre, of all TO, of Freire's praxis, is dialogue, and eventual action in the world. Boal developed Forum explicitly to generate, invite, and provoke immediate public dialogue–often within minutes of the event's beginning. Dialogue happens first in the community itself, and then in making the Forum Theatre scenes. The play is not hatched full blown from the brain of one master mind, but by groups of people—often not experienced in the theatre—who are using theatre as a pedagogical and political way to express not only their desires but the desires and contradictions of their community. Dialogue is not the start of the process: dialogue is the process. It is the core pedagogy. Eventually scenes are presented before an audience, hopefully an audience that shares the concerns represented on the stage. Interventions intensify the dialogue and locate the focus of the Forum in the audience. Spectators are transformed into spect-actors who put their physical selves into the dialogue by replacing the struggling protagonist in order to propose change. Then comes the open discussion about an intervention to evaluate the proposal collectively, followed by more interventions and evalua-tions. As Boal said to me many times, "I much prefer a good discussion to a good scene. And I want the best scene possible!"

I am uneasy with the multiple protagonist project because it places so much emphasis on the scene and interventions, which, in turn, muddies the subject. The foundational purpose of TO and of Forum Theatre is not games, scenes, not even interventions and proposals. These are all means to the end: dialogue and action, which are also the process. Furthermore, the subject of Forum is oppression, in all its manifold appearances. Recall the words of the *Oxford English Dictionary*: "to keep in subjection ... harsh ... cruel ... unjust ... tyranny ... trample, smother, crush, overwhelm." These are the kinds of social and political relationships Freire saw as core to anti-oppression work. If we are confronting genuine oppression, then debate about who is oppressed and who is the oppressor is irrelevant. It should be very clear. And we need to dialogue about concrete oppression, oppressor, and oppressed in a focused way, so as to generate actions and ideas that can resist and transform oppression. Forum—with its single protagonist—has a remarkable ability to do this. It does not "empower," but "brings out the power" already present in communities and individuals who experience oppression, and that is based on dialogue.

Nearly ten years ago, I wrote:

> So what kind of Theatre do I find most effective? Theatre that creates dialogue, invites audience interaction and intervention, [invites] people to imagine and enact their solutions, and goes on to create even more dialogue. In other words, the remarkable theatre of Augusto Boal. (Paterson, 2001, p. 67)

If we forget that central objective, we have forgotten the central reason Paulo Freire wrote *Pedagogy of the Oppressed* and the reason Augusto Boal, inspired by his friend and countryman, invented and developed Forum Theatre with its protagonist capable of transforming the world. If we remember their basic principles, we honor their work in all the TO we do.

References

Boal, A. (2002). *Games for actors and non-actors* (2nd Ed.). (A. Jackson, Trans.). New York, NY: Routledge.

Cohen-Cruz, J., & Schutzman, M. (1994). *Playing Boal: Theatre, therapy, activism.* New York, NY: Routledge.

Diamond, D. (2007). *Theatre for living.* Victoria, BC, Canada: Trafford Publishing.

Freire, P. (1968). *Pedagogy of the oppressed.* New York, NY: Continuum Publishing.

Oppression. (n.d.). In *Merriam-Webster online dictionary*. Retrieved from http://www.merriam-webster.com/dictionary/oppression

Oppression. (2002). In *The shorter Oxford English dictionary*. New York, NY: Oxford University Press.

Paterson, D. (2001). The TASC is: Theatre and social change. *Theatre, 31*(1), 62–93.

Paterson, D., & Weinberg, M. (1996). We are all theatre: An interview with Augusto Boal, with an introduction by Doug Paterson. *High Performance, 19*(2), 18-23.

CHAPTER TWO

Marc Weinblatt with contributions from Cheryl Harrison

Theatre of the Oppressor
Working with Privilege Toward Social Justice

KABUL, AFGHANISTAN, OCTOBER 2009. A dinner excursion after leading a Theatre of the Oppressed (TO) training session with Afghan applied theatre practitioners. After dark.

Our vehicle had gotten stuck in a deep rut on the edge of the street as our driver, Amin, tried to squeeze through a narrowing in the intersection. (Ninety percent of the roads in Kabul are in various states of rubble, mostly due to the brutal civil war of the 1990s that leveled much of the capital city.) As the rear right wheel spun freely in the air, Amin, a magician with cars, was attempting to free the car when two armed security guards approached us. In Kabul there are hundreds of young men contracted, then stationed at apartment buildings, restaurants, and other barricaded private sites–peppering every half-block around the city's central districts. They are paid the equivalent of $60.00 (USD) per month, handed a semi-automatic weapon, and instructed to "watch this building." The two guards were particularly unsympathetic to our plight, gruffly telling us to leave the area immediately, without the car. Through the skillful negotiation of several of the Afghan colleagues in our group, we were finally allowed to continue our attempt to free the vehicle. When Amin managed to get all four tires back on the ground, I got back in the car in preparation for a swift departure. In that moment, I was unclear about what happened next. I only knew that tense words were exchanged and I could see Amin hoisting several large stones, which I had used to help level the car, out of the sewer water in the rut where our tire had been stuck. Our friend and colleague, a former freedom fighter turned actor and joker, whom we called simply "The Doctor," got back in the car, visibly upset.

"I am so angry!" he blurted. "Those men are terrible. I had to stop myself because it would not have been safe for you."

"What happened?" I asked.

"They made him take the stones from the water because he is Hazara. They used racial slurs in Pashto. They didn't know I spoke Pashto. I just had to leave!"

I tell this story not because it was a particularly dramatic moment for me in Afghanistan, (which it was) but because of the conversation, which followed, in the car—a conversation that concretely illuminates an element of the TO adaptation I sometimes refer to as "Theatre of the Oppressor."

Amin, who spoke only Dari, is Hazara, a traditionally marginalized minority ethnic group in Afghanistan. The guards were Pashtun, the majority, traditionally dominant ethnic group. The Doctor is Pashtun. What could or should I have done? Had I known what was going on, what could my action have been, as a white foreigner from the currently occupying United States? What could the Doctor have done, as a fellow Pashtun, in support of his Hazara friend? Or others in the car, both Afghan and foreigners? The answer to these questions is not particularly relevant. Perhaps just getting away from the situation was the best choice in that moment. But our discussion of possible actions in that situation was riveting and was enlightening for us. In essence, we engaged in a theoretical Forum—Boal's problem-solving structure in which the protagonist of the scene is replaced by audience members to suggest alternative solutions (1992, p. 242). But in this case, the main protagonist—the truly "oppressed"—was Amin. In more classical interpretations of Theatre of the Oppressed, we would analyze his role and possible actions one could take in his situation. Part of what we do with "Theatre of the Oppressor" is analyze the role of the potential ally from the dominant social group—in the case of the Doctor, his own social group. The Doctor was fascinated by this analysis and was, I believe, forever changed by looking at what people who carry more societal rank can and perhaps ultimately must do to end oppression (Mindell, 1995, p. 28).

Historical Context and Theoretical Background

The moment described here took me full circle. My path as a TO practitioner has unfolded in ways I could never have foreseen when I began nearly two decades ago. I started in the early 1990s by leading traditional TO workshops and Forum Theatre performances with marginalized populations such as homeless youth, refugees, Native American tribes. More recently, I have worked with villagers in Afghanistan and the Republic of Congo. Yet, even with my early projects, I often broke classical form by inviting audiences to replace any character in a Forum scene—as long as they could identify how that person was struggling with the oppression. Long before developing TO adaptations for working with privileged people, I was convinced that all of us are culpable and responsible for uprooting social injustice—not just the "oppressed." We must all be protagonists and, therefore, activists. We must all be willing to look at where we are (even if unintentionally) part of the problem and potentially a more effective part of the solution.

Like Boal, I have adapted my work to the socio-political environment and circumstances in which I have found myself. I am a straight, white, able-bodied man, raised upper middle-class, living in the United States—a person of some privilege in a country of tremendous privilege. In anti-oppression jargon, I possess much "agency" (Adams, 1997, p. 20). Symbolically, and, in ways, literally, I am the oppressor. It is important to be clear that this work is not about bashing straight, white, able-bodied men of means as the source of all problems. It is important for all people to feel good about who they are. How else can we be authentic and compassionate members of society as well as effective citizen activists? Shame breeds frozenness, an inability to act, which helps no one. Our work does not point a finger, nor does it attempt to oversimplify human beings into the binary of either oppressed or oppressor. People are inevitably complex in ways that are impossible to define with labels.

A valued colleague of mine, Dr. Leticia Nieto, a scholar in Systematic Oppression Theory, has suggested that if ninety percent of women in the United States think they are too fat, then that is not just an issue for individual women. It is societal and it is the result of Systematic Oppression, the historic, institutional, and socially pervasive disempowerment of a social group (called "targets") by another social group (called "agents") or society at large (Adams, p. 20). Systematic Oppression drives the "isms" and is defined by societal (as opposed to personal) power, privilege, and access to resources, education, employment opportunities, etc. So, according to this theory: racism equals racial prejudice + power; sexism equals gender prejudice + power; classism equals class prejudice + power, etc. (See Appendix for a handout developed to use in workshops; it describes the roles typically played in Systematic Oppression.)

Systematic Oppression can include overt bigotry and mistreatment, but often it is unintentional and/or unconscious. Its manifestations can be deceptively subtle—almost invisible, except to the targets of the oppression. It carries assumptions based on the values of the dominant culture. By definition, all people are agents and targets of various forms of Systematic Oppression.

Because we want to see the humanity in all people, we can be significantly resistant to this way of viewing the world. Even (sometimes especially) within the progressive community, there is a tendency to focus primarily on our similarities and avoid our differences. "Why can't we get beyond all that and just get along?!" I have heard comments like this countless times in "diversity" workshops. In a perfect world, perhaps. Systematic Oppression Theory, by itself, is a gross over-simplification. However for many people, acknowledgment of social group memberships is a critical piece of the puzzle. Until we have a perfect world with "liberty and justice for all," it is a mistake to skip over these divisions, which are a painful reality for so many people. Heterogeneous groups can, in fact, come together more genuinely and heart-fully if these divisions are acknowledged. In order for us to be true anti-oppression activists or agents of liberation, it is our responsibility to learn to become effective allies to those people/groups who are treated as "other" or "less than" by society. Systematic Oppression dehumanizes and hurts us all.

To help people grapple with this concept, Dr. Nieto identifies a duality: the difference between truth and reality. The truth is, we are all one people. We all bleed, we all love our children, we all want respect, we all die. At the same time, the reality is that some people are treated differently than others are, in part, due to their identity group membership. Some groups have more societal power than others. The culture of those with power is the dominant culture of society and its social values are considered "normal"—while other groups of people are marginalized, less valued, invisible, "other." The truth of unity and the reality of division exist simultaneously.

Though I experienced success conducting TO workshops with marginalized populations, I ultimately came to realize that my most valuable work might be with my "own" people, those with significant social privileges. I kept returning to the classic image of oppression that Boal describes—of the man lying on the ground with another man's foot on his chest. Asked to recreate the image as an ideal image, the man on the ground simply removes the foot from his chest but does not stand up. While the self-empowerment of the oppressed is indeed critical work, how much easier might it be if the oppressor removed his own foot from the man's chest? Sometimes the one standing is not even aware that his foot is figuratively on the other's chest. However well-intentioned that person may be, he may still be inadvertently "oppressing." It must be possible for agents of oppression to re-invent themselves as agents of liberation, to "use their privilege" for social justice (Mindell, 1995, p. 73). This is more than just "magic," Boal's term for changing the essential truth of a character (1992, p. 267). Those with more power have the ability, access, and perhaps the duty to be a part of the solution. However, even for people with the best of intentions, this can be a remarkably challenging process. Who of us wants to think of ourselves as part of the problem?

Cheryl Harrison is a longtime colleague, TO joker, and anti-oppression activist as well as on of my mentors about Systematic Oppression Theory. We have been developing and co-facilitating TO-based diversity/anti-oppression workshops since the early 1990s. In a recent e-mail conversation about our work, she offered the following:

In my experience, no one wants to be viewed as the "bad guy," particularly if you identify as a member of a historically marginalized social group. I think it is also important to keep in mind when doing work around issues of Systematic Oppression that we are talking about social groups that humans are either born into or grow into over time—that this is not about "good" people versus "bad" people, an idea which seems to surface often when exploring these issues. For example, in one workshop, we were using a non-TO structure called the Power Shuffle,[1] in which people are invited to cross the room based on social identity group membership, followed by an Image Theatre structure to illuminate the idea of "target" (marginalized)/"agent" (dominant) social group membership. One African American male was stunned at the idea that, although he was a member of at least one marginalized group and was conscious of often being targeted in various ways by racist assumptions and attitudes, bigoted behaviors and unwarranted suspicion by police officials, he did not consider that he also carried the privilege of being an adult, straight, university-educated male. Having to admit this reality can be uncomfortable for those who usually identify as marginalized because it places them in the role they are usually frustrated with—the person who can't see her or his privilege. (personal communication, January 4, 2010)

As co-facilitator of the workshop Cheryl describes, I recall the moment of this man's awakening. It was a delicate journey for him and the group, but, ultimately, it seemed to significantly impact his worldview, both as an activist and as a person. So, the challenge of working with privilege is (1) bringing awareness to the notion that you may have your "foot on someone's chest," (2) unlearning embedded historical patterns of dominance and superiority including an attitude of "we know best," and (3) learning new ways to share power and becoming effective allies to other people. Theatre of the Oppressed can be adapted and used toward these ends.

Stories from the Field

Though we have used "Theatre of the Oppressor" concepts in a wide variety of contexts and around many issues, Cheryl and I have by far applied it most often in working with racism—arguably one of the most volatile issues in the United States. Even in our more general diversity/anti-oppression programs, groups often end up focusing on racism. A typical workshop lasts two to three days and includes TO community-building games, Image Theatre explorations of issues, basic Systematic Oppression Theory (not inherent to a classic TO practice), and, depending on the needs of the group, some caucus work in which participants are split into separate groups by their social identity groups. For example, in the United States, when splitting along lines of race (a sociopolitical construct which has little basis in truth but still unfortunately seems necessary because of reality), I generally work with the white people and Cheryl generally works with the people of color. This is sometimes controversial, but particularly the people identifying as members of the targeted social

identity group almost always appreciate it. The few times I have seen significant resistance to this idea, it is almost always, for example, the white people
who take issue with the division and the people of color who breathe a sigh of
relief. I must state with certainty that we are not creating this division. We are
just naming it, working with it, and by doing so, seeking to bridge it. And our
experience is that some things can happen in separate caucus groups that
would rarely, if ever, happen when the group is together. Or it would take an
inordinate amount of time to create the trust necessary for full disclosure to
happen within a mixed group.

   This is not just true in the United States where the "isms" are often at the
forefront of the discourse. When I was working with a group of mixed gender
victims of ethnic cleansing by the Taliban in the village of Yakowlang, Afghanistan, it was ultimately apparent that the women were much quieter and
more reluctant to participate than the men. I finally asked the women if it
would be easier for them to participate freely if the men were not in the room,
and they immediately replied, "Yes, absolutely." They knew who held systemic
power in the group; it was not safe for them to be free in that mixed gender
context. They indicated that it was agreeable for me to work with them
separately. (As a foreigner, I apparently posed less of a threat.) When working
without the men in the room, the women lit up and displayed a stunning level
of power and honesty.

   Whether working separately in caucus or together as one group, a few specific "Theatre of the Oppressor" adaptations of TO techniques are notewor-
thy. One, referred to earlier, is the use of Forum Theatre to analyze and
propose actions for potential allies. In classic TO we replace the most oppressed—the disabled person in a scene about ableism, the teen in a scene
about adultism, etc. Again, this is important work. But the work of the ally,
the person from the agent or dominant social group who does not have the
historic wound and might even be taken more seriously by those instigating
the oppression, is equally important. A recent performance on elder issues by
the Poetic Justice Theatre Ensemble (our Port Townsend-based multi-
generational theatre troupe which employs both TO and Playback Theatre
techniques) included a Forum scene depicting an oppressive situation at their
senior assisted living facility. The play came from stories the audience told of
their experiences living under the thumb of absent owners and a disconnected
manager. For many reasons, they felt powerless to change things. The Forum
yielded not only possible solutions for the elder residents but also invited one
younger adult advocate in the audience to explore what he might do as an ally
in support of his friends. He put himself on the spot by telling a story of his
sister advocating for their aging father at a different senior facility. As joker, I

seized the opportunity and invited him to play essentially himself, a potential ally, instead of an elder—the "oppressed," which might have only served to be what Boal (1992) has sometimes called "theatre of advice"(p. 269). I asked him what he could do for his friends. He took the challenge and tried several alternatives. Most touching was when he first asked his elder friends what they wanted him to do. He found out that they were scared of repercussions, that they did not necessarily want him to storm into the manager's office demanding change. And they certainly did not want him to take action immediately in response to the theatre performance. The elders needed a very sensitive handling of their struggle, but they did want his help. The most profound revelation for all was the importance of checking in with the elders first before jumping to action, a subtle but important layer to consider in ally work.

"Theatre of the Oppressor" invites often-silent witnesses to break their silence and take action. Knowing how to do it without disempowering the targets of the oppression is tricky. How better to explore options and generate valuable dialogue than through the experiential process of Forum Theatre? But to discover the best supportive actions, it helps to allow people to replace characters other than the "oppressed." It also may be valuable to replace the character that we think is causing the oppression—particularly if we relate in any way to the motivation of that character. We learn much about ourselves by playing the characters we do not want to be. Perhaps, in part, because we are those characters.

Some of the most profound and transformative moments in our work have come via an adaptation of the Cop-in-the-Head structure. As developed by Boal for TO, the Cop-in-the-Head is used to investigate internalized oppression. In TO the Cop-in-the Head brings to life the inner voices that replicate societal messages of oppression. For example, a common voice of internalized classism operating in a person raised poor might be personified by an image of someone covering her mouth and saying, "You're not good enough." In Theatre of the Oppressor, we have adapted Cop-in-the-Head to investigate internalized privilege. A person raised upper class might create a counterpoint image to the "You're not good enough" image that looks like a supportive hand lifting up the person raised poor and saying, "You deserve it."

In one "diversity" workshop that Cheryl and I co-facilitated with high school students, the youth created a scene in which two friends, one White, raised with money, and one Black, raised poor, look on the school bulletin board to find the results of their final exams. Both got a "C." Without any specific instruction from us, these teens added a Cop-in-the-Head for each character. The White student's internal cop said, "You've got to complain; you deserve better than that!" The Black student's cop said, "Doesn't matter;

you're just going to go to community college anyway." Same grade; different experience. The voice of internalized oppression keeps us down; the voice of internalized privilege keeps us up. These are not just personal messages specific to that individual. They are often archetypes that permeate the experiences of people from those social identity groups. Not that the voices of internalized privilege always feel good. In fact, many of those voices cause tremendous pain and suffering. And sometimes the voices look and feel exactly the same as the voices of internalized oppression. The difference is that internalized privilege includes benefits.

For example, one Cop-in-the-Head process with White people included a Forum that engaged a classic voice of internalized privilege. This voice confronted a well-intentioned White protagonist in a moment in which she recognized but did not speak up against an act of overt racism. It was a shushing finger to mouth image and spoke something to the effect of "Don't say anything; you're going to sound stupid." This is a painful voice, creating much distress in those who know and have lived with it. A successfully silencing voice, however painful, keeps the protagonist away from risk. So the assignment in the Forum was to attempt to disarm, silence, neutralize this cop-in-the-head of internalized privilege. With the participants of color invited to witness, the White people in the group proceeded to do battle with the voice. Person after person attempted, with little effect, to disarm this voice. After a dozen attempts by different participants, the young White actress playing the cop-in-the-head broke down in tears sobbing, "Why can't anybody stop me?!" I will never forget this moment. The woman knew this voice very well. She took her role very seriously and she desperately wanted to find a meaningful way to stop it. After a long pause, finally someone came up and did what was perhaps the obvious choice. She simply ignored the voice and spoke out loud against the act of racism. The woman playing the cop-in-the-head immediately dropped to the floor, dead. The voice no longer had a use. It was too late. The action was taken; the deed was done. What was most remarkable was how difficult it was for the White people to find a solution, how confounding this voice of internalized privilege was. The simple lesson experienced was clear to everyone in the room. Take action. Risk your privilege and gain deeper humanity for all.

Another moment is from a similar internalized privilege process with a group of White people who explored a common desire—reaching out to a person of color and saying, "I want to be your friend." After a long and delicate process collectively exploring possible cops-in-the-head of internalized privilege, two significant ones emerged: "Stay away; you're going to get hurt!" and "Shh. Don't let them see you; they're going to find out that you're a racist." There is no doubt that these voices would not have come to the surface if there were people of color in the room. I know this because when I asked the White people if they would be willing to show these voices to the other caucus, the people or color, they spoke with embarrassment, "I don't think we should show this to them." I gently responded, "I think they already know." Ultimately the group agreed to share the results of their exploration with their colleagues of color who responded compassionately, "Yes, we already knew. Thanks for admitting it." Targets tend to be the experts of their own oppression. Agents often have to work very hard just to see the deeper truth below the surface. From this moment, the groups grew closer. By naming the division, a bridge was built on a foundation of greater honesty. It is breathtaking how much work it can take in diverse groups to get to the real truths about a highly polarizing issue. Working with their privilege can help people inch forward towards greater authenticity, humanness, and the possibility for true solidarity.

This approach does not come without challenges. There are significant risks and potential pitfalls, particularly when working with mixed (race, gender, class, etc.) groups on the "isms." I have, on occasion, seen very progressive groups completely polarize around race, gender, or sexual orientation. Even when cautioned in advance, people sometimes cannot help but slip into the "Who's the better White person?" game of political correctness. Though painful to everyone, these polarizations tend to have particular cost for the target groups due to cumulative, historical re-wounding. Some colleagues question whether most people are even ready to work on these issues in mixed groups in a healthy way. Even when splitting into separate caucuses, there can be resistance. I once heard a White participant say as I led her (White) caucus into a break-out room, "I don't want to be here with the White people. I want to be in the other room; I'm an honorary Black person."

We were greeted before one "diversity" workshop even started with a comment by a participant, "I don't even want to be here; I feel like I'm being forced to go to somebody else's church!" We handled some of these moments well; some not as well. I have said the wrong thing, spoken when I should not have, not spoken when I should have, and lived through many "nightmare" joker moments. Does this mean that one should not do the work? Of course not. But I would encourage jokers heading into the fire of diversity/anti-oppression material, particularly attempting to facilitate work on privilege, to simultaneously be working on themselves, to "burn one's own wood" (Mindell, 1995, p. 208). Among other things, it is important to be aware of one's own social/identity groups and how these affect one's experience, awareness (and lack thereof), and also how one is perceived by others. However distasteful and dehumanizing they may be, societal rank, privilege and history do matter in how people interact. Our work is, in part, to transform that.

Conclusion

The "Theatre of the Oppressor" adaptations continue to be the most challenging work Cheryl and I do, and it calls for a fine balance between compassion and accountability. Theatre of the Oppressed demands revolution—justifiably calling for the marginalized to rise up and reclaim their power in the face of oppression. I worry that, alone, this revolution will flip, a role reversal, still leaving us with a world in which one group is on top and the others below. Theatre of the Oppressor, in conjunction with traditional Theatre of the Oppressed, invites everyone to be the protagonist with full responsibility for his/her part in an oppressive system. I believe that working for change from both/all roles is the most sustainable and perhaps least bloody path to the equilibrium that Augusto Boal regularly spoke of: a world where no one is oppressed, creating a true liberation for all.

When people say, regarding our anti-oppression work, "You are preaching to the converted," I respond by saying that there is no such thing as the converted. No one has graduated this course. We all have more work to do in playing our roles as agents of liberation. I will continue to explore this work, in part, so that I can learn to be a better ally, a better advocate for a more just world, a better person. I give particular thanks to brilliant colleagues like Ms. Harrison, Dr. Nieto, and also Qwo-li Driskill, two-spirit/queer writer, scholar, activist, and TO practitioner, among many others, for taking the time to educate and push me into deeper self-reflection.

As someone living in a body suit that possesses significant agency, I am aware that I could use my privilege and quit being an activist at any time. If I were doing more traditional activism as a community organizer, I worry that indeed I might quit. I am deeply grateful to Augusto Boal for providing Theatre of the Oppressed, which embodies, enlivens, and nourishes as much as it challenges. Boal's passing throws the gauntlet to all of us, his potential multipliers, to take the work further and boldly into new directions.

Appendix: Roles in Systematic Oppression*

Targets are members of social identity groups that are historically and systematically disenfranchised, exploited, and victimized in a variety of ways by institutions and society as a whole. Agents are members of dominant social identity groups who carry unearned (and often unconscious) power, privilege, and access within institutions and society as a whole. The following is a format for identifying agent and target groups.

Category	Agents	Targets
Age	Adults (21-59)	Children, youth, elders
Disability	Able persons	Persons with disabilities
Religion	Christian	Non-Christian
Ethnicity	Euro-Americans	People of Color (including African, Asian, Arab, Latino/a, & Native peoples)
Social Class	Middle and Owning Class (enough or more than enough resources)	Poor & Working Class (less than enough resources)
Sexual Orientation	Heterosexuals	Gay, Lesbian, Bisexual, Queer
Indigenous Background	Non-native	Native
National Origin	U.S. Born	Immigrant
Gender	Male	Female, Transgender, Gender Queer, etc.

(*Adapted from "ADRESSING" model by Pamela Hays with thanks to Dr. Leticia Nieto.)

Please note: This is a model specific to the United States. Socio-political structure should be analyzed and categories may need to be adapted for other countries. In addition, human beings are obviously more complex than this simplistic "hierarchical binary" would seem to indicate. Please think of this as just a piece of the puzzle with agents representing a society based on the dominant culture and targets as "other."

Note

1.   See Creighton and Kivel's *Helping Teens Stop Violence* for a complete description of this exercise.

References

Adams, M. et al. (1997). *Teaching for diversity and social justice: A sourcebook*. New York, NY: Routledge.
Boal, A. (1979). *Theatre of the oppressed*. New York, NY: Urizen Books.
—. (1992). *Games for actors and non-actors*. New York, NY: Routledge.
Creighton, A. & Kivel, P. (1990). *Helping teens stop violence*. Alameda, CA: Hunter House.
Mindell, A. (1995). *Sitting in the fire: Large group transformation using conflict and diversity*. Portland, OR: Lau Tse Press.
Nieto, L., Boyer, M. F. Goodwin, L., Johnson, G. R., & Smith, L. C. (2010). *Beyond inclusion, beyond empowerment: A developmental strategy to liberate everyone*. Olympia, WA: Cuetzpalin.

CHAPTER THREE

Brent Blair

The Complex
Theatre of the Oppressed, Trauma, and the Seventh Shift

Where does the other come from? Who is the other? I wear myself out, I shall never know.
—Roland Barthes, A Lover's Discourse, p. 134

While rhetorically the indigenous movement may be encapsulated within the politics of self-determination, it is a much more dynamic and complex movement which incorporates many dimensions, some of which are still unfolding.
—Linda Tuhiwai Smith, Decolonizing Methodologies, p. 110

Nothing is absolutely identical to anything else. All inanimate things and all living beings are always unique and unrepeatable, even if cloned.
—Augusto Boal, Aesthetics of the Oppressed, p. 11

THEATRE OF THE OPPRESSED was born of complexity. Boal's original explorations into what later became Forum Theatre came about as the result of what he viewed as his failed previous ventures into a more binaried[1] form of political theatrical intervention. Through the early years of its existence, TO evolved from agit-prop, with an externalized, professional control of the community narrative, toward a reassignment of the tools of authorship to within the community itself—simultaneous dramaturgy (Boal, 1995, p. 3). It was born of complexity, so by extension we might posit that the work of TO can relatively easily be threatened by simplicity, by a stagnant withdrawal into concretized games, techniques, and presentations which do not continuously adapt themselves to the ever-shifting cultural environment. Never satisfied with the lure of simplistic solutions, Boal's growing community—the founding jokers of the Center for Theatre of the Oppressed Rio (CTO Rio) and the subsequent practitioners and participants of TO around the world—have continued exploring this shifting *locus* of power relationships.

Many in the TO community have identified and categorized this shift through the years from the early protagonist/antagonist structures of TO in its Latin American origins to its more complex forays in other parts of the world, including Cops-in-the-Head and Rainbow of Desire techniques.[2] In my own desire to put complex things into neat categories, I identify TO's movement towards complexity as *shifts* which seem to respond to an increasingly intersubjective field;[3] shifts which challenge traditionally held notions of subject/object or oppressor/oppressed relationships in the work.

Looking over nearly forty years of the development of TO, I am drawn to observe the following adjustments which have affected the core techniques and therefore impacted the very structure of performances and—most notably—the lives of many thousands of participants whose stories may otherwise have been lost in the "Manichaean equation suggested by the terms 'oppressor' and 'oppressed'" (Adrian Jackson, in his introduction to Boal, 1995, p. xix). These appear to me best represented by shifts in: 1) authorship, 2) agency, 3) locus, 4) scope, 5) creative domain, and 6) assignment.

If the first shift as described in the story of the rupture with agit-prop and the landless workers movement[4] is viewed as a *shift of authorship*—from the professional, external control of a theatre company back to the people themselves (simultaneous dramaturgy), then the second shift must be Boal's discovery in Peru that although the text was controlled by the audience, it was the professional actors who still interpreted it,[5] therefore betraying the very voices for which the play proposed to speak. This seems to represent a *shift of agency* after the humorously disastrous consequences of the Peruvian woman who finally represented her own story by essentially replacing *herself* (Boal, 1995, p. 4). Here, we see the practical genesis of the spect-actor.[6]

The third shift appears years later in Sweden, Finland, and Paris with the birth of *Flic dans la Tête* (Cops-in-the-Head) after Boal realized that internal antagonists could be just as threatening to human life as external cops or soldiers; perhaps we can identify this as a *shift of locus*, from external to internal antagonists (p. 8).

The evolution of TO after Boal's election as *vereador* (comparable to city councilor) in Rio de Janeiro afforded him the opportunity to employ his dissolving theatre company as newly employed community advocates.[7] These partnership ventures became a proving ground for community-based Forum Theatre around issues that needed something more than spect-actor interventions; indeed, many of the plays told the story of daily oppressions that were apparently impossible to resolve through audience interventions. In these cases, only a change in fundamental legislation would seem to offer a pathway to liberation. This fourth shift of TO practice turned ordinary spect-actors into the ranks of citizen legislators, endowed with an even greater sphere of influence than that experienced within the Forum Theatre event. We may consider this to be a *shift of scope*—the spect-actor shifts from witness of the Forum to author of new laws.[8]

In the years following his legislative tenure, Boal again turned his attention to the democratization of all the arts—indeed, the democratization of all roles. TO participants may be not only citizen-legislators, but also citizen-artists, citizen-poets, citizen-musicians—a fifth shift, a *shift of creative domain*, moving people from positions as passive consumers to more active creators in this body of work known worldwide now as Aesthetics of the Oppressed (Boal, 2006, p. 4).

In the final years of his life, Boal had become increasingly interested in the growing complexity found within organizational relationships, particularly those within and among liberatory groups who, despite their common cause, may find themselves suddenly at odds with each other over internal ruptures.[9] Though the techniques of TO can be used to settle such disputes, the power dynamics are complex since both participants are, in effect, "protagonists"— meaning that neither holds power over the other, yet each is antagonistic to the other. In a post-session interview after just such a workshop addressing a similar rupture between two jokers in 2007 at CTO Rio,[10] Boal perceived three types of Forum: 1) *Foro Antagonistica* (Antagonistic Forum) "where the battle is strong, defined, and conflictual. The antagonist clearly doesn't want to help the protagonist, is somewhat static, and the protagonist must fight strongly against the antagonist" 2) *Foro Protagonistica* (Protagonistic Forum)—where it is not clear that the struggle is so antagonistic. The "antagonist" may be someone known and loved by the protagonist, but there is more or less a will that intentionally or not interferes with or obstructs the protagonist's desire. Examples of this model include Rainbow of Desire scenarios. Nonetheless, there is a hierarchy—the antagonist has the institution of power behind him/her—that is to say a mother, father, teacher, etc. and, finally, 3) *Foro Psicológico* (Psychological Forum) where the two (participants in conflict) are colleagues, there is no hierarchical binary necessarily defined, but the obstruction of desire is presently felt, just as the one we had witnessed between the two CTO Rio jokers during that 2007 workshop (personal notes, March 13, 2007).

Boal saw psychological forum as a movement from the protagonist/ antagonist binary toward a more subtle relationship between protagonist and another protagonist. During that workshop in 2007, Boal and the *curingas* (Portuguese for joker) of CTO Rio were exploring what we might describe as a sixth shift, a move away from the antagonistic conflict between two opposing forces to a protagonistic conflict between two otherwise aligned forces. In effect, each protagonist was assigned a new role to play—including her own desire, while confronting an opposing desire from a colleague. This partner could not be the antagonist, as she had no hierarchical advantage over her peer—neither from salary, position, status or other subtle or overt power structures that we typically assign to the antagonist. Here, though, each protagonist is behaving *antagonistically* from the perspective of the other. Each, then, has been assigned a new role by their partners, that of "antagonist"—even though they previously viewed themselves only as *protagonists*. Thence, the sixth *shift of assignment*.

In both the "Forum Theatre" and the "shifts" evolutionary model there is a development away from the simpler binary toward a more complex structure. A fair warning here is in order: Boal would not likely have seen these systems or methods as belonging to any kind of linear narrative toward something or away from something else, despite this rather natural conclusion if only looking at their historical development; on the contrary, the Tree of TO suggests a more organic and fluid model—any part of the tree offers different types of the same essential fruit, depending on which branch of TO is being practiced. Legislative Theatre works in some instances while only Rainbow or Cop-in-the-Head may work in others. Though Psychological Forum appears on no "official" branch of this tree, it seems useful to imagine this complex relationship between two protagonists existing side by side with Newspaper Theatre and the era of agit-prop. Though used simultaneously and ubiquitously, the linearity of their evolution seems itself to tell a story that now—with Legislative Theatre—invites citizens to "transgress, to break the conventions, to enter into the mirror of a theatrical convention, rehearse forms of struggle and then return to reality with the images of their desires" (Boal, 1998, p. 8).

These six shifts of TO paradigms lead to a nearly infinite variety of techniques within the body of TO worldwide, and most of these techniques are in wide use in the most diverse sets of circumstances. Still, there remains a vulnerable experience to which few of these techniques by themselves seem well-suited; that is, the experience of collective trauma within, between, and among populations burdened by the complex reality that survivors and perpetrators cohabit the same system. This seventh shift can be called the *shift of significance*. Let me offer a few examples of complexities that have occurred during theatre workshops over the years which have given rise to an acknowledgment that this may be still another shift in TO worth investigating.

The Seventh Shift: A Semiotic Dance in Two Parables

Perhaps part of the next shift for those of us working in complex circumstances in which lines between victim and perpetrator, oppressed and oppressor, are becoming more and more blurred is to acknowledge that the stage itself, the frame of our collective camera lens, reveals only a small part of the complex picture. During the same workshop in 2007 in Brazil, Boal invited an adjustment within the psychological forum he referred to as "zoom in," but when I ascertained that he intended this structure to widen the frame of the dialogue, I suggested the term "pan out" instead. At this moment, the peripheral context of the selected scene (the anti-model) was added to frame the narrative and better depict its complexity. For example, if the anti-model scene is between an abusive husband and his wife, the "pan out" moment may add the characters of the man's abusive family, and perhaps the wife's own family story as well. When we only see the scene between husband and wife, we have the simplified version, but perhaps not the more complex circumstances needed to understand their situation.

This kind of abstraction of concrete notions of character and the subsequent expansion of reductive narratives is found throughout the techniques of Rainbow of Desire (Boal, 1995)—"Image of the Images" (p. 77), "Image of the Word" (p. 87), "Kaleidoscopic Image" (p. 96). The difference in this seventh shift is not so much that the *protagonist* is transformed by projected invisible characters organized around her narrative, but rather that the *mise en scene* itself is "invisible." In the complexity of people trapped in issues of collective trauma, the setting is unclear: On which landscape are we operating? What is the stage for this dialogue? More than to whom are we speaking, we must ask, Where is this conversation taking place? Internally? Externally? Historically? All of the above? And most significantly—since we are all prone, as jokers, spect-actors and participants alike—to become something of our own *memory entrepreneurs*[11] without even recognizing it, what is our investment in this setting? For example, a woman in Rwanda is having difficulty being intimate within her married relationship, but is this dialogue happening in the kitchen with her husband, or on the killing fields in 1994 during the genocide? If the joker is not a direct survivor of the genocide, might (s)he be inclined to romanticize the narrative of the genocide or focus on one aspect or another of this play to the exclusion of some of the other narratives in this complex field?

In this seventh shift, we move the camera lens far back from the original binary of oppressed/oppressor to investigate the nature of the binary itself. In a world where globalization produces more agitation propaganda toward the construction of new Wal-marts and the demolition of old growth rain forests to fill more orders for McDonald's beef consumption, agit-prop remains a viable response. But it is just the first layer of response. As TO encourages us to imagine, there is more, always more. Psychological forum invites a process of meta-narratives to which Chela Sandoval refers in her book *Methodology of the Oppressed* (2000). Here, I offer, the seventh shift appears as a *shift of signs*; it is a semiotic shift, away from the narrative—"this vs. that"—to the meta-narrative—"what does 'this vs. that' mean?"

To illustrate the need for a seventh shift, I offer two examples: first, when the narrative of the protagonist/antagonist binary is complex and invites a more perforated, interactive response and second, when teen dating and domestic violence TO workshops ask more questions than they answer.

Case 1: The Hardest Day–the Protagonist/Antagonist Who Were Neither

In 2003 I was immersed in volunteer work building theatre projects in and out of Juvenile Hall and looking for new theatrical avenues in the arena of restorative justice. I wanted to work with both crime victims *and* the family members of those accused of violent behavior. I especially wanted to work around the rupture of loss—bereaved loss of a slain loved one and the loss of a youth incarcerated for life in the adult prison system.

Reyna and Herminia[12] were both women in their mid-forties who were volunteers in the Catholic chaplain's prison program, whose lives had been forever interrupted by violence. Reyna's brothers were both killed. While still a teenager, Herminia's son was incarcerated for thirty years to life for a crime for which he, Herminia, and their entire family vigorously proclaim his innocence. The women knew each other through the Los Angeles Archdiocese Prison Ministries program and seemed open to the idea of working together. I interviewed them separately and transcribed the entire process. I began with Reyna, whose narrative, though muted by many years of coping, was still a source of great emotional difficulty for her. I then interviewed Herminia, who was in such pain that we had to stop the session several times. I went home and spent several weeks typing the transcriptions of their accounts and embarked on a journey to put these two narratives in dialogue with each other, seeking points of commonality and exploring conflict and difficulty. After three weeks of arranging their words into a scripted dialogue, I returned to the women individually. We read the dialogue together, with me reading the part of the other woman. Each in her own way was brought to tears. There was no articulated antagonist, just the experience of loss, and the awareness of the other woman's story lingering in the background. The women were neither antagonists nor present tense allies. They were simply "there," on the periphery; somehow distinctly unreal, traumatically *vague*.

The two women came together to perform this double narrative for an audience of 500 youth involved in a restorative justice conference in 2003. By the time they were ready to perform, not only did they become real to each other, but it was clear that there was a third voice emerging between these two women—a voice of the meta-narrative, the voice holding out rebelliously against the trap of the binary, insisting on the new rupture that went beyond "who killed/ who was killed" and into the shared, collective experience of loss and grief.

Grief is personified and present, much in the same way Boal typically understood fear as a powerful starting impetus for constructing images of oneself in the introspective techniques of Rainbow of Desire (1995, p. 118). In the latter case, of course, fear is the quality that is made manifest in the images of the protagonists, as reactive statues to the concretized and oppressive phantom antagonist. In the former case, as with Herminia and Reyna, Grief seemed an active protagonist, a respondent "other" that paradoxically unified these two women.[13] Again, in light of the world of semiotics, Grief and Loss—of Reyna's brothers and Herminia's son—caused the women to depart the *mise en scene*, if only during the performance, in order to see themselves, together, in another scene. Not only were they seeing themselves outside of themselves, *in-situ* (Boal, 1995, p. 14), but in fact the shared aspect of Grief itself presented a sort of platform whereby the women could see themselves through the eyes of Grief, both bearing witness to their loss.[14]

"THE HARDEST DAY"

I: Both of my brothers...

II: I'll start with the hardest day of my life ...

I: Both of my brothers and a cousin were killed.

II: The hardest day of my life, the day he was sentenced.

I: Why is this going on?

II: When I heard that the judge gave him 30 years to life, I felt like my whole life was gone.

I: Both of my brothers and a cousin were killed, and my nephew lost his whole left leg due to a drive by shooting.

II: I felt like screaming, crying, getting up and asking the judge, "Why?"

I: I was angry.

II: I was lost.

I: I wondered, Why is this going on?

Opening excerpt of the script developed and produced for a Restorative Justice conference at Loyola Marymount in Los Angeles in 2003.

Case 2: "Cigarette" –Whose Story Is It, Anyway?

In a sixteen-week theatre project for teens on the issue of teen dating and domestic violence known as TELA (see Blair, 2010), there was no end to the complexity that came up as a result of the participants' stories. I refer to this section with the subtitle "Whose story is it, anyway?" because the Russian-born teen who told this story of abuse titled "Cigarette" ended up dropping out of the program halfway through. She left, ostensibly, to spend time with her father on weekends; her parents, divorced, were both negotiating for their daughter's time. Those of us in the workshop always wondered about the timing of her departure, just one week after sharing this traumatic story with the group. What I am left to wonder is whether the story itself, along with the response of the jokers and the group, which she may have interpreted as judgmental, contributed to a landscape of trauma whereby she felt either unclear or unsafe in this workshop.

The story itself was simple, if torturous. The girl, Lilly, before coming to the United States, had been dating a boy in Russia for several months. She was attracted to him and, quite possibly, afraid of him at the same time. One day, among friends, he offered her a cigarette, which she refused. "You know I don't smoke," she protested, to which he replied, "I know, but it's okay— treat yourself." They went back and forth for a few moments, after which she took the cigarette and took a drag. The boyfriend slapped the cigarette out of her mouth and then hauled off and slapped her across the face. This was her scene.

My first impulse as joker was to abort the scene: "This is not oppression," I decried, "but *aggression*. How are we going to invite the spect-actor to come up and replace her?" Co-jokers Ada Palotai, Christine Manley, and I led a long and deeply heated discussion about this in the group, circling our passionate wagons around familiar territory, and it raised many questions. For my part, I could not imagine a woman—any woman—staying in such a horrible relationship. Then again, I acknowledged that I had not experienced this situation myself, so I relied on the other participants who knew about such situations to respond. To my surprise, other women in our group acknowledged that they felt the situation was more complex than "should she stay or should she go."

Just after I expressed my confusion and my desire to abandon this scene on the grounds that violent scenes should not be forumed with spect-actors, I noticed the abject silence of the protagonist, matched by the crest-fallen eyes of one of the co-facilitators of the workshop, who also happened to be a woman. In the conversation that ensued, it became clear that we, as a community, were about to banish the voice of one of our participants because it did not fit into our prescribed formula for transformative TO work.

Of course, we were wrong on many counts. As the dust settled and we gathered together to contemplate how to honor this material without violating the principal ethics of TO, we realized that this story of violence was perhaps less insurmountable than we may have imagined. Furthermore, it merited an audience if it represented real situations faced by real teens on a daily basis. Finally, it was perhaps less outside the realm of historical TO practice than we may have imagined. At this point, many questions arose in our group. Here, in brief, is a list of some of the questions that surfaced:

- What are we asking of the protagonist in this situation? Are we suggesting that women should be able to come up with a solution to situations of dating and domestic violence on their own? Is it always that simple? What of the man's responsibility?

- If we do not show this scene because of the violence, are we suggesting that no scene that includes violence can be shown on stage?

- If we show the violent scene, are we inviting spect-actors to replace a protagonist in a potentially risky and traumatizing situation? Who would come up to participate in such a scene? If we do show the scene with its violence, would we forbid the spect-actor's use of violence as a response?

- What about the history (violence, abuse) of the perpetrator/antagonist? Are we willing and/or able to hear his story as well?

- If we allow the voices of the oppressed and abused men in the room as well, are we once again diminishing the voices of the women, whose stories are rarely told?

What resulted was a blending of techniques for the performance. We decided as a group to devise a hybrid Cop-in-the-Head and Forum Theatre episode, whereby each character entered the cigarette scene, accompanied by their "cops-in-the-head"–the sole purpose being to "pan out" the binaried story of aggression between the boy and the girl to include the landscape of the boy's history of violence and the environment of the girl's internalized oppression of self-esteem and self-doubt. The mixed scene was prepared and performed before an audience of youth and adults by six actors: the boy, the girl, his two cops and her two cops. At the point of spect-actor intervention, people could replace the boy or the girl against their own cops, but we were disinclined to invite replacement of the girl against the boy. This, too, was problematized by members of the group in long sessions after the opening night performance. I personally felt shy to invite audience members into a situation of violence, imagining that some of our teen spect-actors would haul off and slug the boy. Our co-facilitators argued that this was part of the landscape of the dialogue on teen dating violence, and to omit this opportunity was to avoid the subject all together.

In this arena, we imagine each person in the conflict carrying a very complex narrative, one which both clarifies *and* obscures the process of humanization that typically occurs in TO, primarily because the stakeholders *within* are themselves divided! Just as I have seen in my work with genocide survivors in Rwanda (Blair, 2010), the survivor of collective trauma from racism, sexual abuse, poverty, homophobia or other chronic marginalization, has learned over the years to amass an inner army surrounding the wounded self, both defending against further attack and at the same time holding on to the identity of woundedness.

To shift the internal terrain toward freedom is, perhaps, to disabuse players of their long-held attachments to an identity as *imprisoned*. In these situations, the joker must recognize the traumatized TO participant as attached to a specific, perhaps even reductive and possibly "precious" defensiveness of her state. Paulo Freire's observation seems particularly cogent here:

> The oppressed, having internalized the image of the oppressor and adopted his guidelines, are fearful of freedom. Freedom would require them to eject this image and replace it with autonomy and responsibility. Freedom is acquired by conquest, not by gift. It must be pursued constantly and responsibly. Freedom is not an ideal located outside of man; nor is it an idea which becomes myth. It is rather the indispensable condition for the quest for human completion. (1970, p. 47)

Here, we may say "the oppressed, having internalized the image of themselves *as oppressed*—from which a familiar if ironic comfort emanates—are fearful of freedom." What to do, then, with a group of willing participants who nonetheless struggle with the notion of releasing static images of this identity? And what of external forces, civic, cultural, interpersonal, which contribute to the concretization of this identity? After all, what is a joker, TO practitioner, or participant to do when the very antagonists seemingly behind the systems of trauma and traumatic memory are employed as vendors or entrepreneurs of survival? Though identification as a victim may seem anathema to the cultural fieldworker, it has long been the close ally of the survivor of collective trauma. This presents a unique challenge within the TO community. The idea that a joker, any TO technique or the fellow participants, through games and interventions, will provide the survivor of collective trauma with a transformation may be more than should be expected.

What is a joker, then? Perhaps it is more useful to begin with what I believe a joker is not. A joker is not: an expert; an empowerment facilitator; a therapist; a facilitator; a director, or a participant. I believe that if we summon the ethics of the Tree of TO and consider all the philosophical underpinnings of TO in general, we might sum up a joker by this simple analogy, favored by Boal and Freire alike: a joker is, simply put, a *lover*.

Love is unique, beneficial, patient, kind, curious, boundaried, and active. Lovers argue for the best for each other, respect what the other needs and wants, and provide their truest and most discerning attention for their partner. The joker is consistently curious, attentive, engaged and above all, full of humility and humor. More than anything, of course, the joker must ask questions: constant, heartfelt, curious questions. Without questions, there is no complexity.

The final question around this delicate terrain must always be born of a rigorous, fiercely honest self-reflection: just what exactly am I, as a joker, intending to gain by trying to dislodge these structured systems of survival? Perhaps more importantly, what is my understanding of the nature of trans-formation and the role of theatre in this process? How do I see this protago-nist in her rupture? What is the origin of the conflict we are addressing? On this latter point, there is still much to be written,[15] though many political theorists, economists, and philosophers have multiple treatises on just this question of the origin of experience, and therefore the domain of our cultural fieldwork. Is it internal? Political? Both? If it seems like I am focusing much of this analysis on the role of the joker, it is because I suspect that my domain as a cultural fieldworker begins and ends with my own role in the room. From this perspective, the joker knows only what she/he sees and observes, but does not project into the world of the participant what he/she may or may not need.

At what point does our work in TO addressing the individual (cops-in-the-head) realm need to take on the socio-political landscape of its nascence? At what point is the opposite called for—where the interactive political landscape of our work needs to be suspended to attend to the demands of the trauma-tized individual in the room? If we imagine replacing the protagonist at the moment of her inability or incapacity to speak or act in her own defense, what message are we sending? Are we communicating a subtle hope that she must somehow find a capacity to respond, that it is somehow within her to seek this transformation? Is the group imposing a subtle expectation onto the trauma-tized participant by its very enthusiastic willingness to replace her in the technique, sending a not-so subtle message that the power of transformation lies within her, if only she could find it? How does this apply to our work with victims of domestic violence, survivors of genocide, or people emerging from the chronic collective trauma of racism, gender inequity, the violence of poverty or homophobia?

My experience is that the fundamental ethics at the core of Theatre of the Oppressed which gave birth to the six previous shifts are a perfect match for this branch of "seventh shift" TO trauma work—primarily because of the absence of the "expert" in the room. The joker rejects the mantle of expertise, but rather invites all those involved in the process to a banquet of ideas in which all partake. Here, there is no therapist, no ordained minister or certified grief counselor, yet there is also no simplistic expectation of a replacement of the protagonist to assist her in her battle against the internal or external antagonist. This shift returns us to a more amorphous, less "directed" technique, more like Boal's early Image Theatre and some of the exercises within Rainbow of Desire but without the expectation of transformation of the protagonist; rather, the shift from silence to speaking may be the transformation.

Conclusion

In this world of mounting injustice, where violence is increasingly a symptom but curiously not the root disease, the obligation to "pan out" and look for complexity in context seems ever more necessary. How can we look at the slaughter of Tutsis in Rwanda by only stretching the curtains of history as far back as the perpetration of the Hutus, but not exploring the invasion of the Belgians, the creators of the construct of Hutu/Tutsi? And how can we work within the criminal justice system but continue to use the colonizing language of "perpetrator" and "victim," or, possibly, protagonist and antagonist, without feeding into the very binary created by colonial existence itself? Without "panning out" and allowing for the narrative of the complex, we risk reproducing the very ruptures to which we are attempting to respond.

Creating images of images, observing ourselves *in situ*, stepping back and exploring meta-narratives is not overcomplicating the resistance, but rather *invigorating* it by acknowledging that, in a complex world, widening the frame of TO makes more critical and engaged citizens of us all.

Notes

1. Oppressor/oppressed, protagonist/antagonist, subject/object, or actor/audience. See Jacques Derrida's notion of the "hierarchical binary," for example, or the treatment of the "sender/receiver" relationship in the field of semiotics.
2. See translator Adrian Jackson's note about this account on p. xix of *The Rainbow of Desire*.
3. See Edmund Husserl's work in phenomenology or David Abrams' splendid complication of the notion of subject and object in *The Spell of the Sensuous*. In psychology, see the works of Robert Stolorow.
4. *Movimento dos Trabalhadores Rurais Sem Terra*, the landless workers movement that first encouraged Boal's theatre ensemble to imagine themselves in solidarity without being prepared to actually "spill" their own blood. This rupture inspired the beginning of the writing of the Theatre of the Oppressed text and the launching of this worldwide movement in the early 1970s.

5. Boal invokes the Italian expression "*tradutore, traditore*" (1995, p. 7) or "translator, betrayer" as the paradigmatic impetus for shifting into what became Forum Theatre.

6. Arguably, although the idea of the spect-actor is implicit even in the earlier form of simultaneous dramaturgy, the actual on-stage involvement of audience members (as more than dramaturges and playwrights) began with Forum Theatre.

7. Boal told an audience at Emerson College in 1991 how, faced with artistic cutbacks, his theatre company had faced being disbanded, at the same time he had just won an overwhelming victory as *vereador* when his sole purpose for campaigning in the first place was to gain free TV air time to support the flagging campaign of Luiz Inácio Lula da Silva for President. Newly elected, Boal found himself with a staff budget that allowed him to re-hire his entire theatre ensemble as members of his legislative staff.

8. It seems to be used sporadically around the world in response to specific ruptures, i.e., in Ville de Grasse, France, around the issue of flooding and poor land use, and in Nairobi / Kibera, Kenya, where impoverished youth lift their voices to help develop a new constitution. To date, however, the only sustained experiences seem to have been in Rio de Janeiro, from 1993–1997.

9. See Derrida's explication of this term in *Writing and Difference* (1966, p. 252) as he quotes Freud's fascination with the notion that neurons must be "ruptured" to create new pathways in the brain, which are newly identifiable to us as memories.

10. During a week long "internal training" workshop, two jokers from CTO Rio were in conflict with each other about how each was understanding her responsibilities in the organization. Without going into details, although one was significantly more experienced than the other, Boal considered them both to be protagonists because neither had an obvious power advantage over the other. What looked like a classic Forum Theatre model in fact was Psychological Forum because both jokers were in the room, playing their own parts, and each was antagonistic to the other. Spect-actors could replace either joker in the scene.

11. According to Elizabeth Jelin, author of *State Repression and the Labors of Memory*, memory entrepreneurs "... seek social recognition and political legitimacy of one (their own) interpretation or narrative of the past" (pp. 33-34). In collective trauma such as genocide, the perpetrating state sets up the apparatus of mass murder by playing on false notions of collective memory pitting one group against another; similarly, much conflict surrounds the post-genocide state around notions of memorializing the slain. Whose story is told, whose is left out? This complex arrangement of collective memory frequently plays a part in victim/perpetrator scenarios within prison theatre work. What may be more important than the "literal" narrative is the "exemplary" narrative (p. 42) —what are we to do with each of these stories? Who benefits from each telling? Whose voices are left out?

12. All names used in this article are pseudonyms.

13. This work raises profound questions. Though excited at the possibility of this cross-experiential work, there is a profound grief with one of the mothers that is unshakeable even 16 years after her son was incarcerated. Each time she performs the text, it is as if she were re-experiencing the trauma of loss for the first time. Though she insists on moving through it, there is a strong sense that something is not being lifted, something is not being addressed. Clearly, there is room for more work here, and we stay hopeful for more exploration in this area.

14. Perhaps not accidentally, both of these women were united through a Catholic ministries program, and The Rosary bore no small significance in one of the women's stories. This ancient prayer said with a strand of beads divided into five sets of ten beads ("decades") is

of Moorish influence and was popularized by Lady Godiva. It bears the unique and transcendent quality of inviting the supplicant to see the entire story of the birth, life and death of Jesus as told through the point of view of Mary. Mistakenly thought of as a prayer "to the Virgin," the Rosary more accurately is a meditation through the eyes of Mary. In such a way, then, this theatrical exercise between these two women juxtaposed two texts of commonly experienced grief and transformed an erstwhile victim/perpetrator binary into a third, newly-aligned meta-narrative. The Rosary offers a similar, if somewhat esoteric, third perspective.

15. See the writings on "methodological individualism" and "methodological holism" in philosophical and economic circles for elucidation of the ongoing debates about whether people operate on internally generated or externally driven forces. For the purposes of this article on complexity and TO, I support the notion that both are acting upon us for different reasons, at different times and with varying results.

References

Blair, B. (2010). TELAvision: Weaving connections for teen theatre of the oppressed. In P. Duffy & E. Vettraino (Eds.), *Youth and theatre of the oppressed* (pp. 97-123). New York, NY: Palgrave Macmillan.

Boal, A. (1995). *The rainbow of desire: The Boal method of theatre and therapy* (A. Jackson, Trans.). New York, NY: Routledge.

—. (1998). *Legislative theatre.* New York, NY: Routledge.

—. (2006). *The aesthetics of the oppressed.* New York, NY: Routledge.

Freire, P. (1970). *Pedagogy of the oppressed* (M.B. Ramos, Trans.). New York, NY: Continuum Publishing.

Jelin, E. (2003). *State repression and the labors of memory.* Minneapolis, MN: University of Minnesota Press.

Sandoval, C. (2000). *Methodology of the oppressed.* Minneapolis, MN: University of Minnesota Press.

CHAPTER FOUR

Ellie Friedland

Integrating Theatre of the Oppressed into Higher Education
Transformation or Technique?

> *Radicalization involve[s] increased commitment to the position one has chosen. It is predominantly critical, loving, humble, and communicative, and therefore a positive stance. The [person] who has made a radical option does not deny any other [person's] right to choose, nor does he [or she] try to impose his [or her] own choice. He can discuss [his] respective positions. [She] is convinced [she] is right, but respects another [person's] prerogative to judge [herself] correct. He tries to convince and convert, not to crush his opponent. The radical does, however, have the duty, imposed by love itself, to react against the violence of those who try to silence [her]—of those, who, in the name of freedom, kill his freedom and their own.*
> —Paulo Freire, *Education for Critical Consciousness*, p. 1

BOAL'S THEATRE OF THE Oppressed and Freire's Pedagogy of the Oppressed are both based on the principle that dialogue is the common, healthy dynamic between all humans, that all human beings desire and are capable of dialogue, and that when a dialogue becomes a monologue, oppression ensues. In societies stratified by power and money, many dialogues tend to become monologues by those with power, which creates the oppressor/oppressed relationship, and institutions are structured to perpetuate rather than change the oppressive systems. A central purpose of theatre and education, according to Boal and Freire, must be to critique power inequities and to change them. The educational process, like Theatre of the Oppressed, can and should facilitate a transformation of monologue into dialogue.

Boal and Freire's focus on dialogue is particularly relevant in higher education, where too often teaching is a monologue from professor to students. I fear that too many educators, though sincerely dedicated to encouraging independent critical thought, enable the hierarchical system in which students are at the bottom and professors are above them. The professor has the power to tell students what to do and what not to do, to control conversation in the classroom, and ultimately to give grades that determine whether or not students can progress in their studies. Most students not only accept this dynamic, they embrace it, and go about the business of figuring out what each professor wants so they can deliver it.

Critical dialogue, reflection, and action are especially vital in teacher education, because if future teachers do not learn to understand, analyze, critique, and act for change, they will perpetuate rather than change the oppressive school systems that disrespect and disempower teachers and students. As I go through my day-to-day life as a teacher educator, I do not want to become unaware of or accept this power structure and the impact it has on how I live and learn with my students. I do not want to implicitly encourage students to figure me out and deliver what will satisfy me.

I am committed to integrating Theatre of the Oppressed into education as one form of praxis that allows students to move beyond mechanized thinking to critical dialogue, reflection, and action; I try not to separate the TO tools I apply from their ideological base, and my teaching includes ongoing attention to the theoretical frames of Freire, Boal, critical pedagogy, and constructivist early education (educational practice in which learners actively construct their own knowledge). In this chapter I explore how, as a college professor, I conscientiously incorporate elements of Theatre of the Oppressed into class sessions in my course "Creating Welcoming Environments for Lesbian, Gay, Bisexual, and Transgender Families in Education and Human Service" in ways that honor the intention and integrity of Boal's work.

Theoretical and Pedagogical Integrity

Paulo Freire wrote in *Pedagogy of Freedom* (1988) that "...whoever feels that she/he has something to say, ought to accept, as a duty, the need to motivate and challenge the listeners to speak and reply. It is intolerable to see teachers giving themselves the right to behave as if they owned the truth—and taking all the time they waste to talk about it" (p. 102). I do not want to waste time presenting my "truth" to students, but I do have knowledge, strategies, and also values about children, learning, and education that I want students to engage with, consider, and practice. I want to motivate and challenge them to think, critique, and speak. I have a political agenda: I want to be an agent of change in the educational system, and I want students to leave college ready to be change agents in the systems they will enter as professionals.

I try to practice Freire's idea of praxis—that education must include reflection plus action, and that the two are not separable. "Within the word we find two dimensions, reflection and action, in such radical interaction that if one is sacrificed—even in part—the other immediately suffers. There is no true word that is not at the same time a praxis. Thus to speak a word is to transform the world" (1988, p. 75). My constant challenge is to create educational situations that allow a true dialogic process, within the hierarchal structure of college. I must always ask myself if I am creating an environment for learning in which no one is silenced, in which opposing viewpoints are invited and respected.

TO is the most powerful dialogic approach I know, but when I use TO in my classes I need to be sure I am not taming it by separating the technique from its theoretical and political frame. Boal understood that many practitioners using TO in the United States are taking elements of his work and adapting them for use in new ways in new settings, and he encouraged us to do so. However, I took several workshops with Boal before I felt ready to facilitate any TO processes, and in my classes I do not have the luxury of time to lead students through his involved process that creates so much openness, dialogue, problem-solving, and ultimately, action for change. I cannot make learning TO the focus of my courses in education and human services, but I want to incorporate its power into my teaching.

Integrating TO into a College Course

Graduate and undergraduate students in early education, elementary and special education, social work, juvenile justice, youth advocacy, and child life[1] take my course "Creating Welcoming Environments for Lesbian, Gay, Bisexual, and Transgender Families in Education and Human Services" because they know they will work with LGBT families and individuals, and they want to learn more about them and how to support them. But for virtually all students, some aspect of the course sends them into conflict with the ideas, beliefs, and values they have been taught. Many students who choose to take this course are already struggling with aspects of their identities that the course focuses on. Many who are not already thinking about these issues (mostly those who identify as heterosexual) are thrust into awareness, which causes them to question much that they have previously taken for granted.

The course is always co-taught by one instructor who identifies as heterosexual and one who identifies as LGBT or Q, and we discuss our differing perspectives, experiences, biases, and commitments with students throughout the course. We have found that many students experience the course as emotionally and ideologically challenging, and that it is vital that all students have an instructor with whom they are more likely to feel safe. LGBT and Q students often reach out to my co-teacher for support, and straight students often seek me out. One explicit purpose of the course is for all of us to think about our own beliefs and prejudices, to look at areas in which we are oppressed and areas in which we have privilege, including when we are in the position of oppressor. As a result, many students experience internal conflict, which frequently leads to external conflict with others in class, and in their lives outside the classroom. They struggle with the idea of privilege and with recognizing their own biases and acknowledging the possibility of their own roles in perpetuating oppression.

Students are often torn between accepting and acting on what they learn in the course and their respect for the professionals in their student teaching or internship sites, the public school or human service systems that hold their future employment, and often, their love for friends and families, whose values and ideas clash with those we present in the course. Often students equate respect with agreement. They have few models for dialogue that include respectful disagreement and conflict, especially for topics as charged as welcoming and supporting LGBT families in education and human service settings. I know that TO can provide not only models but experiences of dialogue that lead to action for change, but I have to keep in mind that many students are already frightened by topics in the LGBT course. In addition, they are not theatre students, and many are hesitant to speak in class, much less participate in drama activities. I do not have time for the progressive process of TO games that I know leads people past their habitual, mechanized ways of moving and thinking. Again, I must be sure that I do not rob TO of its power.

Lightning Forum Theatre

One of the most difficult topics we address in the LGBT course is how to respond to objections people voice when teachers and other professionals openly include LGBTQ families and individuals in the environment and curriculum. We use a variety of approaches in the course to understand the beliefs, fears, and lack of information that underlie many of the objections about including and respecting LGBT people and topics. We use role-play to practice how to respond when friends make homophobic comments, when children say, "That's so gay," or when children are excluded or bullied. But the objections that are most frightening to face and most difficult to challenge are based on religion. These objections include statements like "My religion says that being gay is a sin, in fact, an abomination, so you have no right to tell my child that people who are gay are to be respected and accepted"; "You can't read that book that has two fathers in it when my child is in your classroom—it violates my religion"; "I can't accept my child who says she is gay. My religion says she is a sinner and will go to Hell." Students are at a loss for how to remain respectful of people's religious beliefs, yet at the same time maintain their commitment to inclusive practice and curriculum. Role-plays are often not helpful, because students simply cannot think of ways to respond.

Boal's Lightning Forum, a truncated version of Forum Theatre, is the most effective structure I have found to bring students into engagement with this difficult area. I use it in classes, and I even use it in professional development workshops for teachers that are only a few hours long. Using Lightning Forum instead of role-playing seems to make it possible for people to think of and apply responses to arguments that stymie them in role-plays, it also seems to be so compelling that participation comes easily for many people. Lightning Forum has the same goals as Forum Theatre, but includes much less preparation and rehearsal and is shorter and quicker.

In Forum Theatre, a group of community members create a short play that has a protagonist who is clearly trying to accomplish something specific, is thwarted by an oppressor, and therefore fails to accomplish her goal. These actors show the play to an audience of people from their community who also want to achieve the goal and have been trying to accomplish it. Then the actors perform the play again, from the beginning, and the audience members become spect-actors—stopping the play and replacing the protagonist, coming onto the stage and trying a new approaches or actions. The other actors improvise responses to each new intervention, keeping their reactions as true to their characters and to the reality of the situation as possible. The joker's role in Forum Theatre is to call on spect-actors who volunteer and to help each volunteer identify the moment of the play at which he wants to intervene. The joker makes sure each spect-actor gets a chance to enact her intervention fully and asks the audience to analyze what this protagonist did differently, whether or not it was realistic (some interventions may be identified as too easy or as "magical"), and how it worked. Several spect-actors try several interventions, and each is discussed by the audience.

In Lightning Forum, spect-actors come into the scene more rapidly and frequently than in full Forum Theatre, and interventions may play out quickly, without discussion between each intervention. When I use Lightning Forum in my classes, we go almost directly to an improvised scene and interventions by spect-actors. Here is an example from a session of the LGBT course. With guidance from me acting as joker, the class very quickly put together the structure of a scene that included parents coming to their child's school to voice objections about including Lesbian, Gay, Bisexual, and Transgender (LGBT) families in early childhood education curriculum, emphasizing the religious objections. The characters in the scene included two straight parents of a five-year-old kindergarten boy; the boy's teacher, and the school's principal. Students volunteered to play all the roles and improvised the scene.

I set up the activity by saying: "In this scene we have the two upset parents coming to express their concern. The principal and teacher will make this conversation as realistic as they can, respond to the parents, and the parents will then respond, and again the teacher and principal will respond—so they will have a conversation. Does it work if we say that in the scene the parents want the school to stop including any references to homosexuality? They have been happy with the school and the classroom until this very important issue came up, and they are now unhappy and disturbed. Is it realistic?" In this case the group agreed, so we went on. If the group had offered suggestions for change, I would have facilitated a discussion to come to consensus about the basics of the scene before we continued.

"Similarly, do we agree that the teacher and principal want to maintain the positive relationship they have heretofore had with these parents, but they are not willing to change their curriculum?" Again, we talked together until there was consensus. "When you are in the scene, try to make your responses to each other realistic. There are no right solutions. We will see how the conversation plays out, and through that we will see the effects of what the professionals say and do. We want to try as many ways as we can think of to create a positive dialogue here, but this won't be easy. We also want many people to get a chance to try their ideas. Therefore the set up is this: anyone playing the teacher or principal can choose to leave the scene at any time if she runs out of ideas. She just raises her hand and I, in my role as joker, will find someone who wants to replace her. Similarly, anyone in the audience can let me know you want to enter the scene, and replace either the teacher or the principal to try an idea you have.

"It will be my job as joker to let each person's intervention play out, so when you want to intervene, raise your hand, and I will be sure you get a chance as soon as the intervention in process is complete. I may not call on you right way, if the current intervention is still playing out. But I will make sure you get a chance, and then you can replace either the teacher or principal, and you can tell the group where to start the scene over and try your idea. The others in the scene will respond as truthfully as they can. We do not need to replace the parents, but if either of them runs out of ideas, they too can raise a hand requesting to be replaced. And if someone in the audience thinks of a strong argument that the parents don't express, you can offer to replace one of them. They may agree to leave, or they can say they aren't ready to leave the scene yet."

Scene: Parents' Religious Objections to LGBT Inclusive Curriculum

The students set up the scene in which two parents have requested a conference with the classroom teacher and school principal specifically to discuss their concerns about the teacher's curriculum unit on families, which includes LGBT families. The couple enters the principal's office, obviously upset.

TEACHER: Hello, Mr. and Mrs. Jones. It's good to see you again. I think you know Ms. Smith, our principal. [Principal greets the couple.]

MOTHER: I wanted to meet with you because I am so concerned about what Billy tells me is going on in his class! He told me he is learning about gay families! I was shocked, and I have to tell you that our religion prohibits teaching homosexuality. This is unacceptable! I am so upset that my child is being exposed to this. It's disgusting!

TEACHER: Mrs. Jones, I understand your concern and I want to assure you that we are not teaching homosexuality. We are doing our unit on families, as we always do at this time of year, and since there are some children in our class with two moms, we are making sure we include everyone. We have some books about families with same sex parents and some photos that show all kinds of families.

MOTHER: Oh my! There are homosexual parents of children in my son's class! He can't be exposed to that! Who are they? I want to be sure he doesn't play with that child!

FATHER: Those people can do what they want, but they have no right to force it on my child, and neither do you!

The student playing the teacher looked out at the group, and waved her hand to indicate someone should replace her. Another student came in as she exited.

TEACHER: (a new actor): Actually, I believe it is important to include all types of families in our kindergarten unit, even if there are no gay families in our class.

PRINCIPAL: It is important that all children see their families represented in the curriculum. We have a commitment to include all families.

FATHER: Well, I certainly don't want my child exposed to all types!

MOTHER: You aren't respecting our family when you insist on teaching homosexuality. You are not respecting my family or my religion!

The teacher and principal in the scene did not respond, looking nervous. In my role as joker, I asked if anyone had ideas and reminded the class that they could play the scene from here or start at any earlier point in the scene. Some students acknowledged how difficult this was, but a student volunteered to replace the actor in role as the teacher. She asked to begin the scene again, just after the couple enters. I reminded the student playing Mother to begin just as the scene began before.

MOTHER: I wanted to meet with you because I am so concerned about what Billy tells me is going on in his class! He told me he is learning about gay families! I was shocked, and I have to tell you that our religion prohibits teaching homosexuality. This is unacceptable! I am so upset that my child is being exposed to this! It's disgusting!

TEACHER: (new actor): Mrs. Jones, I understand your concern and I want to assure you that we are not teaching homosexuality. We are doing our unit on families, as we always do at this time of year. We learn about lots of types of families, and we focus on how important families are for children.

PRINCIPAL: It is important that all children see their families represented in the curriculum. We have a commitment to include all families.

TEACHER: I'd like to share some of our curriculum materials with you. Here is an example of a book about families. [She pretends to show them pages in a book.] You see, it talks about the people children have in their families—some have a mother and father, some have brothers or sisters, grandparents, and some have two mothers or two fathers, some have a step-parent, and so on. In kindergarten we learn about the important people in children's lives. We don't learn anything about sexuality at all.

[Both parents pretend to look at the book.]

MOTHER: Well, it looks fine to me, except for this part about two men as parents. As I said, that goes against my religion.

Again the students playing teacher and principal did not respond, and they looked to the group. Another student replaced the principal.

PRINCIPAL: (new actor): As you know, it is against the law for public schools to teach religion. I know Billy's teacher respects your religion, but at school we respect everyone.

MOTHER: I am not asking you to teach religion! You'd better not! I am asking you not to expose Billy to things that are just plain wrong!

PRINCIPAL: We do respect your beliefs, but we respect and support all children and their families. I'm sorry that you disagree, but we welcome and acknowledge all families.

FATHER: Well, if you insist on using this book and talking about homosexuality, we certainly object. I am telling you that Billy is not to be exposed to this. If you aren't going to stop this, he is to leave the room during this book and during anything else that smacks of homosexuality.

The actors in the scene and many in the class groaned, and the teacher and principal again looked to the group. At this point, no one had ideas for what to do next, or how to start differently earlier in the scene. Therefore, we moved into discussion, and agreed that we would replay the scene after our discussion (possibly in the next class meeting) if students wanted to.

Discussion and Analysis

In full Forum performances, the joker asks the audience after every intervention what the spect-actor did that was different, and if the intervention was realistic, or if it was too "magical." In Lightning Forum, we try many interventions before we talk about them. By this point, as in this example, participants are usually clamoring to express their ideas and reactions. This group began by expressing their surprise that the teacher's and principal's explanations had been so unsuccessful, as well as their frustration and their fear about what they would do when faced with situations like this. They unanimously said that they did not want to remove any child from any portion of a unit on families, but they could not think of what to say or do in response to the request (or demand) from the parents in the scene.

We then talked about the scene from the beginning, analyzing the relationship that the teacher and principal had established with the parents, and how it broke down when the teacher said that there was a child in the class with two moms. This led to a discussion about whether or not to share that information, in general. One student (who had previously self-identified as lesbian) said that the moms might not be "out" in the school or community, so this could have unintentionally outed them. Others had not considered this complication. Then the discussion focused on whether or not students would include LGBT families in the curriculum unit if they thought there were none in the class, which challenged them to consider more deeply the reasons LGBT parents might not be out, as well as their commitment to this potentially risky and controversial curriculum. They compared this situation to teaching about different races and cultures only when children from those groups are present in the classroom and agreed that neither is adequate.

The students thought that the teacher and principal in the scene made an effective choice by not engaging in a discussion about religion with the parents, but they also said it left the issue hanging and allowed the parents to come back to it. They liked the teacher's strategy of sharing the children's book, except that it created the opening for the parents to request that their child be excused during the study of families. They then discussed whether or not children should be either excused or excluded from certain curricula or school activities. Many of the students had been in classrooms in which children of various religions had to sit out or leave during certain celebrations and were uncomfortable that the children were singled out and left out. But many were also reluctant to say there should be no holidays or celebrations in the classroom. We discussed the difference between festive activities and curriculum and whether children should ever be excluded/excused from curriculum and whether teachers should try to teach curriculum that no one would object to. This led to a discussion of Freire's assertion that education is always political, and what that means for teaching. Students thought about what they would be willing to take a stand about, what the risks would be, and what risks they might be willing to take for what they believe in.

We were still left with the scene in which the professionals had not yet found a successful response. In *Games for Actors and Non-Actors*, Boal addresses the question, "Do we have to arrive at a solution or not?" and says: "I believe that it is more important to achieve a good debate than a good solution .... Even if one does reach a solution, it may be good for the person who has proposed it, or good within the confines of the debate, but not necessarily useful or applicable for all the participants in the forum" (p. 259). However, groups I have worked with, including the class described here, have always wanted to replay the scene after discussion of their initial interventions. It seems important for people to experience more success so they are not left with a sense that the obstacles to successful dialogue are insurmountable.

As usually happens, the students in this LGBT class approached the scene very differently after the first round of Lightning Forum had shown the humanity and sincerity of those on both sides of this highly charged issue. They understood the reality of how difficult it is for professionals to remain respectful of the parents while also maintaining their commitment to ideas with which the parents disagree. However, they also saw the parents as caring, earnest people who want the best for their child. In the second Lightning Forum students began their interventions very differently, and found ways to respond that allowed the parents to stay in dialogue with them. There were no easy solutions, but the Lightning Forum took them past the comfort of their stereotypes of parents, of people who hold certain religious beliefs, and of why parents make appointments with school administrators. It revealed the complexities of establishing and maintaining respectful dialogue with people who oppose us, while taking a stand for what we believe is just.

Conclusion

My teaching partner, Kim Westheimer, and I have been offering the LGBT course at Wheelock College for four years now, and we are consistently moved by how willing students are to change their own ideas and to take action. We always have a mixture of first-year through graduate students in class, as well as students with a range of racial, cultural, religious, gender, and sexual orientation identities. All students create an action for change project as the final course assignment, designed to create change in their worlds. Students have revised intake forms in social work agencies and childcare centers to be more inclusive, they have educated family and friends about the impact of homophobic language, and they have joined and even started activist groups, including Gay Straight Alliances.

Miles Horton, of the Highlander Folk School (an educational center for civil rights activists, now called the Highlander Research and Education Center) wrote, "Many people are trying to adopt Freire's educational system, but it cannot be reduced to a mere methodology; to make his system work you must have a radical philosophy" (Graves, 1979, p. 4). I am committed to the radical philosophies of Boal and Freire, and to teaching courses that create opportunities for students to create change in the world. Therefore, I must continue to critique my practice, and seek critique from students, to make sure that my courses, with their clear political and social agendas, avoid becoming indoctrination. I must not reduce Theatre of the Oppressed to one more "nice" technique. As I operate within established educational systems, I must live a radical philosophy of transformation.

Note

1.   Child life specialists are the professionals who work with children in hospitals, staffing playrooms, and preparing and supporting children and families for medical procedures and hospitalizations.

References

Boal, A. (1979). *Theatre of the oppressed.* New York, NY: Urizen Books.
—. (1992). *Games for actors and non-actors.* New York, NY: Routledge.
—. (2006). *The aesthetics of the oppressed.* New York, NY: Routledge.
Freire, P. (1988). *Pedagogy of the oppressed.* New York, NY: Continuum.
—. (1973). *Education for critical consciousness.* New York, NY: Continuum.
—. (1998). *Pedagogy of freedom.* Lanham, MD: Rowman & Littlefield.
Graves, B. (1979). What is liberating education? A conversation with Miles Horton. *Radical Teacher,* 3-5.

PART II

*Transforming the Context
for Theatre of the Oppressed*

CHAPTER FIVE

Toby Emert

Dramatizing Success
Boal Enters the High School Language Arts Classroom

> *"It's weird how much emotion you can show just with your body and no words."*
> —Sarah, 10th grade English student at McRae High School

NESTLED AT THE END of a city street, McRae High School[1] is a squat building with a nondescript brick façade. Three dirt-brown doors at the common entrance confront faculty, staff, students, and visitors, but in stark contrast, stained glass panels, designed by McRae students, flank the doors: a winged dragon rises up on the left, and below the dragon a rainbow mosaic spells out the school's name in pointy letters. The dissonance between the forbidding doors and the colorful bits of glass that surround them is a striking metaphor for this unique school. Located in a small municipality in a Mid-Atlantic state, McRae is the only alternative public high school in its county's system. It was founded in 1988 to address the needs of students who were struggling to be academically successful in "traditional" classrooms, and its approach to learning, based on William Glasser's Choice Theory, is still considered experimental, even after twenty years of implementation. Glasser, best known as a behavioral psychologist, imagines schools where personal responsibility is the ethos with regard to behavioral choices,[2] mediation is the preferred approach to conflict when it arises, and "quality" projects—assignments that ask students to demonstrate their deep commitment to learning—are the primary assessments (Rose, 2003, p. 53).

A language arts classroom at McRae became the setting for the Theatre of the Oppressed (TO) Image Theatre project described in this chapter. When I conceived the idea for the project, I was honing my understanding of Boal's methods and my skills as a joker by taking monthly workshops at the Theatre of the Oppressed Laboratory (TOPLAB) in New York. My training as an actor and director allowed me to understand how I might use Boal's exercises and structures to develop drama projects that focus on awareness and action, but I was also committed to imagining ways in which the philosophies and practices might translate for use in middle and high school classrooms, especially language arts classes, where I was regularly working as a coach and teaching artist.

The reading I had been doing and the workshops I was participating in at TOPLAB had already begun to transform my thinking about the potential aims of theatre. Before encountering Boal's work, my theatre training had been quite traditional, with a heavy focus on the production values typically associated with a well-rehearsed set of performances for paying audiences: set and costume design, a script written by a playwright, forceful artistic direction, and rich character portrayals based on weeks of analysis. I had considered theatre a competitive art form; only those with the most talent, training, and luck were likely to be successful in getting cast or hired. So, Boal's concept of a democratic theatre practice that privileges the idea of a spect-actor and drama as a mode to develop community awareness and social action challenged much of what I thought I knew. I wondered how I might translate his ideas for use in classroom instruction. Specifically, I began to consider how Boal's dramatic structures could be adapted to help students examine their "classroom" identities—who they become when they enter formal learning spaces—and to question how those identities affect their interest, comprehension, and level of academic achievement.

Public school classrooms in the United States are too often regulated spaces, numbed by routine and intransigence—traits that dull the expectations and educational experiences of students. Boal insists that our bodies have been mechanized by repetitive movements to respond in predictable ways to any number of situations, but that through attentive de-mechanization exercises we can develop bodily awareness that may alter our programmed behaviors. Classrooms are filled with bodies—of both students and teachers—mechanized to behave, unconsciously, in expected ways. Rao (2008) suggests that Boal's Image Theatre, with its emphasis on body-based representations of concepts, can be an effective tool for exploring "embodied meanings" (p. 552). This idea seemed an apt philosophical starting point as I contemplated how to translate Boal's ideas to design an intervention for students that asked them to de-mechanize their bodies and their intellectual and emotional responses to the day-to-day routine of their class, and I especially wanted to give them opportunities to reconsider their sense of power and responsibility within a setting in which they often felt disengaged and disempowered. I understood that I would be re-purposing Boal's strategies for using theatre as a tool for political engagement, but, as an educator, I was interested to envision instructional interventions that incorporated the theoretical and practical structures that undergird TO. I had the sense that Boal's articulation of the idea of "mechanization" might be an important concept, particularly when designing instruction for students who have the demonstrated capacity to succeed in schools,[3] but who are resistant to the familiar paradigms of schooling in American classrooms.

The students attending McRae, though bright, have been academically unsuccessful in traditional high schools. The semester that I introduced the project, one English teacher, Ms. Shelby Wickston, was offering a course specifically to allow students to get a graduation credit in language arts because they had failed to do so in the previous semester. The course, "English Through Choice Theory" (ETCT), had the twin goals of mastering language arts concepts and exploring the practical application of Glasser's theory. Ms. Wickston's students were stereotypically "mechanized" to practice a variety of behaviors that are at odds with academic success: nonchalance, procrastination, defiance, refusal to complete assignments, hesitance to engage with the teacher or the content in a meaningful way, tardiness, absenteeism, and the use of denigrating language to describe themselves and their peers. I wondered if Image Theatre, with its steady emphasis on observation and awareness, might serve as a tool for the students as they examined their roles within the school generally and within this language arts class particularly. I wanted to assist them in looking closely at the classroom-based personas they constructed for themselves, knowing that as Adrian Jackson points out in his introduction to Boal's *The Rainbow of Desire* (1995), "looking at the problem ... is a step toward doing something about it" (p. xx). Consciousness has the potential to generate change.

When I presented the idea of collaborating on this project to Ms. Wickston, she willingly accepted the invitation. Like many of the teachers at McRae, Ms. Wickston felt strongly that her role as a teacher involved helping her students recognize and address the oppressions in their own cultures, especially those oppressions that she suggested may be self-imposed.

Introduction to the Project

Ms. Wickston and I met on several occasions early in the semester to discuss the project and the needs of her students. Ultimately we decided I would design a workshop that would encompass three consecutive 90-minute class periods and that would explore the core ideas of the course: the tenets of Glasser's Choice Theory.[4] We chose to focus specifically on Boal's Image Theatre techniques, hoping to elicit dialogues that encouraged the students to analyze their experience of the course. The workshop had three objectives: (1) to invite the students to generate topics for discussion that stemmed directly from their thinking about the course and, more generally, the school; (2) to offer the students an alternative method (Image Theatre) to reflect on their roles within the classroom and their experiences in their English class; and (3) to assess their understanding of the key concepts of the course (especially as they related to Choice Theory, which emphasizes self-awareness, accountability, and personal agency). I wanted to document the experiences of the students during the workshops and, ultimately, draw conclusions about their perceptions of their individual levels of success in the course. I thought of the work as a short-term action research project with a broad guiding question: "What are the responses of high school students to a drama workshop based on Theatre of the Oppressed games-ercises and designed to address a concept related to the language arts curriculum?" I saw myself not only as the joker for the workshops, but also as a teacher-researcher, testing an alternative instructional strategy—Image Theatre—designed specifically to address ideas of self-evaluation and self-advocacy for a group of students for whom those skills did not come easily.

Description of the Workshops

Objectives and Outcomes: A few weeks before the workshops began, I visited Ms. Wickston's students to discuss the project and offer them an outline of learning objectives for the workshops. I wanted to preview the stylistic tone of the sessions and to set expectations for engagement. In that first meeting with the students, I explained that the workshops would ask them to participate in the class in an unorthodox manner by encouraging them to (1) engage their bodies to express scenarios that relate to the key ideas of the class; (2) share personal stories; (3) improvise physical movements and "skits" about designated concepts; (4) observe and reflect orally and in writing on their reactions to the improvisations; and (5) respond to the "skits" through guided group discussion and in writing. I offered a brief introduction to Boal and the history of Theatre of the Oppressed, but only as a frame for the workshop objectives. I told the students they would be participating in an "interactive theatre workshop." I wanted them to understand that the work I would be asking them to do in the sessions was theoretically grounded, but I did not want them to envision themselves as the "oppressed," a term which carries, in the United States, a connotation of helplessness.

In fact, the students in Ms. Wickston's class were attending a school that was designed specifically to support them in being academically successful. Though there were institutional forces that provided tensions—district expectations about performance and achievement, for example—the students were not, in Boal's use of the word to signify those who are politically and socially disenfranchised, "oppressed." (See discussion of this term in *The Rainbow of Desire*, 1995, p. xix.) They were however, as I learned during the workshop sessions, "defeated" by the realities of the larger educational system in which they were participating, and they were struggling to demonstrate a sense of personal power that would foster academic success.

General Overview of the Workshop Design: The workshop spanned three consecutive ETCT class meetings during the last month of the school year. In each session the students worked on a series of acting games adapted from Boal's book *Games for Actors and Non-Actors* (1992). I played the role of Boal's joker, explaining the games, facilitating the process, and encouraging the students to problem-pose (to construct a question and then to explore the question in a variety of ways), especially as they considered their participation in ETCT. The workshops were designed to complement the work that was already taking place in the classroom, and each session served as a regular class meeting. However, honoring the ethos of "choice" that pervaded the school's policies and practices, students had the option of electing not to participate in any given exercise or in any portion of the workshop sessions.

At the conclusion of each workshop session, I asked the students to respond in writing to a survey about their experience of the games, and I ended each session with a short conversation in which they talked with each other and with me about the day's work. I wanted to model the process of reflection for the students, and I wanted to record their reactions to the exercises for later review, as I considered the impact of this instructional intervention. As they talked I made notes and asked clarifying questions. This allowed me, as a facilitator, to make purposeful connections between the sessions, translating some of the themes that emerged from the games and the dialogues. I want to note here that I was aware that my role in the process was not neutral, as is typically the case for Boal's joker; rather, I offered the students a constructed experience of interacting with Boal's games, at times playing the traditional role of "participatory researcher." I had questions about the students' experience of the course that I was interested to answer; at the same time, I wanted to promote dialogues that authentically honored the students' voices, musings, and concerns.

Workshop Session I: Session I began with discussion of a set of guidelines for participation in the workshops, "The Ground Rules for an Interactive Theatre Workshop," which I posted in the classroom so that we could refer to them during the course of the sessions.

1. Speak from your own experience.

2. Respect others in the room—assume there will be disagreement.

3. Come to the discussion as a protagonist, not an antagonist.

4. Step up, step back.

5. Think well of each other.

6. Be aware of the physical and emotional safety of each participant.

7. Call each other by name.

8. Try! Step a bit beyond your safe line.

After the students discussed and agreed to abide by these guidelines, as warm-up for the later work, we moved into a round of "Energy Clap," followed by "Clap Exchange," "Columbian Hypnosis," "Draw Your Own Body," and several variations of "Complete the Image."[5] I wanted to provide an introduction to the idea of Image Theatre that felt both safe and inviting. In the first round of "Complete the Image," the students worked in pairs. As is typical for this game, each pair began the game in a still-life pose of two characters shaking hands, and then continued by improvising a number of two-person poses. Once it was clear from their fluid movement from one pose to another that they understood the basic premise of the game, I asked all of the pairs to freeze. I then explained that we were going to do a "transformation" in which the individual pair-sculpted images would "meld" into one whole group image. I clapped my hands six times, asking the students to take six "steps" toward an improvised collective image. This exercise served as an introduction to the subsequent phase of the workshop: sculpting images in response to a discussion of concepts related to their class. We concluded Session I with an improvised group sculpture of ETCT, in which each student chose a location within the room and simultaneously auto-sculpted a pose for a character/persona representing her- or himself as a student in the class. The result was a collage of individual images that, when observed together, offered a representative picture of the group of "characters" the students tend to play. After the final images were created, we discussed the work the students had done, their reactions to the images, and commented on the characters they had developed.

Workshop Session II: In Session II, we continued the dialogue about the previous day's final images. Initially the students were reticent, but as we moved into a new set of games, they entered the conversation more freely. In the first segment of the session, we played "French Telephone," a game in which the participants stand in a circle and, focusing on the actions of one other person in the circle, begin to emulate those actions. This exercise often leads to a greater sense of connection and group cohesion. It also invites close observation and reflection, key components of the work we would engage in later in the session. We then segued into a round of "Complete the Image" and followed that with an introduction to other sculpting games: "Illustrating a Subject with Your Body" and "Illustrating a Subject Using Other People's Bodies."[6] Using these three primary techniques of Image Theatre, we addressed four key concepts about the students' perceptions of the ETCT classroom, generated in a brainstorming session: argument, conflict, contradiction, and choice. Again, as in the first session, we concluded with a conversation about the day's workshop.

Workshop Session III: Session III continued the image work introduced in Session II. Building on the dialogues from that session, we added dynamizations to the image-making and worked through several transformation exercises. In addition, as the joker, I played the role of "orchestra leader" with several of the images, inviting the students to delve deeper into the characters they had created by improvising short lines for the characters to say. We used those lines as a way of making further meaning of the sculptures. Students played out a number of potential scenarios and "flash" skits—very short scenes, sometimes only a few lines long, based on Boal's idea of Lightning Forum.[7] We focused entirely on ETCT as a concept in this session, exploring the students' perceptions of the course, their frustration with not meeting their own or others' expectations of them academically, and the complications of trying to negotiate the course requirements successfully. Ultimately the images the students created and the subsequent dialogues began to reveal a series of themes that seemed representative of their experiences in ETCT. Words that were repeated in the discussions included argument, conflict, frustration, fear, boredom, escape, regret, and isolation. As the students talked about their images and as they observed each other in the process of sculpting, they began to notice and respond to a prevailing theme that we later labeled "disengagement." The students agreed that they often found reasons to disengage during ETCT.

We constructed images that depicted their perceived "reality" of the classroom situation. I explained that one of the methods for using Image Theatre involves creating images of the current reality and then transforming those images to represent a more "ideal" picture of what the reality could potentially become. To prepare us for the sculpting work, we began with a "Complete the Image" exercise in which each of the participants formed a pose that represented their individual interpretations of the "reality" of ETCT. In jokering the exercise, I suggested that the students create personal images that reflected their current experience of participating in the class.

Once the students had developed their poses, I asked them to freeze, and we titled the final group sculpture, "English Through Choice Theory." Within the group image each pose represented the students' individual reactions to the course. I asked the students if the sculptures seemed representative of their experiences in the class, and they responded that they did. When I asked them to observe and analyze the poses of their classmates, they also suggested that they recognized themselves and others in the class in the sculptures. "That is so our class," one of the students offered as a response to the collective poses. In the ensuing analysis and dialogue, we discussed the overarching issues—such as disillusion, frustration, and lack of motivation—implicitly suggested by the group sculpting exercise.

Identifying Emerging Themes

Later, after the workshops concluded, as I analyzed my field notes, the surveys that the students had completed, and the photographs I had taken, a number of significant themes emerged. Dominant phrases continued to be repeated in the students' responses and in my notes: self-protection, distraction, discon-nection, intensity, resistance, suspicion, struggle, isolation, and desire. In the post-workshop discussions, the students had revealed their growing frustra-tions with the course. At first I did not understand the specifics of their concerns. I recognized the lack of engagement in many of their poses, and we all acknowledged that the images they had created often suggested discon-tented, restless, and unmotivated characters, but I did not initially compre-hend the reasons for the disengagement. The students had selected the course, and the syllabus had been designed to address their particular concerns. This framework suggested that they should find many reasons to interact success-fully with the content of the class and with each other.

The students identified several sources of frustration. They were having difficulty integrating the Choice Theory-based decision-making model into their understanding of themselves as learners, and they were continuing to rely on habitual strategies that had proven unsuccessful for them in other settings and in other classes. As Ms. Wickston had explained to me in our initial meetings, the students in ETCT came to the class with assumptions, beliefs, and behaviors that had not, in the past, worked in their favor. When we discussed these issues, the students expressed feelings of powerlessness. "I'm just afraid that even if I do the work [for the course], I'm going to find out that I didn't do it right, and I won't know until it's too late," one of the students asserted.

Another concurred, "It makes it hard to get motivated, knowing that I could just be wasting my time."

The students explained that it felt as though they could be heading in the wrong direction and that, at any moment, someone could suggest they were not accomplishing what was necessary to complete the course successfully. They used the analogy of building a wall of bricks, only to discover when they finally reached the top, someone was there waiting to push the wall over. It would fall on them, nullifying their hard work, and crushing them in the process. "It's like just waiting to be crushed under the weight of it all," one student offered. This was a potent metaphor for me as I tried to understand the complexities of the issues the students were voicing.

They acknowledged, in the theatrical images they generated and in the conversations that followed, that part of the responsibility for their success lay in their own hands. They articulated concerns, however, that despite their good faith responses to the assignments, they would be penalized at the conclusion of the semester, that some authority figure would deem the work they submitted unacceptable and that ultimately they would fail.[8]

The students' resistant and isolating behaviors, coupled with their tendency toward resignation, left them struggling to imagine viable choices that might change the current reality of their situation as they perceived it. One student's response during the dialogue after the students had created an image of their desire to succeed in the course summarized the prevailing sentiment: "Even though I hate the class, I don't know if I will be able to do anything very differently." The ambivalence in this statement typified the thinking of the students in the workshop. They understood at some level that they had the power to change the circumstances of their educational experiences, but they could not fully envision how to wield that power in ways that would assist them in reaching their goals of academic success.

Drawing Conclusions

In the follow-up conversation I had with the ETCT students when I returned to their classroom a few weeks later to show them the photographs I had taken of our work together and to share my observations on our interactions, they confirmed that their experience of the Boal-based workshops had been significant. They felt they had been able to voice their concerns about the class, that they had comprehended their roles in the classroom in more nuanced ways, and that the themes that emerged during the workshops had mirrored their feelings about their experience of ETCT. They were somewhat surprised that they were able to generate clear and relevant visions of their classroom through the dramatic tableaux they developed. They were, however, in agreement that the ideas that surfaced from the images did, in fact, represent the "reality" of their experiences. The messages of the body became extraordinarily revealing when examined in critical detail. Repeatedly the students pointed out, particularly in the images we created of ETCT, that they saw themselves clearly represented in the sculptures. They expressed their surprise at how obviously the characters they were constructing mirrored the characters they often played in the classroom. They also recognized the behavioral choices that their peers were exhibiting and, by extension, began to explore how the roles they chose to play affected other students in the environment.

I was not surprised that overarching issues for the students were fore-grounded in the workshop. I have seen this phenomenon in other settings in which I played the role of joker and have come to expect it as part of the process. What was confirmed for me as a "researcher," and what is especially relevant for other educators who would consider incorporating similar exercises in their classrooms, is that Image Theatre, as a drama-based class-room activity with its attention to de-mechanizing the body and representing concepts kinesthetically, specifically invites analysis of and reflection on the issues that surface. This is not necessarily the case with other familiar class-room drama interventions—creative dramatics or readers theatre, for example—which rely less on a dialogic response to the work that is generated by the students and more on ideas about illustration and interpretation of composed texts. The creation of the images of content concepts, like Choice Theory, not only required the McRae students to demonstrate their current understanding of the concept, but also to consider the implications of that understanding. In addition, they had the opportunity to witness the images that their peers created, adding both alternative perspectives and nuance to their evolving knowledge base. As one of the students in the workshop responded in the reflective comments he wrote at the end of the second day's activities: "Now I actually see what our class is about."

As we talked about the ETCT classroom experience and the issues affect-ing the learning environment, the students revealed that, in general, they found the dynamics of the classroom contentious. They viewed their peers and themselves as unmotivated and prone to procrastination. They mentioned specific incidents in which students chose behaviors that affected the morale of the entire group: disrespectful interactions with the teacher and/or other classmates, an unwillingness to come to class prepared to engage and exhibit genuine effort, confrontations and arguments, and a tendency to distract and be distracted. And they did not exonerate themselves; they admitted that, in a variety of ways, they each displayed "problematic" behavior that hindered the momentum of the class.

The three workshop sessions, however, revealed the students' capacity to interact in significant ways with each other and with me. They played the games that asked them to collaborate to create integrated portraits of the issues we explored, with a sense of cooperation and connection. They de-signed images in which the characters were close to each other physically; they exhibited a spirit of curiosity and inventiveness; and they talked with each other in relatively sensitive and active ways during the discussion periods. In addition, the conversations generated as a result of the workshops allowed the students to express their personal and collective concerns to each other. As common themes emerged, the students were able to ask each other questions and verify information that had previously puzzled them. At a number of points they came to consensus about important concerns. Ultimately, they left the workshops having conversed with each other in civil and structured ways, marked by candidness. One student commented on the final survey that "this [workshop] has been some kind of life-enriching experience."

The games-ercises in the Theatre of the Oppressed canon draw on the rehearsal techniques used by actors (especially exercises that "de-mechanize" the body and the imagination) to engage the processes of recognition, discovery, empowerment, critical inquiry, and action. The goal of the work is to generate dialogues about important issues for the community who is engaging in it. Boal asserts that everyone possesses the ability to "act," and that theatre has the power to produce deep comprehension and awareness, as well as to encourage action that may transform individuals, and, by extension, the social and cultural situations in which they find themselves tangled.

It seemed clear to me, and eventually to the students, that the Image Theatre workshop invited them to address some of the very real questions that frustrated them. The images encouraged a dialogue that would likely not have occurred without the impetus of the TO-based intervention. The students had an opportunity to compare perceptions about collective concerns and to brainstorm potential action steps for obtaining answers to questions that, unacknowledged and unanswered, might continue to impede their motivation to succeed in the class. They left the workshop with a better understanding of the roles they played within the classroom and with the ability to re-imagine those roles and see themselves as "characters" capable of academic success.

I left the experience with a renewed commitment to how I, as a teacher, artist, and activist, can continue to re-imagine classroom interventions that draw on, but also re-purpose, Boal's canon of techniques. Conducting the workshops with the McRae students confirmed my intuition that the principles of Theatre of the Oppressed can be adapted for classroom experiences that demand a more engaged and critical dialogue from students. And it offered me evidence of the transformation in my own thinking, behavior, and ability to see myself as a co-learner in the classroom spaces I enter.

Notes

1.   The name of the school and the names of all teachers and students are pseudonyms.

2. Students apply for acceptance to McRae, and they must complete the required number of credits each year in order to continue their education there.
3. McRae students routinely score high on IQ tests, for example.
4 Glasser's theory is explained in several books, including *The Quality School* (1998) and *Choice Theory in the Classroom* (1998), but an overarching theme, simply stated, is the belief that humans are responsible for the consequences of the choices they make. Ms. Wickston had articulated a learning goal for ETCT that was specifically related to Glasser's ideas: "Students will learn a great deal of Choice Theory so that they can become leaders at McRae High School, helping new students and faculty understand the theories behind the school, and making use of these theories to improve their present relationships at school and in their private lives."
5. Descriptions of these exercises can be found in *Games for Actors and Non-Actors* (2002) on pages 97, 51, 123, and 139.
6. Descriptions of these exercises can be found in *Games for Actors and Non-Actors* (2002) on pages 176-182.
7. See *The Rainbow of Desire*, (1995) page 63, for a more detailed explanation of Lightning Forum.
8. It is important to note here that Ms. Wickston was not involved in the implementation of the workshop or in the follow-up discussions. She was on long-term medical leave during the final weeks of the semester when the workshop took place. This development in the story of this project is especially significant as it relates to the students' concerns that an "authority figure" would deem their work unsatisfactory. They had lost their teacher, with whom they had built a trusting relationship, and they did not trust that the other adults who might evaluate their assignments would judge them fairly.

References

Boal, A. (1979). *Theatre of the oppressed*. New York, NY: Urizen Books.
—. (1995). *The rainbow of desire: The Boal method of theatre and therapy* (A. Jackson, Trans.). New York, NY: Routledge.
—. (2002). *Games for actors and non-actors* (2nd Ed.). (A. Jackson, Trans.). New York, NY: Routledge.
Rao, R. (2008). The aesthetics of the oppressed/the theatre of urban: Youth and schooling in dangerous times. *Harvard Educational Review*, 78(3), 549-562. Retrieved March 28, 2010, from Research Library. (Document ID: 1575093261).
Rose, S.W. (2003). The relationship between Glasser's quality school concept and brain-based theory. *International Journal of Reality Therapy*, 22(2), 52-56.

CHAPTER SIX

Jennifer L. Freitag, Danielle Dick McGeough, & Aubrey Huber
with Karen S. Mitchell

The Boalian Communication Classroom
A Conversation about the Body, Dialogue, and Social Transformation

KAREN: MARCH 20, 2003: Operation Iraqi Freedom began today. My Performance and Social Change class starts with warm-up exercises and games, but soon it becomes very apparent to me that my students are too preoccupied with the impending war to focus on my planned lesson. Instead of facilitating a dialogue about the invasion in which language is the medium, I ask one of the students to sculpt a group image of how he feels about the events happening this day in our country. He creates an image of USA military forces protecting Iraqi civilians against terrorists. I watch as the students create his image with care and commitment in order for his idea to be seen by the group. True to image theatre, he is never asked to interpret his image; instead, another student silently volunteers to create a different image in response to his. The second student sculpts a figure at the center of the image using two people: one stands helplessly weeping as the other freezes in a crouched position, ready to spring into action, rage evident on her face; they are surrounded by smaller images of violence, death, and torture. After a brief silence, a third student offers an image. Then another student. And another. And another. I witness these achingly beautiful images unfold and realize this is possibly the most profound dialogue I have witnessed in over thirty years of teaching.

In her book *Professing to Learn: Creating Tenured Lives and Careers in the American Research University* (2009), educator Anna Neumann interviews post-tenure professors about their scholarly learning and uncovers experiences that she calls moments of passionate thought. According to Neumann, participants describe these moments "as pockets of deep insight or creation, and of intense 'fulfillment,' 'excitement,' 'exhilaration,' and 'gratification,' instances of beauty frozen in time and space" (p. 62). March 20, 2003 was such a moment for me, a moment made possible through the power that lies at the core of Theatre of the Oppressed.

Over the past fifteen years my teaching and my identity as a teacher have been radically transformed by Theatre of the Oppressed. Through TO, I have witnessed classroom moments of human understanding and critical dialogue that engaged students on intellectual, emotional, and physical levels and in effect changed the thinking of many of my students, a few of whom now use TO in their own teaching.

This essay demonstrates how TO transforms and multiplies, by starting each section with a story from my own experience and then branching out to the stories and experiences of three of my former students who now teach in various parts of the country. All three students encountered TO as undergraduates at the university where I am now a tenured professor. Two of them, in fact, were present in the Performance and Social Change class I described in the opening to this chapter. All three were members of a peer theatre troupe I directed that utilized TO methods, and all three have carried this activist, social justice-centered work forward in their teaching as doctoral students.

This chapter is divided into three sections: Foregrounding the Body, Creating Community Dialogue, and Advocating for Systemic Change. Each section includes a short narrative of my own experience, an introduction to the section written in the collective voice of the three other authors, and an extended dialogue among the three of them describing the tenets of TO and how they incorporate these into their classroom teaching in an effort to create lasting social change. Their discussion is theoretical but always committed to the practical as they share stories, perspectives, and examples of how using TO methods in their classrooms has transformed them and continues to transform others.

Foregrounding the Body

In the body's battle with the world, the senses suffer. And we start to feel very little of what we touch, to listen to very little of what we hear and to see very little of what we look at .... [The body] has to be reharmonised.
—Augusto Boal, *Games for Actors and Non-Actors*, p. 49

Karen: NYC, May 1994. I'm lying on a sofa bed in a hotel somewhere in Manhattan. Every muscle in my body aches, burns, screams to be deadened. I have just experienced my first five hours of a workshop with Boal, five hours dedicated to de-mechanizing the body. As an academic I am aware that I lead a sedentary life—not enough exercise, too many hours at a computer or hunched over a desk grading. I have forgotten my body, but after one session with Boal,

I learn my body has neither forgotten nor forgiven me for this neglect. I hurt to the bone. Just as I am drifting off to sleep I have a thought: if I do these exercises with my students in class, they will drop the course before the second week. A year later, I discover the contrary: the undergraduate students in my Performance and Social Change class, from organizational communication to secondary teaching majors, wholly embrace it.

The three of us came to TO through Karen's teaching. Jenn and Danielle were undergraduate students in communication studies, and Aubrey in education. Jenn began teaching as a graduate student and did not realize until years later that her approach to teaching was critical, liberatory, and directly influenced by Karen's Boalian and Freirian pedagogy. Having grown up in a family of educators committed to cultivating engaged citizens, Danielle was instantly attracted to Karen's interactive methods that link learning with social engagement. As a traditionally trained educator, Aubrey encountered Karen's approach and integrated it into her own teaching, no doubt influencing her desire to study critical pedagogy in her graduate program.

Together, we begin our conversation where Boal's work begins: the body. As the three of us (Jenn, Danielle, and Aubrey) began to reflect on how we use Theatre of the Oppressed to teach undergraduate classes, we were struck by how strongly all of us foreground the body in our teaching. We view the body as foundational for teaching through TO, because without an awareness of the body—of the self—we do not believe true dialogue that leads to transformation can occur. In this section, we discuss the importance of the body for using TO methods in our classrooms. To do this, we make a direct link to Boal's Image Theatre, which literally begins with the body: individuals form frozen images to encourage an alternative kind of dialogue not usually found in traditional classrooms. Boal encourages us to begin in the body as a way to connect viscerally to social problems, and we have found his techniques useful for helping our students not only connect to social problems, but connect with themselves.

Jenn: I believe the first step for using TO methods in the classroom is to consider the body—especially how power operates through the body. I try to acknowledge that my body, depending on how I choose to use it in the classroom, communicates specific meanings. I attempt to embody a self-reflexive pedagogical practice that begins with my body. To do this, I de-center my physical authority, as the person in charge of the classroom, by sitting in a circle with my students and speaking with them as equals. I use my body in ways that create an environment in which my students feel validated and respected as individuals.

Aubrey: In order to teach through the body, it is necessary to re-introduce undergraduate students to their bodies as a way for them to learn to appreciate the value of embodied knowing. We learn with our bodies. Through physical repetitions, we learn bodily memory. This knowledge is stored in one's skin, muscle tissue, and bones. Embodied knowledge is understood through the flesh instead of through cognition. In an undergraduate public speaking or performance classroom, I find Boal's games help students gain awareness of their bodies—how the body moves, how it is disciplined, where it aches, and what it likes. This awareness helps students to first understand themselves and then to help them begin to explore learning through their own embodied experience.

Danielle: For me, the most powerful moments of learning occur through the body because it is so difficult to discipline. In TO learning happens when our bodies fail to hold an image or unintentionally respond to a situation. Two people accidently touch and recognize their interdependence. A repeated hand gesture causes a student to recall a past interaction. A woman feels anger while holding a violent image and is scared by this revelation. Another student is surprised when a tear falls down his cheek. It is the things we fail to discipline (our emotions, memories, and bodily tensions) that leak knowledge and understanding.

In my undergraduate public speaking classes, I instruct students to create sequential tableau images of a selected situation involving public speaking anxiety, the ideal public speaking situation, and the transition between the two. The activity begins with students working in small groups to devise a list of frequently occurring fears surrounding public speaking. Each group then selects a fear from the list and builds a still image of the situation, as well as an image of how the public speaking event would appear if the fear were allevi-ated. Each group presents and discusses their tableau with the larger group. This activity allows those who have difficulty articulating ideas with words to join the conversation. The activity also encourages students to consider how anxieties surrounding public speaking affect the body. I ask students to point out where the body tenses, shakes, or struggles to hold an image.

Aubrey: Sometimes I start with a verbal dialogue to help illustrate to students how experiences are marked on our bodies. For example, we might discuss where we grew up and how that might be communicated nonverbally through our bodies. After students are able to share verbally, they are then able and more willing to show how they feel with their bodies. Instead of talking about the place students live, I ask them to show me in their bodies what that place looks like. The images express many possibilities for further dialogue, human connection, and social change.

Jenn: I vividly recall my first encounter with Image Theatre as an undergraduate in Karen's Performance and Social Change class several years ago: I remember feeling nervous when she asked us to create an image of oppression. I remember the tenseness in my back and shoulders as I held the image. I remember my surprise at the emotional reaction I was experiencing in this frozen bodily position of pain, submission, and fear. I felt anger rise in my chest, and I felt my heart begin to pump faster as my body communicated its connection to previous experiences of violence. And as I took in others' images in the room, I realized things that had not occurred to me before: that I was not alone, that conditions of oppression exist between and across individuals, and that there was great power in the exploration of these conditions through the performance of our bodies in still images. I connected with my own pain, but I also came to understand the notion of the personal as political. I think starting with personal experience helps students to begin to explore how their bodies fit within systems of dominant ideology. These experiences are material realities, and Image Theatre draws attention to the materiality—the concreteness, the real-ness—of power structures and how individual bodies are affected. In Image Theatre, we can ask how our bodies are marginalized and how they might participate in systems of oppression.

Creating Community Dialogue

All the participants in a forum session learn something, become more aware of some problems that they did not consider before, because a standard model is challenged and the idea that there are alternatives is clearly demonstrated.
—Augusto Boal, quoted in Taussig & Schechner, 1990, pp. 61-62

Karen: January 1997. Today is the start of spring semester, and I have already screwed up. Completing one three-day workshop with Boal hardly makes me an expert in TO. I experienced the power in my workshops in New York, but I didn't realize teaching TO would force me to question everything I thought I knew about teaching. Embracing critical pedagogy is time-consuming, emotionally challenging, and scary. First, I change how I view the power and status of the student/teacher relationship. Then I try to unpack the power relationship between student and teacher. My students and I discuss the concept of oppression." As white, middle-class U.S. citizens (which we are), can we truly understand oppression?" I have no answer. We struggle as we analyze external and internal oppressions, explore the inconsistencies in society and culture, and practice TO.

Dialogue cannot occur without the foundation of an engaged body. We view dialogue as an extension of individual bodies communicating with one another in a critical, reflexive conversation. This is where we feel authentic education occurs. A critical dialogue involves brainstorming solutions for societal problems and embodies Freire's (1970) concept of authentic thinking in which individuals work interdependently to transform their reality (p. 58). Boal's Forum Theatre applies this idea to the body by asking individuals to become spect-actors (not spectators, but actual actors) in theatrical scenes to rehearse solutions to societal problems. We apply this idea to our teaching by attempting to create dialogue which engages our students in intellectual, emotional, and physical ways. We see our approach to creating dialogue in our classes as mirroring, if not explicitly practicing, Boal's Forum Theatre. For us, this means we both explicitly use Boal's techniques and employ a Boalian approach in our classrooms that may not explicitly use his techniques, but embodies the soul and foundation of Boalian praxis. In other words, we carry the essence of Boal's praxis into our classrooms through our attitudes and the way we use our bodies in the classroom. We ask: How are we creating community? How are we facilitating dialogue? How do our bodies participate or intervene in dominant ideologies and systemic oppressions? We use a Boalian approach both in practice (explicit techniques) and ideology (attitude and approach that influences our pedagogical philosophy whether or not that includes explicit Boalian techniques).

Danielle: As I reflect on my own experiences as a student, I remember the TO classroom as a space of *communitas*, meaning there was a sense of togetherness and equality. In Performance for Social Change, Karen introduced the class to controversial issues pertaining to race, sexuality, gender, and class. Karen encouraged students to connect course content to everyday life by sharing their own experiences verbally or using Forum or Image Theatre. Through acts of sharing, students were able to teach one another and moments of human understanding were created. A community of mutual respect formed a safe place for diverse and conflicting opinions to emerge. Though subtly, Karen's use of TO changed the student-teacher relationship, inviting students to take control of their own education.

Jenn: I agree, and this is why I try to create community with my students as opposed to imposing community on them. I attempt to engage with my students, not as a teacher, but as a facilitator of a process we will all experience together, one predicated on the connections established among us as a community. This forms the basis for dialogue in which we all are respectful of what is shared, and one in which we can all be challenged to think critically and ask ourselves tough questions. When they feel a sense of community students can be challenged to reflect on their privilege without becoming blatantly disrespectful to others. I have witnessed heated dialogues in my classes between white students and students of color I thought might result in anger and division, but instead I have found these students happily conversing with one another in the hallway after class. This is what community means.

Aubrey: Fostering community in my classroom is integral to my application of critical pedagogy and TO. As a teacher I want my students to be able to dialogue among themselves with the intention of discussing issues that directly affect their lives. As a teacher I want to foster tools, skills, and knowledge that will enable them to change their own lives. To do this throughout my public speaking and pedagogy courses, I work with students so they can facilitate classroom debates, presentations, and discussions. This means at different times during the class, students become facilitators of discussion by raising alternative viewpoints; asking questions about power, privilege, and access; and problem-posing to encourage their classmates to think critically and holistically about issues important to them. Student-facilitated discussions give students the opportunity to understand power on multiple levels from multiple perspectives as well as develop methods of change. This practice is firmly rooted in Freire's (1970) idea of *conscientização* or consciousness-raising in which one locates systemic problems in order to strategize ways of enacting change.

Danielle: I find Image Theatre techniques useful when students are struggling to form their opinion on a controversial subject. Image Theatre is particularly useful for dialogues concerning marriage equity, interracial relationships, or exploring the different positions taken by political candidates. For example, I may ask students to construct an image that represents their feelings about a current event, such as the controversy surrounding the construction of a Muslim mosque near Ground Zero. A student creates, then plays with and/or alter the image until it portrays what (s)he is feeling. Then another student may choose to alter the image further. First year students, for example, may not have had many opportunities to express their positions on difficult subjects and therefore may struggle to articulate their ideas. I find image work, such as this, helps students express opinions still forming because it does not require the same specificity or commitment as a persuasive speech or opinion paper. Moreover, the images never belong to one particular student but to the entire class, and this helps the class to participate and interact as a community. Individual participation is necessary to make the activity progress, but the product is always a community creation. Students who have reservations about verbally participating in classroom discussion have approached me after class to express how much they enjoyed the activity because it allowed them to participate using new, nonverbal modes of communication. Through the use of Image Theatre in the classroom, students are able to nurture the modes of communication with which they are comfortable while developing other modes of expressing themselves.

Jenn: When I facilitate dialogue in my classes, I attempt to play the Boalian joker in various ways. I avoid manipulating students to accept certain perspectives, I play devil's advocate with my students to promote critical thinking, and I watch out for magical solutions or discussion closers that offer answers that are too easy or simplistic given the issue we are discussing.

Aubrey: For the reasons Jenn mentioned, I find Freire's problem-posing useful for facilitating dialogue. In my public speaking classroom I invite students to bring in current events that illustrate problems prevalent within the community. As a class we create scenes that highlight community issues and feed into oppressive systems, and in the process reveal the messiness and complexity of oppression. I ask for one volunteer to share an image. That person creates an image in the middle of the classroom, and one by one six to ten students add to the image. The remaining students and I walk around the image describing what we see. Through this embodied image and description students are made aware of their dual roles as the oppressed and those that oppress others.

Jenn: I also use problem-posing in my public speaking courses, although not always as explicitly as Aubrey has described. For example, I encourage my students to create speeches to communicate something that needs to change in society and to generate possible solutions. I challenge them to speak out on social issues in which they have a stake. Students' speeches function as prompts for dialogue and potential social action that may occur outside the walls of the classroom. On the surface, it might seem I am just assigning run-of-the-mill motivational speeches, but as a class we are actually embodying Freirian and Boalian ideals that change the goal of these assignments from skill application to social transformation. This begins with the way I assign the speech: I encourage students to choose an issue they are passionate about wanting to change, and I require them to offer a specific call to all of us in the class toward action on that issue with ways we can meet that invitation. We also discuss the speeches after they are given to question the likelihood students will actually take action on that issue when they leave the classroom. I have noticed a large difference in students' intentions to take action than when I do not use a problem-posing strategy for this assignment. Students' topics are much more geared toward social change, and students seem more motivated to do something about these social issues when they leave the classroom. Most recently, some of the topics my students have addressed include environmental issues, human trafficking, diamond purchasing, and various topics that deal with policy change. I ask my students to think critically, propose solutions to societal problems, and start dialogue with their classmates about how to make change occur. So even when I'm not utilizing TO methods explicitly in my classroom, my approach reflects TO's philosophy of engagement, dialogue, and social transformation.

Advocating for Systemic Change

In Theatre of the Oppressed, reality is shown not only as it is, but also, more importantly, as it could be. Which is what we live for—to become what we have the potential to be.
—Augusto Boal, *Games for Actors and Non-Actors*, p. 6

Karen: April 14, 2010. I am sitting in a classroom on a beautiful spring afternoon listening to my colleagues discuss our department's outcomes assessment plan. I think about the goals and outcomes listed on my syllabus for my Performance and Social Change class, and I know the most important goal I have for my students is they become lifelong advocates for social justice. This goal is not listed because it cannot be documented. I bring TO into my classroom because I believe the process and practice of Theatre of the Oppressed has the potential to change me, my students, our campus, and our community. As I continue my work semester after semester in hope of transforming individuals and society, I know I may never have concrete proof of the change my students make in the world. Systemic change takes years, lifetimes, generations. I simply continue to trust Boal's method and believe lasting social change is possible, even if it isn't listed on our outcomes assessment plan.

Just as Boal's goal in Theatre of the Oppressed work was to "reshape the human objective" (1985, p. 14), so is our goal in the classroom. As the bodies of individuals become demechanized and more socially conscious, and as they begin to engage in critical, transformative dialogue, they become a collective that shifts cultural norms and social conditions. Boal's (1998) Legislative Theatre makes such change tangible as it attempts to reshape laws and policies. Although transformation may not be as easily measured in our classrooms, our work is always inspired by Boal's dedication to actualized change on the systemic level. Not only are we interested in transforming the lives of individual students, but we also strive to radically transform the contemporary educational system.

Danielle: The idea of facilitating systemic change in the classroom is overwhelming, so I try to start small. I ask students to be self-reflective about their everyday behaviors and language choices and to consider how those choices contribute to either social equality or oppression.

Jenn: Regardless of the class I am teaching, I always focus throughout the semester on the ways language structures reality. For example, I ask students, in groups, to generate a list of all the synonyms or descriptive words used to describe men, and then all those used for women. We analyze the lists to locate patterns that tell us something about the way discourse functions to either reify or resist the system of gender. As students make realizations about how our language is intertwined with cultural attitudes and behaviors, they begin to speak out against words used to describe gender identity. The next class period, students tell me they talked about our exercise with friends or family. As we begin to dialogue and intervene in oppressive systems beyond the walls of our classroom, our intervention is no longer rehearsal but actual action toward the transformation of our reality.

Aubrey: I think dialogue itself is transformational. Boal's work is about creating revolutionary dialogue. TO allows groups to move out into the community to facilitate change. Through student-facilitated discussions and image work, I have witnessed students' recognition of their white privilege. I have witnessed students' revelations about how they benefit from heterosexual privilege, and I have seen students sign petitions, vote in elections, and join social justice campaigns for the first time.

Jenn: Boal's approach embodies hope for change. In many ways this potentiality underlies everything I do as an educator. I view classrooms as spaces in which Boal's "rehearsal for transformation of reality" (Democracy Now, 2005, para. 8) can occur. The classroom becomes a space actively disrupting what Freire refers to as the banking system of education, a space in which the teacher's power is de-centered and collaborative dialogue is the approach. It becomes a space in which minds and bodies become engaged in education; it becomes a space in which self-reflexive dialogue is practiced so that it might begin to transform communication inside the classroom and beyond it. In my public speaking class, I ask students to situate their bodies on a "disagree—agree" continuum as I read value statements such as, "McDonald's does more harm than good for the world" or "Men are stronger than women." They situate their bodies in relation to how they feel about the statement, and then we engage in verbal dialogue about where we place our bodies. As we articulate various positions, we move along the continuum as we become persuaded by arguments offered by one another. Not only are students asked to learn and utilize skills for persuasion and public speaking (an objective of the class), they also are encouraged to reflect on their own opinions. Most importantly, they are given permission to—encouraged to—amend their position when they feel inclined to do so. They move their bodies, and this movement is the foundation for realizing how individual social consciousness leads to collective social transformation.

Danielle: It is difficult to find ways to measure whether a seed for social change was planted or if students learned a new way of moving their bodies, gained new perspectives, or became cognizant of a social issue through critical dialogue.

Jenn: I do see evidence of individual change in my course evaluations, anonymous informal feedback, and emails from my students. Their feedback reminds me of how revolutionary these methods are in the traditional United States educational system. I am often told by students in my classes that I am an unconventional teacher, and that what we do as a class not only helps to create a community in which they are comfortable interacting with and speaking in front of one another, but it helps them to learn things about themselves. They reiterate the importance of building community, engaging bodies in the classroom, and facilitating dialogue that matters in their lives. I also see the evidence of TO's ability to promote social transformation through my life and the lives of others who were introduced to these methods through Karen's classes and are now living these in our own classrooms.

Danielle: Exactly, Jenn. I trust TO because I am acutely aware of the impact of having been taught by someone using TO methods in the classroom. As a student who was exposed to Boalian techniques as an undergraduate and graduate student, I can say Boalian methods drastically challenged the way I learned, and now challenge the way I teach. TO engages students intellectually, emotionally, and physically, and offers educators the tools to link knowledge with social transformation.

On March 29, 2009 Augusto Boal gave his last public address for World Theatre Day. He spoke eloquently about the transformative power of theatre:

> When we look beyond appearances, we see oppressors and oppressed people, in all societies, ethnic groups, genders, social classes and casts; we see an unfair and cruel world. We have to create another world because we know it is possible. But it is up to

us to build this other world with our hands and by acting on the stage and in our own life. (Boal, 2009, para. 7)

When coupled with actions rehearsed through TO, passionate thoughts such as this may very well change the world.

The four of us believe in the power of Theatre of the Oppressed in the classroom because we are living proof of its transformative potential. All of us have been changed by the work, and its impact can be seen in the ways we carry TO forward into our classes, as well as how we witness its impact on another generation of students. The movement from body to dialogue to social change is foundational for our continued commitment to pedagogy that is passionate, engaged, and liberatory. Our conversation may end here, but we hope the dialogue about this work continues far beyond these pages among teachers and social justice activists around the world.

References

Boal, A. (1985). *Theatre of the oppressed* (C. A. McBride & M. L. McBride, Trans.). New York, NY: Theatre Communications Group. (Original work published 1974).

—. (1998). *Legislative theatre: Using performance to make politics* (A. Jackson, Trans.). New York, NY: Routledge.

—. (1992). *Games for actors and non-actors.* (A. Jackson, Trans.). New York, NY: Routledge.

—. (March 27, 2009). World theatre day message. September 6, 2009 from http://www.iti-worldwide.org/theatredaymessage.html

Democracy Now! Web Site. (2005, June 3). Famed Brazilian artist Augusto Boal on the "Theatre of the Oppressed." June 1, 2009 from http://www.democracynow.org/2005/6/3/famed_brazilian_artist_augusto_boal_on

Freire, P. (1970). *Pedagogy of the oppressed.* (M.B. Ramos, Trans.). New York, NY: Continuum Publishing.

Jackson, A. (1992). Translator's postscript to the first edition (pp. xxii–xxvii). *Games for actors and non-actors* (2nd ed.) (A. Jackson, Trans.). New York, NY: Routledge.

Neumann, A. (2009). *Professing to learn: Creating tenured lives and careers in the American research university.* Baltimore, MD: The Johns Hopkins University Press.

Taussig, M., & Schechner, R. (1990). Boal in Brazil, France, the USA: An interview with Augusto Boal. *The Drama Review, 34,* 50-65.

CHAPTER SEVEN

Jenny Wanasek & Mark Weinberg

The One-Line Play
Elaborations on Image Theatre

THE ONE-LINE PLAY, a Theatre of the Oppressed innovation we developed through our work at the Center for Applied Theatre[1] (CAT) in Milwaukee, is a process that modifies Boal's Image Theatre and dynamization techniques. It also draws on elaborations of TO taught to us by the many practitioners from whom we have learned over the years, the transformative language techniques outlined by Kegan and Lahey (2001) in their book *How the Way We Talk Can Change the Way We Work: Seven Languages for Transformation*, and our many years of traditional theatre training.[2] CAT, founded in 2003, began as a TO performance company focused on developing and touring Forum plays about problems faced by school age youth. That arm of the Center still exists, but its community-based work—with a wide variety of student, educator, worker, advocacy, and service groups—has relied increasingly on Image Theatre based techniques, and the One-Line Play has become the primary technique we use in our work.

Grounded in the pedagogical theories of Paulo Freire and the analysis of cultural identity and politics proposed by Giroux and Grossberg (1994), hooks (1994, 2006) and others, the One-Line Play process is designed to guide participants in the (re)definition of issues and the development of problem solving techniques and public agreements based on their emerging belief in personal and group agency. Many of our recent workshops have focused on participants breaking out of cycles of conflict and under-achievement, and on difficult dialogues surrounding issues of power dynamics, racism, and ethnocentrism.

Often TO work begins with the presupposition that the participants have identified a known oppressor. The goal of the work at these times is to develop strategies to fight the oppression—usually by thwarting the desires or actions of the oppressor. Although undeniably useful, at times such work can result in the relatively simple structuring of melodramatic narratives in which the villain/oppressor must be defeated by the aware hero/oppressed.

One of the differences between our work and that kind of battle planning is that most of the time the people with whom we work have not yet defined the causes of their problems (i.e., there is no clearly known or understood oppressor), and perhaps because of that, they feel powerless to effect change. At other times, the issue for groups is a lack of awareness about perceptions and biases rather than the need to strategize responses to a known, pre-existing oppressor. We use the One-Line Play process to encourage awareness of perceptions and analysis of causes. This frequently includes looking at ineffectual choices participants previously made in the face of difficulties, but it does not necessarily include finding specific solutions. Another use of the One-Line Play process is to help participants identify skills for handling pressures they will probably have to face in the future, such as students entering high school concerned about the pressures to drop out or halfway house residents concerned about staying out of prison when they are released.

This is not to say that concrete action plans do not result from these workshops. When we work in long term association with non-governmental organizations (NGOs), or other groups, there is usually a need for an action plan. In those cases we share a process by which participants can develop specific public agreements for action. However, our first steps are to raise questions that reveal beliefs and assumptions about others and to challenge those beliefs, thereby preventing participants from becoming inadvertent oppressors or abusing power.

While problem-solving is the ultimate task, an essential prerequisite is promoting a sense of agency. We do that in three ways: treating all contributions with respect while subjecting them to honest inquiry; providing physical ways of discovering the nature/causes of difficulties (which bypasses complaining and leads to meaningful dialogue); and increasing options by sharing problem-solving tools and techniques.

Theoretical Underpinnings

Put simply, we believe that the great power of TO is that it promotes people using and hearing their own voices to critically analyze their own perceptions, their statements about those perceptions, their actions based on those perceptions, and the consequences of those actions. We base these assumptions on the central premises about dialogue and democracy propounded by Augusto Boal and Paulo Freire. Both assert that the road to transformation begins with learning through dialogue, which must itself begin with the beliefs of those seeking change. This assertion assumes the ability of everyone to create knowledge and then to question and use what they have learned (Freire, 1995, p. 69; Boal, 2002, pp. xxiii-xxiv).

We assert that social transformation is only possible if those who desire change see themselves as having agency. Only then will they invest the energy in analysis and take the risk of action to make changes in society (and often in themselves). In the Acknowledgments section of *Between Borders: Pedagogy and the Politics of Cultural Studies* (1994) the editors note that "the production of knowledge, values, and cultural identities takes place within particular social, historical, cultural, institutional, and textual formations" (p. ix). We also assert that these "formations," and the ways in which people use language within them, establish restrictive, and often oppressive, power structures which are supported through narrative and representation. Lack of agency (oppression) can be understood from this perspective as a learned understanding of one's self, molded by these pressures.[3]

TO, and particularly the Image Theatre based work that CAT does, challenges the concept of inevitability, embodies learning, embraces ambiguity, and promotes what Freire called "conscientization." The One-Line Play process promotes the primacy of the body and the senses, opening paths to discovery that are often blocked by the very structure of verbal language. The words that participants use in response to the images created as part of the process are grounded in immediate experience and are both visceral and reflective—a stimulating amalgam of observation, interpretation, discovery, and desire. As Boal puts it in *The Aesthetics of the Oppressed* (2006): "Art is the search for truths by means of our sensory equipment ... rather than only using the symbolic language of words dissociated from the concrete, sensible realities, to which they refer" (p. 5). Every image, constructed without signs and language labels, provides a new context for examination of power and position—it is an articulation of both "is" and "what if."

The One-Line Play Process

The One-Line Play process encourages participants to explore and challenge oppressions by re-assembling elements of their social structure through images. While it is based on Image Theatre as Boal describes it in *Games for Actors and Non-Actors* (2002), it differs significantly in animation and the dynamization of images to delineate the nature of difficulties and determine possible solutions. The One-Line Play approach is a vehicle that assists jokers and participants in the process of problem definition. It is very flexible and often quickly reveals the core difficulties with which participants are dealing. We have used it in brief workshops with students—which have focused on everything from violence to self-advocacy to educational success to healthy choices—and in multi-day workshops with cultural workers and faculty on topics as varied as racism, difficult dialogues, worker/management relations, and student engagement.

The One-Line Play begins with an image followed by one line of dialogue from each person in the image and a single shift of position by everyone in the image at the same time to activate it. In the sections that follow we describe the One-Line Play process and then trace its use in a particular multi-visit experience. Finally, we describe our method of co-jokering which, while not a necessary element of the One-Line Play process, provides a significant enhancement to the work of CAT.

Our process for working with a group always begins with a brief welcome and then games and exercises, some of which are drawn from the arsenal of TO, such as "Fill The Space," "Car and Driver," "Colombian Hypnosis," and "Complete the Image" (Boal, 2002), and others which challenge groups to balance individual and community responsibility, such as "Line Races," "Chain Tag," "Everybody's It," and "Cross the Circle."[4] Physical play before work affords us the opportunity to demonstrate and foster joy in expression and delight in discovery. We conclude the games segment with "Image Circle," in which everyone self-sculpts simultaneously in response to a word or phrase.[5] Then we move to group image building. In this phase of the workshop, we suggest a topic and the group creates an image in the center of the room in response to the suggested topic. One person begins by taking a static position, and one by one, other participants join the image by taking positions in relation to the people already in place. We remind participants that the images must be static and that if they change to accommodate someone who enters after them, the group loses their original unique contribution. We also emphasize the importance of silence.

We often begin with a demonstration, asking the participants to create an image of a birthday party. After a few participants have entered the image, we ask those watching to tell us what they see in the image. There is usually general agreement about the situation, but the varied descriptions of the roles of individuals provide the participants with a focus for debate and analysis. The people in the center are not given the sole right to explain the role and function of the characters they have created, and the people outside the image become contributors to the implied narrative and its meaning. After the participants note what they see, we ask two questions: "What do you see that makes you think that?" and "What else might it be?" These questions keep the discussion open-ended and remind the participants that they are the creators of meaning in the room. This simple example illustrates technique, de-centers power, and begins the dialogic process in earnest.

We then ask participants to break up into small groups to begin the One-Line Play process. We ask them to create a group image in response to a suggestion from us. As part of the planning process we try to create a phrase that will relate to the issue we were hired to examine, but not tell the participants how to respond or what to sculpt. We have used phrases like "someone doesn't know what to do because someone is being hurt" (the issue was unintentional emotional violence), "someone can't get what they need" (self-advocacy), "someone has been made to feel small" (violence and bullying), "the communication process breaks down." We encourage participants to sculpt their group images without words—sculpting in response to each other in silence disrupts existing power struggles. The images must be shown to other participants without words, movement, or explanation.

After all images are shown to the other participants, we begin to dynamize them one at a time. The first step is to have every person in the image speak a single line–the One-Line Play.[6] As in Boal's "Image of the Word" and its dynamization, we invite the people in the image to speak a line of dialogue that fits with the character they believe they are portraying. Next, we ask a specific question of those in the image and ask them to respond to the question by making a single move, all making only one change in position. All participants in the image move at the same time. Our dynamizing questions are based on the issue and the image. Some questions we have used are: What would make things better? What would make them worse? What will happen next? What happened 30 seconds before this image? What would it look like if everyone in the image got what they want? We find this one line and one move a fruitful ground for observation on our part and the participants. We ask them questions about the result of their moves and invite everyone to analyze as well.

We sometimes vary the process, making it similar to "simultaneous dramaturgy" in which those outside the image "write" one line for each of the characters they see in the image. Those lines (instead of lines they created for themselves, as in the previous description) are delivered by the "characters" before each person gets to make one movement, taking into account their original position, the line of dialogue written for them by someone outside the image, and the question asked by the jokers. After the image shift, those not in the image briefly describe and interpret what they see. This writing of lines from the outside is often a useful second step in creating new One-Line Plays after those in the image have created one from the line they chose themselves. The process is repeated with every other group image in the room, but the dynamizing questions vary. By the time four or five groups have made their plays, the room is filled with the implied dialogue of comparison and contrast of images and changes. In other words, the participants have already begun a dialogue which is grounded in the images and the perceptions gained from analyzing them. The creation of this participatory aesthetic space allows the ensuing exploration, whether through discussion or reworking of images, to focus on the specific words and actions of the *characters* in the plays and to extrapolate from them to the reality of the participants. This kind of interaction circumvents individual blame and personal friendships or animosities that had developed from the unexamined problems before the workshops began.

The process continues by developing the images that resonate the most with the participants. Often they want to re-sculpt images, provide entirely new but contrasting sculptures, or try new lines of dialogue. As Jokers we problematize the work by asking questions, often about causes or consequences, and usually couched in terms of "what if?" Participants speak in their own voices and with their own bodies and are heard. They experiment and problem-solve, not simply blame external causes or succumb to what they see as narrative inevitability. Suggestions from participants come so rapidly that it feels like a creative explosion in the room as people shout out new suggestions, argue about consequences for actions they've seen, and challenge one another's opinions. Our function as jokers at this time is to channel this creative frenzy so that as many of the opinions voiced can be tried and analyzed as possible. We choose the plays that have generated the most intense reactions and attack them one at a time, trying as many of the suggestions as we can. Without a doubt, the most challenging work on our part is to make sure we're listening to—and hearing—what the people we're serving want to explore and making observations which suggest to participants how the relationship of events in the room might reveal associations between actions and consequences.

We believe that their rapid and active processing of ideas and affirmation of voice and agency is more significant than any particular problem/solution pairing. In every instance it is the role of the jokers to keep dialogue open and to support each individual's right to see, speak, and transform. More elaborate dynamization and Forum techniques can extend the discussion, but the structure and performance of the One-Line Plays provides a short and intense path to meaningful and public exploration of issues through an embodied, engaging and empowering discourse.

The Case of "DJ"

DJ, a young man in an alternative high school for kids who could not or would not function in the "traditional" classroom had constructed an image of his current situation in response to our suggestion that he sculpt "what prevents you from achieving your goal." He said that after bouncing around to different schools he "really wanted to graduate from this one." He sculpted an image of friends who distracted him, family members who weighed him down with their own needs, and others who promised quick rewards selling drugs. He put Mark into the image (even though he was co-joker), hand extended, presumably with a diploma. He took his position with his many antagonists a short distance away. Following our usual process, each person in the image spoke a single line and then moved. The result was that DJ was more deeply ensnared by, and responsive to, the antagonists. Several participants outside the image gave DJ a new line or suggested different ways he might move during the single-move animations, but each one led to the same result. When DJ's frustration began to show, and in response to a comment that the problem is too big to be resolved all at once, Jenny suggested she could count to five and he could make a movement toward achieving his goal with every number. With each count the antagonists increased their pressure on him—literally blocking his way, climbing on his back, wrapping around his legs. He twisted and turned from one to the other, desperately trying to negotiate with them to get them to stop. Jenny reached five and he had made no progress toward his goal. She stopped at fifteen. He had made no progress. Other participants began to yell instructions and advice to DJ. More counting, but still no progress. DJ sat down, tired but vindicated that he had proven the difficulty of his situation. "See," he said, "It's really, really hard."

As we discussed the image with those who had been in it and compared each change that had been suggested, DJ asked Mark, "Why didn't you do something?" Mark simply said, "You never looked at me." It was true—the entire time the image was dynamized DJ had focused all of his energy in battling or appeasing the antagonists—and had missed graduation. He said he was shocked to realize that regardless of how he wanted to live his life, he was "totally wrapped up in" his problems—never focused on his goal. The mood in the room changed drastically. Students who had been quick with complaints and excuses for not succeeding in classrooms were suddenly quiet and thoughtful. The whole group acknowledged that it was easy to blame others—much harder to focus on goals or look for help in order to make meaningful change.

On another occasion we were working at a school to which students were granted admission if they asserted that they were abused or mistreated in regular schools. The student population included many LGBT youth, Goths, and others who had been ostracized or mistreated. When we asked them how they liked their new school, they said that the curriculum and teachers were great, but that they were still mistreated by other students. Near the end of a three-visit workshop, small groups created One-Line Plays about physical or psychological violence.

One image was of a young woman lying on the ground while several people were pulling her jacket and boots off. Lines written by those in the image included "Give them here, bitch" and "You think you're all that." The protagonist just said, "Help." In discussion of the image someone said, "She probably stole those boots." Another group made an image of a young woman being ostracized by a group. Some people were pointing at her disparagingly, others turned away; still others pushed her away. The lines offered—like "Get outta my face" and "No one wants you here"—did not point to a cause for her rejection, but when the image was animated by moving it back in time, participants showed the victim flirting with another woman's significant other. After they interpreted a third image in a similar way, (and knowing they had all felt victimized at the school) we felt moved to ask, "Did everyone who was blamed or abused deserve it?" The students immediately answered "No!" but still defended their interpretations. Some, though, began to re-examine the images based on their own experiences of bullying, using phrases such as "Maybe they thought the only way she could get boots like that was to take them" and "They didn't know her and she had boots like their friend's that had been stolen." When asked about the girl and the boyfriend image someone said, "Maybe someone got jealous and turned people against her," "People don't mix with new people here," and "People think that just because you talk to someone you're trying to get something." When one person asserted that "Everybody just follows the group," the participants acknowledged that they were part of that "everybody." We asked, "Why do you think everybody blamed the victim when you first interpreted the images?" The impact of this question on this group of very verbal, high energy, self-identified victims was startling—sudden silence, glances between each other, embarrassed shoulder shrugs.

While the specific question about blaming came from the jokers, it arose naturally from the sequence of events and was really more of a re-articulation of what the students were saying than an insertion by the jokers. Questions from the jokers are truly that—questions. We maintain that the comparison of all the One-Line Plays and their animated images during the workshop session allowed the students to engage in an analysis of their own situation and behavior in ways they would not have been able to even in the most open discussion. It is hard to deny what you have discovered with your body.

An Extended Workshop

Some other ways in which we use the One-Line Play process can be illustrated by looking at an extended workshop we conducted for a specialty Job Center providing re-employment and retraining services for dislocated workers.[7] The case managers at this NGO are a dedicated group whose focus is serving clients who are often desperate for help. We were asked to provide 12 hours of workshops to explore recurring tensions over leadership, creative power, divisive attitudes, and racism—a full plate.

During the three-day workshop, which included well-known TO games[8] as well as a process of exploring conflicting personal commitments,[9] we used several variations of the One-Line Play process as both exploratory ventures into problem definition and problem solving. In one instance the One-Line Play process provided an unusual path to discovery of one of the core difficulties in the way the group functioned. We gave each of six small groups a different word or phrase garnered from earlier exercises and asked the groups to sculpt an image of the issue. The list of words was posted, but the groups did not know which words the other groups had. Each small group showed its image to the larger group, who guessed which word on the list was being illustrated.

One image was of someone who barricaded herself behind a desk. No one could get to her, yet it was clear that without contact she could not begin her work. Another image was of a meeting in which no one would accept or focus on a leader. In another image a person was pulled in several directions by several people and was unable to focus on his own job. In another, pairs of people were unable to connect with other pairs. In yet another image, women in the group were unable to have meaningful interactions with a domineering male. During the guessing process, group members applied every topic on the list to every group. Not one image was seen as providing a specific focus on a single issue.

We animated the One-Line Plays in a variety of ways to explore concerns raised in the guessing process. When the "barricade group" moved toward intensification of their actions (a dynamizing technique that often reveals both self-oppression and complicity), each person made the barrier more impenetrable. One person lifted her chair in front of her face, while another pushed the person in front of her towards the desk, and a third made a phone call. Suddenly it seemed as if the isolation of the protagonist was not of her own doing.

The "meeting image" became chaotic when the dynamizing question was "What happened next?" People made phone calls, had irrelevant conversations, left the image, one started putting on makeup while another began to point and whisper. We asked people in the image, "Pairs who were unable to connect," to dynamize toward "Getting what you want." Rather than moving together, each individual tried to talk to someone different, further fragmenting the image and isolating the participants. When participants re-sculpted the "domineering male image," they were able to decentralize power, but their improvised extension of the scene was about complaints rather than change.

As several of the images devolved into progressively more frustrating situations, participants pointed out parallels between the action of the One-Line Plays and power dynamics at work and noted their own recurring modes of self-protection. Exploration of what seemed to be highly differentiated problems began to cluster around certain causal structures in the culture of the group—especially feelings of disempowerment because of fear about negative response to suggestions for change and assumed hierarchical impediments to open communication. During additional One-Line Plays focusing on the communication patterns of the group—and of conflicts that surfaced in the workshop—personal experience was made public and visible in a non-aggressive manner. Participants shared that they had a clearer picture of the causes of tension, the apparent limits to creative change, and openly questioned their own roles in the perpetuation of current difficulties.

Because of the nature of our charge, the composition of the group, and the clients they serve, we spent much of the third day examining racism, whiteness, and privilege. One of the techniques we used was a variation of the One-Line Play process we call "Deconstructing the Image." Although based on Boal's work, it is an extension of image techniques to a particular exploration of the difference between representation and experience. It uses contrasting images—one based on observation of cultural stereotypes and one based on individual experience—to examine stereotyping.

Participants made a list of labels associated with their clients—unemployed, rural, undocumented, etc. After dividing into smaller groups, half of each small group was asked to make an image of a stereotype associated with the label as it is portrayed in popular or mass culture. The other half was asked to sculpt a particular example of someone to whom that label might be applied.

One highly charged pair of images had to do with "rural" as a label. The stereotype showed lazy and bumbling "hayseeds" and the lines for the characters were right out of old TV shows. The image informed by the actual experience of two of the participants was of hard-working and resourceful people who, during the dynamization, worked as an efficient group to accomplish tasks. The participants raised questions about how the stereotype developed, and the discussion expanded to representations of race and ethnicity. There was a creative tension in the room as participants verbalized parallels between their own thinking and the stereotypes and how that affected their treatment of clients.

The final segment of the workshop was development of an action plan. We believe that if members of a group have committed to at least one very specific action, they will have a concrete example that will provide rich learning material about the dynamics at play in the organization and an impetus to attempt greater change. We call these "public agreements" (borrowing from the language of Kegan and Lahey, 2001). The nature of such agreements is simple—everyone agrees to certain actions or behaviors in a particular type of situation.

This group adopted public agreements based on discoveries made during the One-Line Play process. One agreement adopted was a simple sequence for reserving public spaces for each teams' needs—an issue that had previously been mired in suspicion and the "claiming of turf." Another was the agreement about steps to take when individuals come into conflict. The steps laid out served the function of diffusing personal emotional reactions and laying the ground work for constructive learning—both about the nature of the problem and individuals' ability to cooperate with the agreements themselves. The act of developing public agreements reaffirmed the goals of the group and made clear the role individual choice plays in transformation. It was, in ways, the final removal of us as jokers from the process and an assertion of agency by the participants.[10] We believe that if everyone in the group commits to a test of assumptions, then everyone will be rehearsing a larger change—the very aim of Theatre of the Oppressed.

Transformation Through Co-jokering

Everyone does what they do for a reason, jokers included. Oppression is not arbitrary. If we explore inequities and oppressions as consequences of actions taken to fulfill culturally, socially, or institutionally influenced needs and desires, then we undermine the easy demonizing of the oppressor and avoid a good/evil dichotomy—opening the door for intervention designed to achieve change rather than victory. Without such awareness, we battle within the confines of the system and often inadvertently reiterate or become complicit in oppression.

To challenge the economies of power and position, we have tried to develop procedures which de-center power. Partly de-centering is done by organizing workshops so that the germinal ideas for each step or image are found in the previous step—not in the suggestions made by the jokers. We make every effort to begin with ideas from the participants and go where they want to go with honesty and curiosity. It is only after people feel that they have been heard that they are ready to question the consequences of what they have said or done. This is our road to problematizing.

A significant enhancement to the de-centering of power—and to the process as a whole—is our method of co-jokering, which relies on dialogue both before and during workshops, thereby modeling the very process the One-Line Play techniques are meant to engender. We try to model critical behavior—to assist and challenge each other. While we assign primary responsibility for an activity before the workshop begins, it is understood that we can contribute to each other's work as it is happening. We offer, when appropriate, our response to the work in the moment—and then respond openly to yield, support, or challenge one another as we see fit. This is particularly valuable when one of us notices the other pursuing a line of questioning that speaks to, often inadvertently, his or her own concerns and not necessarily those voiced by the group.

This often generates some surprise from participants who expect facilitators to know the exact contour of the road to be traveled and to direct them to what they should find rather than share in the process of dialogue and discovery. Co-jokering is an embodied and active rehearsal of critical praxis—of "engaged pedagogy" (hooks, 1994). It is in the rigorous interrogation of one another's kneejerk reactions when crafting and guiding One-Line Play and other TO workshops that we have found a most fruitful ground for our own development as Boal practitioners. Far from undermining confidence in the process, this demonstration of respect for the work and for one another invariably encourages the participants to follow suit with even greater honesty and courage than before. And because we're married, it amuses them as well.

The technique—and we believe this is true of all participatory art—requires a particular attitude be held by the jokers/facilitators. We do not think of ourselves as teachers or helpers. It is our responsibility to learn and to promote learning. We firmly believe that the only knowledge that will generate action is knowledge that is created by the learner. We try to avoid "the elitism of intellectuals [which] comes, not merely from our assumption that we already know the answers, but even more from our assumption that we already know the questions" (Grossberg, 1994, p. 20). The shared responsibility, support, and challenge of co-jokering allow each of us to more fully enter workshops as curious participants engaged in the learning and discovery process.

This concatenation of identity exploration, personal development, ongoing interrogation, and social action has, we think, made us more useful members of the community of persons seeking social justice, more engaging and effective teachers in the classroom, more inquisitive and inventive theatre collaborators, and better jokers.[11] We believe in the work we do and the techniques with which we do it—but we realistically acknowledge limitations in our knowledge and our ability to create transformation. We do not acknowledge any limitations in the power of the people.

Notes

1. We will use the acronym CAT from this point on even though CAT is closely associated with the Creative Arts Team—a leading force in the development and pedagogy of Applied Theatre in New York City.
2. Weinberg has a long background in politically charged theatre as a member of the Other Theatre Company collective and researcher in collective theatre-making. (See his *Challenging the Hierarchy: Collective Theatre in the United States*, Greenwood Press, 1992.) Wanasek has created and directed plays with Milwaukee Public Theatre about the lives and problems of inner city youth.
3. Some critiques of Boal's thought have focused on the implication that the actions of creative individuals are more significant in social change than the collective action of oppressed groups. We feel that a focus on individual empowerment does permeate Boal's theory, but that his work in the past several years has been driven by a growing commitment to the concept of the individual as a social and cultural construct whose actions can be examined as indicators of transformative group actions rather than as stand-alone personal choices. One need only look at his last few Rainbow-to-Forum and Legislative Theatre workshops to chart this change.
4. In "Line Races" teams try to line up in order based on attributes called out by the jokers [a game originally learned from Philippine Educational Theatre Association (PETA) and taught again to us in another form by Chris Vine]. In "Chain Tag" each person tagged becomes part of a group "it" while in "Everybody's It" each person tries to tag but not get tagged. "Cross the Circle" is a game which begins with simple walking movements but leads participants to wildly individualized stepping and sound sequences.
5. This is similar to an image technique in *Games for Actors and Non-Actors* (p. 177), but we have everyone sculpt simultaneously. Boal is very clear that he feels it is only appropriate in small groups and that the preferred method is to have individuals enter the center in response to the word. We feel however, that such a pressure to "perform" is quite disruptive. It reduces the opportunity for full involvement, invites the most extroverted to dominate the activity, and produces imitation and response to the previous image rather than to the word or concept.
6. We insist that everyone speak at the same time first, otherwise each person tends to "write" their line in response to what the previous person says rather than to their position in the image. Then the lines are delivered sequentially.
7. We do not include the name of the group to respect the privacy of its workers.
8. We try to choose warm ups that take into account the particulars of each situation. The games we chose allowed us to introduce labor and diversity issues gently and provided small moments of physical touching and the sharing of personal details which eased tensions in the group. Since there had been some finger-pointing and blaming during the first day, we modified our plan to veer away from any game that might encourage someone to escape responsibility by claiming powerlessness.
9. Based on Kegan and Leahy's "internal languages" (2001).

10. While public agreements are not always appropriate—e.g., when the group has come together around an issue but will not remain together after the workshop—it is always essential to return to the group as the agents of change—as the makers of the future.

11. We would be remiss here if we did not mention some of those from whom we have learned and under whose jokering guidance we have enjoyed the spect-actor experience. Chief among them, of course, are Augusto and Julian, but we owe much as well to Doug Paterson, Michael Rohd, Chris Vine, Chen Alon, Norma Bowles, Jan Mandell, Brent Blair, the participants in the international jokers workshop facilitated by Marc Weinblatt and David Diamond several years ago, and the inspirational work of Mohammed Waseem in Pakistan.

References

Boal, A. (1995). *The rainbow of desire: The Boal method of theatre and therapy.* New York, NY: Routledge.

—. (2002). *Games for actors and non-actors* (2nded.) (A. Jackson, Trans.). New York, NY: Routledge.

—. (2006). *The aesthetics of the oppressed.* New York, NY: Routledge.

Cohen-Cruz, Jan. (2006). Redefining the private: from personal storytelling to political act. In Cohen-Cruz, J. and Schutzman, M. (Eds). *A Boal companion: Dialogues on theatre and cultural politics* (pp. 103-113). New York, NY: Routledge.

Freire, P. (1994). *Education for critical consciousness.* New York, NY: Continuum.

—. (1995). *Pedagogy of the oppressed* (20th anniversary ed.). New York, NY: Continuum.

Giroux, H. (1994). Living dangerously: Identity politics and the new cultural racism. In Giroux, H. & McLaren, P. (Eds). *Between borders: Pedagogy and the politics of cultural studies* (pp. 29-55). New York, NY: Routledge.

Grossberg, L. (1994). Introduction: Bringin' it all back home–pedagogy and cultural studies. In Giroux, H. & McLaren, P. (Eds). *Between borders: Pedagogy and the politics of cultural studies* (pp. 1-25). New York, NY: Routledge.

hooks, b. (1994). *Teaching to transgress: Education as the practice of freedom.* New York, NY: Routledge.

—. (2006). *Outlaw culture.* New York, NY: Routledge.

Janmohamed, A. (1994). Some implications of Paulo Freire's border pedagogy. In Giroux, H. & McLaren, P. (Eds.). *Between borders: Pedagogy and the politics of cultural studies* (pp. 242-252). New York, NY: Routledge.

Kegan, R., & Lahey, L. (2001). *How the way we talk can change the way we work: Seven languages for transformation.* San Francisco, CA: Jossey-Bass.

Ohmann, R. (Ed.). (1996). *Making and selling culture.* Hanover, NH: Wesleyan University Press.

Schutzman, M. (1994). Canadian roundtable: An interview. In Schutzman, M. & Cohen-Cruz, J. (Eds.). *Playing Boal: Theatre, therapy, activism* (pp. 198-226). New York, NY: Routledge.

CHAPTER EIGHT

S. Leigh Thompson & Alexander Santiago-Jirau

Performing Truth
Queer Youth and the Transformative Power of Theatre of the Oppressed

IT WAS A MUGGY summer afternoon and the concrete stairs outside the Lesbian, Gay, Bisexual and Transgender Community Center (the Center) were packed tightly with young queers,[1] sweating in the gritty New York City heat. They were waiting for the Center's youth program to open for the day and rather than sit inside the Center where staffers shush noisy patrons, they collected outside, drawing community borders in public space. The young people gossiped, shouted, and laughed as white thirty-somethings hurried by or crossed to the other side of the street rather than walk in front of this rowdy crowd. We passed unnoticed—our last afternoon of anonymity—on our way to begin the first session of what would become Performing Truth. Utilizing Theatre of the Oppressed (TO) techniques, we were about to begin work to develop Forum Theatre with a group of queer youth from the Youth Enrichment Services (YES) program of the Center. We hoped to provide them the opportunity to move beyond heartwarming stories of queer pride or tragic displays of queer devastation to develop Forum performances of the oppression they face that would stimulate dialogue and positive action for change.

Our experience would culminate in Forum Theatre performances for youth in several YES programs that explored experiences of oppression that queer youth tackle daily—experiences of school bullying, restrictions on gender expression, and family disapproval. The oppressions that queer youth face are familiar to us, as both of us were once young queers fumbling to forge our identities in resistant, sometimes hostile environments. But while we were connected to this community, we recognized that as co-jokers we needed to understand the distance between us as adults and the group of young people and their unique historical, political and social perspectives.

Queer youth culture is evolving and today's queer teenagers are less in-clined than youth growing up in the 1990s to regard their sexuality as their biggest hurdle or their most important personal quality (Savin-Williams,

2005). Definitions of queerness have become blurred, with young people today reconstructing concepts of gender and sexuality, and creating more complex and layered identities. This new cultural landscape is challenging adults—including queer adults—to rethink notions about queer adolescents, to move beyond the rigid limitation of labels. As adult queer jokers we knew that we needed to allow the shifting and developing voices of queer youth to infuse and drive our work.

All young people struggle to understand themselves as independent individuals in an adult world, but queer youth face unique struggles in this process. Like all teenagers, young queers look for guidance and support as they grow into social and political consciousness; but because many adults do not share or support their understanding of sexuality and gender, these young people often find themselves isolated. Our heterosexist society often dismisses queer youth as being confused or just "going through a phase." By discounting the validity of the youth's identity, adults create expectations of certainty, implying that people are allowed to identify as queer only if they are absolutely sure of being queer. Thus, these young people are discouraged from questioning their understanding of their queer sexuality or gender.

In our experience, this unreasonable expectation can often have one of two effects. First, it pushes many young people deeper into the closet, which can hinder the vital emotional and sexual development occurring during puberty, stalling growth until the person is later capable of making an assertion regarding personal sexuality. In other circumstances, young people may be forced to come out and stay out, which does not allow for gradual, flexible self-exploration. Instead, it reinforces the notion that young people must be rock-solid in their gender and/or sexuality if it strays from the norm, and that they must hide all reservations. Any display of doubt can be used to dismiss their identities, so queer youth often present a solid front, refusing to acknowledge any confusion about their identities, even though it is typical for all teenagers to have doubts and confusion.

Out youth often deny that they experience difficulty or hardship, especially if they think showing fear could cause someone to question the validity of their queerness. They refuse to admit any oppression they face in order to portray complete confidence. Often, they do not ask for assistance and they dismiss any concerns, which can be detrimental to their development. In our work we have observed that young queer people rarely turn to straight, non-queer adults for help or guidance. As queer adults in the role of co-jokers for this group, we wanted to respect their uncertainties and doubts, as well as support their confidence and pride.

Using Theatre of the Oppressed as a Tool for Youth Action

Theatre of the Oppressed offers queer young people the opportunity to go beyond the exploration of their identities and provides structures for under-standing the larger political dimensions of their personal oppression stories. We hoped that our Forum Theatre workshop and performances could help our actors and their peers acknowledge and fight anti-queer harassment and violence. In *The Rainbow of Desire* (1995), Augusto Boal wrote:

> Theatre is born when the human being discovers that it can observe itself; when it discovers that, in this act of seeing, it can see *itself*—see itself *in situ*: see itself seeing. Observing itself, the human being perceives what it is, discovers what it is not and imagines what it could become. It perceives where it is and where it is not, and imagines where it could go. (p. 13)

In our work we sought to create situations in which participants could excite their imaginations and begin to discover possibilities that challenged the prevalent images presented of queer youth: as victims, worthy of ridicule, abuse or neglect. Through TO, queer youth would not only explore their identities and personal oppression stories, but also develop possibilities for future action. Above all, we wanted the participants to locate hope.

Adapting Theatre of the Oppressed: Developing "Performing Truth"

Our project with YES began in August of 2008. YES is a free and confidential program for young people between the ages of thirteen and twenty-one who identify as queer, lesbian, gay, bisexual or transgender or are questioning their sexuality or gender identity. YES provides community support to foster healthy development in a safe, affirming, sex-positive, alcohol- and drug-free environment. We were approached by YES programming staff to offer a theatrical workshop for YES's Arts in Advocacy track and to develop a performance for an upcoming YES-sponsored conference for queer youth. We agreed to joker a TO process working toward several Forum Theatre perform-ances. Our intention was to provide tools for the young people and their peers to begin dialogues about the important and often overlooked issues they face. While the youth performed on several separate occasions, in this chapter we will focus on one performance at YES, at which the audience was comprised only of other queer youth and YES staff.

After an initial discussion with YES staff, the group "Performing Truth" was born. The young people self-selected to participate, and the group re-mained open for new participants to join for the first three weeks. After the third meeting, the group was closed to new members because we needed to establish an ensemble dynamic with the group and solidify our actors as they created Forum Theatre scenes from their personal stories of oppression. The group met every Friday afternoon for twelve weeks. Due to competing groups and commitments, attendance fluctuated throughout the weeks. We started with ten to fifteen participants during the early sessions and finished with a core group of six. Each session consisted of two hours of work followed by thirty minutes for a community meal, which gave us an opportunity to continue the dialogue and connect. As co-facilitators we worked together to support the youth and each other. Our different styles and energies allowed us to tailor the facilitation to respond to the immediate needs of the group, and each of us relied on our partner to step in during challenging moments.

We began by working to establish trust and group investment. One way we worked toward common trust was by enthusiastically participating in YES community standards. We utilized portions of the YES structure to provide program continuity and familiarity for the young people in our workshop. During the first group we established a series of ground rules necessary for participants to feel safe in the environment, which we recited before each group session began, a YES standard. The ground rules included "Step up/step back," "Take care of yourself," and "Take risks." These were added to a list of YES programmatic rules that we adopted, which the participants playfully referred to as CRABS Ass:

Confidentiality

Respect

Attentiveness

Be open

Sensitivity and

(No) Assumptions

We also incorporated YES check-in questions in our routine, so each of us answered a brief question while introducing ourselves, offering our names, ages, borough of residence, and our Preferred Gender Pronouns (PGPs).[2] During these check-in moments we all became participants in the process and shared equally. The PGP check-in is central to our approach.

We believed that in order to successfully engage the young people in the work we had to queer Theatre of the Oppressed. In other words, working in a queer space, with queer-identified youth and queer-identified facilitators was not enough to make the work liberatory. We had to figure out how to intentionally adapt TO activities to serve our youth's needs by expanding the practice of TO to recognize a wider gender spectrum. We carefully selected activities from Boal's repertoire of games that did not require any one individual to be singled out. We used games like "Good Day," "Two by Three by Bradford," "Colombian Hypnosis," "Walk Stop" series, "Circular Rhythms," and "Circle of Knots."[3]

We tried to stay away from games or game instructions that reinforced the gender binary, and we accepted that the young people would incorporate into the games elements of queer youth culture. They constantly challenged our perceptions of how the games are played. For example, participants included elements of dance and voguing in a "Walk Stop" game. This was an exciting challenge for us as jokers. During this game, as well as many others, we needed to determine if group members were adding or changing the games because they were engaged and fully participating or if their changes served as protection that allowed them to stay distant from the issues we were exploring, and from themselves.

Like many queer youth, some participants kept themselves tucked behind performative masks—some even utilizing performer pseudonyms—which function to protect the innermost feelings and identity of the individual. Such performative behaviors serve as survival techniques and "are the armaments such children and the adults they become use to withstand the disabling forces of culture and state apparatus bent on denying, eliding, and, in too many cases, sniffing out such emergent identity practices" (Muñoz, 1999, p. 37).

Within the queer movement there has been much work to establish the concept of pride to combat widespread feelings of shame. This often becomes the primary goal: one must escape shame and become proud. With little direction on how to achieve this objective, many young people believe that to escape shame and gain pride they must deny that they face oppression.

Many of the youth we worked with performed pride unwaveringly, another layer in their armor. Although they were able to identify stories in which they were punished or attacked for being queer, they still had trouble recognizing these situations as results of oppression. As the functions of oppression are insidious and often lay hidden, it was our aim to help the participants develop consciousness of systems of oppression and how they affect their lives, so they could develop the tools to take action to address oppressions they face.

Their performative behaviors were a source of power for many of our group members, but also became barriers to establishing deep connections. Breaking through this armor became a goal of our TO process as we worked with the group to create Forum pieces. We worked toward getting past performative masks by demanding one performative expression after another until the "actor" stepped off the stage and the person within surfaced. In one instance, we played a long series of games and provided little time for discussion. After a barrage of performative displays, when we finally did gather for discussion, the participants were content just to sit in a circle and be honest with each other, sharing their personal stories.

Establishing the trust necessary for participants to be willing to address the shame that came with their recognition of oppression was not easy, and our progress waxed and waned. While group members were generally enthusiastic about the program and the work, at times individuals in the group would push back, which we read as an effort to reclaim power over the group and space. Sometimes this happened in overt ways, with participants resisting an activity's structure, refusing to complete an exercise or refraining from dialogue.

Other times the pushback was subtler and quite possibly unconscious. One such incident involved an Image Theatre exercise. We worked on the topics of "family," "community," and "education." Groups of four silently built their images as we introduced the topics. After the groups completed their sculptures, we showcased each one and asked the viewers to comment. In their analysis, a few viewers began to explain what they saw in the images in sexual terms, professing to see everything from sexual acts to elaborate pornographic storylines. More and more participants joined in this new game of subverting the process. As jokers, we interpreted this as the group flexing its autonomy and attempting to gain power by steering the conversation toward topics and issues that might have been intended to make the adult jokers uncomfortable. It was a challenge we answered in the true spirit of community.

For the next image, we called out the topic, "Sex." The group stalled. "Sex?" they asked. "What do you mean?"

"Just like before. In your same groups, create an image of the word, whatever that means for you." The groups moved slowly at first, unsure how to approach the subject directly. Eventually, the thrill of the activity won them over, and each group presented images that reflected their own experience or understanding of the word. Sex was no longer subversion, but an outward and acceptable topic for exploration.

While many of the participants sculpted images of sexual acts, others added themselves into these images in portrayals of shock, prayer, and disapproval. Even though the youth communicated a narrow view of sex when they were subverting the activity, when they had an opportunity to truly approach the subject, they showed a wide variety of understandings of the topic. The subsequent analysis of the images led to a rich discussion. The young people noted that many straight people see queer youth as constantly acting out sexually, and talked about how those perceptions can push them into sexual behaviors that play out the stereotype.

This exercise helped build trust and create an ensemble in several ways. Focusing on sex as a topic for dialogue was a way for the group members to take charge of the conversation and to share power in the workshop. By allowing and encouraging the discussion, we as jokers established a connection with the group and lessened the gap between us. It also allowed participants to purge much of the tension; by calling out the elephant in the room we were able to decrease our focus on it. By using Boal's Image Theatre and utilizing physical rather than verbal expression, participants were able to address an important issue in the queer community with honest reflection. After this moment, the group members were more open to dialogue and more willing to discuss other frightening and taboo topics with vulnerability.

The Forum Scenes

Once the group members trusted each other and us, we continued to work with Image Theatre so they could begin to establish a language of aesthetics, as they focused on how to communicate their personal stories to the group and to an audience. We had conversations about oppression and how it functioned in society and in our lives. While we, as leaders, participated in most of the discussions, we were careful not to misdirect the group's attention to our issues, but instead only offered our own openness in exchange for theirs.

Our Forum scenes were short, only five to ten minutes long, but each explored a moment or multiple moments of clear oppression on the basis of sexual orientation and/or gender expression. The first scene, "*La Familia*," was based on three separate stories of different family members enforcing a young person's normative gender expression. The second scene, "The School," explored the epidemic of often-violent anti-queer bullying and harassment in schools.[4]

In "*La Familia*," the young protagonist, D, is in his room getting ready for school when Mama comes in to prepare him for the day. She is happy and enthusiastic until she notices a bottle of nail polish sitting on his bedside table. "AY DIOS MIO!" she screams, "My son has NAIL POLISH! I'll never have grandchildren!" D tries to explain, but Mama hurries out of the room. D, determined to have a good day, leaves his room with a designer shoulder bag, and is greeted by Auntie, who announces she will take him to school. Then Auntie notices the bag. "That's not a bag, that's a purse," she tells D. "Boys don't wear purses. Are you some sort of faggot or something? Wait until your father hears about this!" The scene ends and next D appears again at the end of the school day. His father is waiting in a car outside his school. Mama and Auntie have told Dad about what happened with D in the morning, and as they drive home he tells D, "Boys don't wear nail polish. And boys don't carry purses. Do you see me carrying a purse to work? No." Although D protests, Dad eventually gives D an ultimatum, "So here's how it's gonna be. If I catch you doing anything girly like that again you are outta here, cut off! You hear me?" D, defeated, agrees to the demand and they drive home in silence.

In the second Forum piece, "The School," the young people told the story of a queer student bullied daily at his high school. On this day, the oppressed student decides to confront his bullies. "You know, every day I pass by, and you say something mean, and I don't say anything. Well, not today." An argument ensues and the violence escalates until the bullies attack the student. The scene ends with the student on the floor, about to get punched, having failed to convince the bullies to leave him alone and stop their homophobic taunts. The student's final words "I'm sorry!" are shouted as a blow from the bully freezes in mid-air. It was important to the group to depict in the scene the level of violence to which bullying and harassment can escalate in schools. The participants were well aware of the consequences of anti-queer bullying in schools, especially after the recent murder of a middle school student in California.[5]

As they developed the scenes, we as jokers chose to leave a majority of the aesthetic choices up to the actors. We explained the possibilities and options that we saw, but wanted them to make the final decisions on their stories' representations. To decide on staging, those not performing in a scene would discuss what they saw as they viewed both objectively and subjectively, using tools from our work with Image Theatre. We would ask questions to provide clarity, and the scene's actors would make decisions based on this dialogue.

Queering TO

In some Forum Theatre performances that we have seen, actors often rely on stereotypes when making aesthetic choices for their characters. This issue became the focus of exciting dialogue in our group, as the actors disagreed about how to represent their characters. The most heated discussion was about the character Auntie in *"La Familia,"* who was played by a gender-nonconforming male-assigned youth with a beard. Some said it was important for the actor to shave the beard off; others questioned this, asking why couldn't Auntie have a beard? This evolved into a larger discussion about images and representation. What does an aunt look like? Who is or is not a bully? Why would we want an aunt who is a stereotype if we are criticizing these characters for stereotyping us?

This is an example of how we found that Boal's emphasis on archetypal representation did not serve these youth, whose understandings of gender and sexuality break the rigid boundaries of known archetypes. In a community in which identity is proclaimed, not prescribed, each person has a right to self identify, and that must be respected. Theatrical representation can rely more strongly on a similar proclamation of character. In the end, the group decided that each actor would present one costume piece or prop that would represent the character, and it would be used only if agreed upon by the whole group. In addition, each character would wear a name card to show the audience who the characters were without resorting to stereotyping.

This process showcased the group's willingness to give something up (making costumes) in order to serve a better goal (destroying stereotypes). Our discussion of costume and stereotype was another conscious attempt at queering TO and challenging stereotypical representations on stage.

During our performances, the scene of violence in "The School" became physically and emotionally demanding for the actors. It was difficult for the participants playing the oppressor roles to maintain the level of aggression necessary for the scene, but they noted that by taking on the role of the oppressor, they were in some ways taking control of their own oppression, giving its expression validity and visibility. It was equally difficult for the participant playing the protagonist to play a scene in which he was constantly reminded of the threat of violence for queer youth. The scene rang true with the audience as well; many dabbed at tears as they watched, and several spect-actors took a moment to compose themselves after they intervened in the scene. Many had experienced similar situations in school or had heard stories from friends; all were familiar with the type of name-calling and harassment presented in the scene.

The protagonist's final shout, "I'm sorry!" rang through the audience, a haunting scream that reflected the shame that queer youth often feel. We noticed that most of the interventions to the violence in the scene were also violent in nature. Some of the spect-actors wanted to confront the bullies and were willing to fight to defend their dignity. "Hit me if you really are so tough," one spect-actor said. "Ok, you want to fight? Let's fight!" said another. One spect-actor never uttered a word, and just began swinging. It was not until one of the young spect-actors, tired of the violence, intervened by using his cell phone to call for help, that we were able to begin addressing other possible responses to the bullying.

"*La Familia*" was also a difficult scene for spect-actors to tackle. The family's structure provided a strong web of oppression that seemed difficult to escape. Spect-actors faced particular difficulty as they attempted to confront Auntie. The actor playing Auntie had difficulty yielding power in front of his peers, and so spect-actors faced greater resistance from this oppressor. Spect-actor after spect-actor tried to reason with Auntie, pleading to her logic and emotions. One explained how a purse is like a bookbag, comparing their common base elements—cloth, zipper, handles. Another pleaded, "If you care about me, you won't focus on the bag so much." Auntie just pushed harder and harder and, in reaction, the spect-actors pushed harder back. One challenged Auntie's femininity, using the same oppression against the oppressor. Another threatened blackmail. And one spect-actor pulled the purse out of her hand and began to beat her with it.

While we, as jokers, never condoned the use of violence, and often challenged the violence used in interventions in the discussion afterwards, many young queers saw violence as a true and honest option that could support their liberation from the oppression. Additionally, many were willing to accept homelessness as a viable route toward becoming free of family dynamics and living authentically as out and proud queer people. In many interventions addressing Dad, the spect-actors chose to come out as gay, telling the father off and walking out of the scene. One such spect-actor came out to Dad, screaming the words, and then stormed off, which yielded hoots and cheers from the audience. When we asked him what the consequences of such a tactic would be, he shrugged off homelessness. "Oh, I went to a shelter," he said. "For me it's a solution."

While this was disheartening to us as the adult facilitators, homelessness was not only an option for the queer youth participating, but it was quite common in reality among their peers. It is estimated that as many as forty percent of New York City's homeless youth identify as lesbian, gay, bisexual or transgender, according to Nicolas Ray (2006) of the National Gay and Lesbian Task Force. Leaving home is not a foreign concept to young people who see so many of their friends take this road. As with violent interventions, we did not moralize about this option, but rather asked the audience to consider the consequence of homelessness. As the audience began to discuss this question, spect-actors began to explore alternate interventions. One person asked the Dad to support his logic, "So you think everyone who wears nail polish is gay?" Then he followed with refocusing on Dad's role. "You're supposed to be wiser than me. We need to have a conversation!" Though this and other interventions, the youth began to identify the power in dialogue.

There was at least one YES staff person at each performance by our group, and we met with the entire YES staff to debrief and talk about how they could build on the Forum performances. They were struck by how frequently youth chose violence and homelessness, and questioned how their own programs might be able to better address violence and homelessness in the community.

Boal (1992) encouraged us to resist providing heroic characters in Forum performances in order to encourage audience members to take action. "What I want is for the spect-actor to take a heroic stance, not the character" (p. 28). By creating protagonist roles born out of their own experiences, our actors gave focus to their positions in oppressive systems in which others exploit power over them. In our two scenes, the protagonists were not presented as heroes, but rather as real youth responding to difficult situations. Lack of queer representation in society can alienate young people as they struggle to assert their adulthood. Muñoz (1999) states: "It is crucial that [queer] children are able to look past 'self' and encounter others who have managed to prosper in such spaces. Sometimes a subject needs something to identify with, sometimes a subject needs heroes to mimic and to invest all sorts of energies in" (p. 38). Although we started with theatrical anti-models, actors during the rehearsal process and spect-actors during the Forum performances all experienced the protagonists' potential victories, thus actively envisioning and creating the possibility of liberation.

Conclusion

Several of the youth with whom we worked still collect outside the Center in the late afternoon, rowdy as ever, but often the tone shifts—from distancing performances to engaged dialogue—and the topic changes to community issues and strategies for action. Now as we walk by the Center, performers and spect-actors call out our names and invite us to sit and continue the discussion we began two years ago. These discussions are often infused with language that reflects strengthened critical thinking. Through their experience with Theatre of the Oppressed, the youth with whom we worked played more than characters in a scene; they embodied the roles of teachers and experts for a diversity of audiences, roles that they continued long after they stepped off the stage.

Ultimately, the process of working with youth at YES was as transformational for us as it was for the young people. Throughout the process the participants made us rethink notions of agency in our work. They reminded us to be flexible, to meet each challenge as an opportunity. They helped us to recommit ourselves to the cause of equality for queer people all over the world—a cause that, if it is to succeed, must include youth voices in the fight against youth oppressions. They challenged our understandings of theatrical representation and encouraged us to rethink the divide between the actor and the individual within. Augusto Boal reminded us that to be a citizen, it is not enough to live in society; instead he called for us to transform society. Through our experiences as queer activists and theatre artists we have discovered that this transformation begins with youth. We are committed to helping them perform their truth.

Notes

1. For the purposes of this chapter we are utilizing the term "queer" to denote anyone who does not experience gender or sexuality within the boundaries of societal expectations. This includes those who fall within the LGBT acronym—those who identify as lesbian, gay, bisexual and/or transgender—but also it reflects a growing consciousness of fluid gender

identities, presentations and sexual orientations that do not necessarily adopt the assumptions of a static identity captured within those labels. Queer also reflects an understanding that when gender escapes the bounds of the binary, terms that rely on gender distinction—such as "lesbian," "gay" and even "bisexual"—become less concrete. In addition, queer includes individuals who are not yet certain of their sexual orientation or their gender identity. This group is often termed as "questioning" and is common among youth who are still attempting to understand themselves in terms of gender, sexual and/or romantic attraction.

2.   PGPs, are the set of words individuals prefer others to use for them. These include she/her/hers, he/him/his, or the gender-neutral ze/hir/hirs or they/them/theirs. One can also choose a multiple of these or no pronouns. Since gender identity should not be something prescribed or assumed by others, asking PGPs offers the opportunity for all participants to self-identify, feel recognized and respected.

3.   See Boal's *Games for Actors and Non-Actors* (2002) for complete explanations of these games.

4.   According to the Gay, Lesbian and Straight Education Network's (GLSEN) 2009 National School Climate Survey, nearly 9 out of 10 LGBT students reported experiencing anti-LGBT verbal harassment and 2 out of 5 reported experiencing physical harassment in school within the past year (Kosciw, 2010).

5.   On February 12, 2008, 14-year-old Brandon McInerney entered E.O. Green Junior High School in Oxnard, California and in the middle of a computer lab pulled out a gun and shot 8th grader Lawrence "Larry" King twice in the head in front of a roomful of students. Larry was an openly queer teenager who defied gender boundaries and had begun to wear makeup, jewelry, and high-heeled shoes to school. He was frequently taunted and called names. Eventually Larry learned to defend himself from the harassment by utilizing their bias to his advantage—Larry flirted with his bullies. Unfortunately this tactic worked against him; some say Larry asked Brandon to be his Valentine a few days before he was shot.

References

Boal, A. (1995). *The rainbow of desire: The Boal method of theatre and therapy*. New York, NY: Routledge.

—. (1992). *Games for actors and non-actors*. New York, NY: Routledge.

Kosciw, J. G., Greytak, E. A., Diaz, E. M., & Bartkiewicz, M. J. (2010). *The 2009 National School Climate Survey: The experiences of lesbian, gay, bisexual and transgender youth in our nation's schools*. New York, NY: GLSEN.

Muñoz, J. E. (1999). *Disidentifications: Queers of color and the performance of politics*. Minneapolis, MN: University of Minnesota Press.

Ray, N. (2006). *Lesbian, gay, bisexual and transgender youth: An epidemic of homelessness*. New York, NY: National Gay and Lesbian Task Force Policy Institute and the National Coalition for the Homeless.

Savin-Williams, R. C. (2005). *The new gay teenager*. Cambridge, MA: Harvard University Press.

The Lesbian, Gay, Bisexual and Transgender Community Center: About Youth Enrichment Services (YES). Accessed December 4, 2009, from http://www.gaycenter.org/youth/about.

CHAPTER NINE

Sonja Arsham Kuftinec

Rehearsing for Dramatic Change in Kabul

I ENTERED MY ADVANCED acting class in senior year of college with some trepidation—the professor had a reputation for eliciting sharp performances from students without an excess of nurturing. As I skimmed the skeletal syllabus on the first day of the course, she announced that there would be no assigned textbooks: "Instead, you'll read *The New York Times* or a similar weekly newspaper." She had a B.A. in history from Berkeley, several years of experience performing with the San Francisco Mime Troupe, and impatience with actor bullshit. Her ideas about "intentions" and "obstacles" extended far beyond the theatrical stage. "An actor who is not informed about the world doesn't deserve a platform to speak about it," she asserted, pacing the room and looking each of us in the eye like a drama drill sergeant. She then passed out a few cryptic pages of text copied from a book that featured on its cover a dynamic man with a flowing mane of hair. "Not only will you read the newspaper," she explained, "but each week you'll create original theatre pieces responding to what's between, beneath, and outside the lines of the news. Your task is to expose the conflicts and contradictions that frame how the events of the world become legible to or hidden from us."

Thus was I introduced to the work of Augusto Boal through the techniques of Newspaper Theatre. Boal developed this technique of popular theatre to foster critical thinking with "actors and non-actors" in Brazil.[1] Over the course of that semester, I learned not only to read the news critically, but also to read the world as changeable. I later discovered this to be the fundamental principle of Paulo Freire's pedagogy of liberation that had inspired Boal's development of Theatre of the Oppressed.[2] In the meantime, for me in 1988, everything about what it meant to be an actor in the world had radically transformed.

I spent the next year as an intern in a corporate regional theatre environment, coming to realize how the potentially radical technology of theatre could so easily become commodified. At the same time, I struggled through *Theatre of the Oppressed* at coffee shops. I marveled at the difference between Boal's theatre that strove to produce a more just, equitable society in which anyone could act and the theatre I worked at which seemed more interested in sustaining the status quo. I pondered this difference as the global society shifted tectonically in 1989—the Berlin Wall and the Soviet Union collapsed, Chinese students confronted government tanks in Beijing, and Serbian leader Slobodan Milošević grew increasingly nationalistic in his rhetoric. Yet, the theatre produced *Harvey*, *Peter Pan*, and *A Christmas Carol*. Something seemed awry—so much seemed missing between the lines of the political and theatrical stages. Where was theatre as an agent of investigation, amplifying and lending depth to the concerns of the present? Where was Augusto Boal?

These questions remained with me in graduate school in the early 1990s where I struggled with even denser theoretical texts, which I read while experiencing a gnawing sense of responsibility towards the emergent conflict in the Balkans where my father's family still lived. In 1995 I worked in Croatia and Bosnia-Hercegovina adapting Boal's techniques to create theatre with youth in refugee camps and small towns. In 2000 I began working as a facilitator for Seeds of Peace, a U.S. organization founded in 1993, that works towards conflict transformation in the Middle East, the Balkans, and South Asia by bringing together youth for dialogue and summer camp activities in Maine. Seeds of Peace also runs follow-up programs staffed by local residents. In the spring and summer of 2004, I traveled with my husband throughout Asia and the Middle East to facilitate a series of workshops through these programs.[3] This chapter chronicles moments from that work, with particular focus on a workshop in Kabul, Afghanistan.

TO with Seeds of Peace

I began to introduce Boal's Image Theatre techniques at Seeds of Peace as a way of moving beyond verbalizations that seemed at times only to rehearse established narratives rather than to propose ways of transforming conflict.[4] I adapted Boal's techniques to model and explore some of the challenges of such social transformations. At a yogic retreat center outside of Bombay, Indian teens analyzed the caste system along with what they perceived of as systemic apathy. A group of fifteen Seeds from Lahore, Pakistan, discovered ways to "dismantle mental borders" while exploring the spiritual and physical aspects of power. In Ohrid, Macedonia, theatre became a forum for Kosovar Serbs and Albanians to begin difficult conversations about recent violence in the region while exposing entrenched nationalist beliefs. In Jerusalem, Israelis and Palestinians experienced insight into each other's communities after almost a year of conversational impasse.[5]

While Image Theatre in Jerusalem clarified the competing ideological paradigms through which Israeli and Palestinian youth understood the conflict situation in their own communities, images in Kabul centered on undoing a culture of violence—highlighting the commonality of concerns among Afghan youth—while also offering strategies for addressing those concerns. The Seeds of Peace workshops provided a space for reforming relationships and understandings initially forged by acts of violence.

In addition to the shared desire to undo a culture of violence, the multi-ethnic Pashtun, Tajik, and Hazara youth in Afghanistan who attended the workshop were united by tensions between their deep uncertainty about and hope for the future of their society. Working under the guidance of an Afghan-Australian teacher, Noor, this group of young men and women had already established ways of thinking critically about their recent history and proposing new visions and actions for their shared future. I had spoken with Noor about these issues, yet I was unprepared for the visceral details of their shared suffering and their capacity to analyze and envision its transformation. I learned a great deal from this group of young men and women during the few days we spent together at a Women's Center on the outskirts of Kabul. Walking down dusty Chicken Street towards the Center, my head and shoulders swathed lightly in a scarf, one of the young women participants slowed her pace to walk beside me and show me her hand.

Images of Everyday Violence in Kabul

Weda told me her story matter-of-factly. She had received a markedly visible scar on her hand from a sharp slap with a splintered ruler while protecting a cowed school friend. Under the Taliban, Weda had secretly continued her studies and could easily transmit the rote answers required by her newly employed teacher while her friend could not. The scar spoke as powerfully as her story about the legacy of brutality in Afghanistan: while the Taliban had been overthrown, a culture of violence remained in Afghanistan, grounded in an obedience that both recognized and constituted authority.

Yet, the eleven Afghan youth in the workshop, aged sixteen to eighteen, created images animating the internal complexity of their society, culture, and history alongside impassioned, and often risky, commitment towards change. Seeds of Peace had provided them with a vision of a future less determined by capricious authority and violence; they felt a duty to enable that future, and enacted their vision through four extremely powerful and dynamic images.

Boal proposes that embodied images uncover essential truths about society and culture without resorting to spoken language. The process of working with images short-circuits cerebral censorship, silencing the "cops-in-the-head" put into place by experience or social education. While images generated in this way can be concrete, metaphoric, or allegorical, Boal encourages partici-pants to search for poetic rather than literal truths, emphasizing the polysemous nature of images—their multiplicity of meanings. According to Boal (1992), images do not function as charades with a one-to-one correspondence between an idea and its "correct" interpretation as determined by performers. Instead, they offer a screen onto which a participating group can project a variety of ideas and interpretations (p. 174). Image Theatre thus engages social rather than individual problem-solving. The process works particularly well with a group marked by varying levels of verbal articulation, leveling the playing field so that active participation does not require verbal skill. Boal's proposals were manifested in Kabul via interactions with and dynamic discussions prompted by a series of images the youth entitled "Education Killer," a title that embraces a multiplicity of interpretations.

Given the explicitly *non*-linguistic character of images, it is difficult to capture in words their expressive nuance absent of interpretation. In fact, Boal advises that the facilitator ask for physical observations prior to subjective interpretations, encouraging the "spect-actors" (his preferred term for a participating audience) to really *see* what they are looking at.[6] That said, I will attempt to conjure a semblance of the images presented in Kabul: 1) a girl stands looking at a book while a male youth points what appears to be a weapon at her; 2) a third party pushes away the weapon; 3) a seated boy studies a sheet of paper beside the still standing girl, while a turbaned youth reaches to strike the girl and the boy; 4) all three figures sit together with books, the girl reaching over to point towards a passage in the boy's book. Taken together the images provoked dynamizations and imagined transformations as well as a number of astute physical observations from the youth spect-actors.

Observations and Dynamizations

In standard techniques of Image Theatre, participants read the images first objectively, noting what they see, then subjectively, proposing various interpretations. The Kabul youth additionally noted what was strikingly absent for them from the images. "She is not wearing a *burqa*." Another youth pointed towards the "invisible forces of foreign influence" that allowed the weapon to be present. Some participants perceived a visible and imminent threat, while others pointed toward the book-reading as an act of resistance. A lively debate ensued about the reality of the image, and whether it existed primarily in Kabul, the only city in Afghanistan at the time where rule of law trumped rule of might.

While the first image provided a forum for verbal analysis, the second image, in which a gun was pushed away from the studying youth, prompted physical dynamizations and interventions. The spect-actors added to or shifted the image to indicate their ideas for change or resistance to change. Theatre of the Oppressed has impact, Boal insists, only if it becomes a rehearsal for transformation, where participants struggle to enact change while also acknowledging the real forces of oppression. Thus, Mir stood up to assist the anti-gunman while Ahmed leapt up behind the gunman, rendering visible the external support that he believed still existed outside the image's frame. An energetic crowd of spect-actors gathered behind each of the interventions, asserting belief in either the power of collective resistance or of external force that sustained violent threats in the city. Still, the attention remained focused on the gunman; Parnian remained alone holding her book. Finally Weda, attentively observing the chaos from a distance, gathered a handful of pens and folders lying about the floor and bounded up behind Parnian. Mustafa, cautiously watching from another corner of the room, arose and offered a book to the gunman, while Noor proffered imaginary tools for a job insisting, "Stop violence first—then jobs, then education." Parnian nodded sagely at the weary but engaged spect-actors. "This shows," she offered, "that it takes a lot of people and effort and time to change a gun to a book."

The third image provoked fewer physical interventions and more debate about why the seated boy didn't resist the threats of the turbaned youth. "He is weak, the Talib are powerful." "He doesn't care." "He thinks about only his future." "During Talib rule, when you saw someone being beaten, no one helped out of fear for themselves." "Because the people were not united!" "Is the population more powerful or is the Taliban?" "People can't oppose the army, even when united—unity plus arms equals power." "But a person needs equipment and books and security to really learn; in the picture the boy has none. He is only studying a sheet of paper, not a real book. His studying was only for the Talib, not for himself."

They all agreed that under the Taliban there was "study but no education."

Rehearsing for Change

While the discussions provoked by the first three images emerged from multiple interpretations and spect-actor interventions, Boal's techniques work most effectively when an image becomes dynamized—transformed by the spect-actors—suggesting the changeable nature of society and the possibilities for individuals to influence that change.[7]

The final image that the Kabul youth created emerged as a proposed "image of the ideal."[8] I asked the group to first note any physical distinctions from the other images: "The studying girl is finally allowed to sit down," noted Weda. Then others chimed in.

"No guns are present."

"They are all physically on the same level."

"The turban has been replaced with a baseball cap."

"They are using pens and not guns."

I then asked another question that Boal maintains is essential for Image Theatre's effectiveness. "Is it a possible or only a 'magical' future?" I had the group physically place themselves into a spectrum of positions from "possible" to "magical" and speak from these places. An extraordinary conversation emerged about the "reality" of the Taliban. "The switch from turban to pen is real," stated Khabir, "people who were forced by the Talib to wear a turban and enforce rules have switched to the side of education—this happened in my family." Others proposed that the turban was "real" but the change "faked."

"People can be judged by what they do when they are in power," insisted Parnian.

Mir then told a story about his mullah, a man who initially supported the Taliban because he wanted the good Islamic government they professed to bring. Once he witnessed their methods of enforcement and concern for outer manifestations of Islam rather than inner conversion and belief, he worked from within the regime to undermine the state by not forcing his congregation to sign the Taliban prayer log as a symbol of their devotion.

The group sat in silence for a moment, absorbing all they had heard and learned, until an impassioned Weda asked them what they could now do. A number of ideas emerged—working in their schools and families, and especially continuing to learn together—as a group of young men and women seated on the same level, with Weda's provocation like a finger underlining an important passage in a common book. In this environment one is not chastised for cooperative education, for learning with others. The socially mechanized body transforms: from a template for the visible marks of punishment to a screen for dreaming and rehearsing dramatic change.

Reflections

In *The Rainbow of Desire* (1995), Boal theorizes about how Theatre of the Oppressed techniques allow for social and individual transformation (pp. 25-26). He proposes that the aesthetic space offers spect-actors the opportunity to create an imagined yet embodied representation, one that is connected to and yet separate from their existential reality—a place to see themselves seeing and to envision change. In Kabul, the aesthetic space offered the opportunity for a group of young men and women to reflect on and reform an image of violence grounded in their experiential understanding. The image-making provided the youth with a way to both create distance from and illuminate the ethos of violence in which they were steeped. This imagistic representation also allowed for social analysis and for the rehearsal of transformation. The images activated the youths' imaginations in ways that supported their ongoing actions to educate themselves in a multi-ethnic, mixed gendered group. The modern state is predicated on the idea of the body politic, characterized by the relationship between individual citizen bodies and the state's political body. Acts of violence can reinforce ethno-national alignments while at the same time drawing attention to how the discourse of identity is often vigilantly controlled. Theatre of the Oppressed offers a means to reflect on and re-imagine this control, puncture received narratives, and suggest ways to forge new kinds of social relationships with the state.

The transformation of violent conflict will require a great deal more labor than a few Image Theatre workshops. But Image Theatre offers a way to manifest perspectival difference, a step towards the possibility of imagining a shared vision of a just future built neither on symbolic nor on physical violence. Thus the directive from my college theatre teacher persists: to reconsider the ethics of acting, to generate a space to envision and rehearse the transformation of the world, and to do so as a way of enacting participatory citizenship. For, as Boal reminded a group of us gathered at the annual Pedagogy and Theatre of the Oppressed conference in North Carolina in 2006, to be a citizen is not to live in society—a citizen is one who transforms society. And a Theatre of the Oppressed practitioner is one who continues to transform the work of Boal in a variety of contexts towards the always essential goal of generating a more just, equitable, and less violent society.

Notes

Special Note: This article is adapted from "Dramatic Changes in Afghanistan," *Community Arts Network* on-line publications Dec. 2004, which can be found at www.communityarts.net/ readingroom/archivefiles/2004/12/rehearsing_for.php.

1. Boal first mentions newspaper theatre as a technique in *Theatre of the Oppressed* (1985, p. 143). He elaborates on the form and techniques in *Legislative Theatre* (Routledge, 1998, pp. 234-246). The phrase "actors and non-actors" refers to Boal's proposal that the separation of actors and audience in Greek theatre signals a move away from communal creation and political equity. Theatre of the Oppressed is designed to include those untrained in professional theatre with the goal of activating everyone's agency to act in the world.

2. Boal has frequently noted that *Theatre of the Oppressed* is, in part, an homage to Freire's *Pedagogy of the Oppressed* (Continuum, 2003).

3. As with all Seeds of Peace events, I conducted workshops in English, a shared if not entirely neutral language that allows participants of different cultural and linguistic backgrounds to communicate together. This seeming neutrality is of course modified by education systems that teach English with varying degrees of enthusiasm, as well as by a youth and media culture dominated by the United States. In this context, Image Theatre has the advantage of working without as much resort to spoken language.

4. I write more about the practice of working with groups in conflict with Chen Alon and Ihsan Turkiyye in "Viewpoints on Israeli-Palestinian Theatrical Encounters," in *Youth and Theatre of the Oppressed*. Eds. Peter Duffy and Elinor Vettraino. (Palgrave, 2010, pp. 83-96).
5. For further reading on these workshops see "Violent Reformations: Image Theatre with Youth in Conflict Regions," in *Violence Performed*. Eds. Jisha Menon and Patrick Anderson. (Palgrave, 2008, pp. 223-43).
6. In *Games for Actors and Non-Actors* (1992) Boal discusses the multiple interpretations that an image makes possible. He refers to this as the "multiple mirror of the gaze of others" (p. 175).
7. In *Theatre of the Oppressed* Boal speaks about the aesthetic space as a site of "rehearsal for revolution"—a space to both try out ideas and practice for later action (pp. 141-42).
8. Boal refers to the "Image of the Ideal" multiple times in *Games for Actors and Non-Actors* (1992), most prominently on pages 185 and 204. Being able to express an "ideal" reality suggests a direction towards which a group can move their thinking and actions.

References

Boal, A. (1992). *Games for actors and non-actors* (A. Jackson, Trans.). New York, NY: Routledge.
—. (1998). *Legislative theatre* (A. Jackson, Trans.). New York, NY: Routledge.
—. (1985). *Theatre of the oppressed* (C. A. & M. Leal McBride, Trans.). New York, NY: Theatre Communications Group.
Freire, P. (2003). *Pedagogy of the oppressed.* 30th anniversary edition (M. B. Ramos, Trans.). New York, NY: Continuum.
Kuftinec, S. (2004). Dramatic changes in Afghanistan. *Community Arts Network Reading Room.* Retrieved from www.communityarts.net/readingroom/archivefiles/2004/12/rehearsing_for.php
Kuftinec, S. (2008). Violent reformations: Image theatre with youth in conflict regions. In J. Menon & P. Anderson (Eds.), *Violence performed* (pp. 223-43). London, England: Palgrave.
Kuftinec, S., & Alon, C. (2010). Viewpoints on Israeli-Palestinian theatrical encounters. In P. Duffy & E. Vettraino (Eds.), *Youth and theatre of the oppressed* (pp. 83-96). London, England: Palgrave.

CHAPTER TEN

Richard J. Piatt

Faith Acts
Exploring the Possibilities for Theatre of the Oppressed and Liberation Theology

I FIRST ENCOUNTERED THE work of Augusto Boal in 2003 though a workshop on Forum Theatre facilitated by Adrian Jackson's London-based Cardboard Citizens. I was drawn to the week-long session because of my work in theatre, my role as a Catholic priest and Augustinian campus minister involved in social justice work, and the strong emphasis Cardboard Citizens has on issues of justice for the homeless community. We (a variety of participants— professional actors, social workers, activists, advocates, educators, and theatre students) explored issues of oppression in contemporary contexts; topics included religious discrimination, child neglect, and economic and racial injustices. The workshop experience was revelatory and prompted me to reconsider how my experience in theatre and theology might be more advantageously combined. The work we did in the TO workshop was concerned largely with the same priority I held as an Augustinian priest, namely, the elimination of human oppressions.

I wondered how Theatre of the Oppressed might be adopted in a predominantly religious setting without being reduced to a tool for proselytizing. I began to consider the compatibility of TO and Catholic theology, specifically Latin American Liberation Theology, a method which engages the poor in the process of alleviating their own indignity, suffering, and oppression. Since that first encounter with TO, I have been attempting to create connections between my work as a priest and educator and Boal's theory and practice. In this chapter I lay the philosophical groundwork that guides me as a Catholic TO practitioner, and I describe the process of developing TO-based workshop for the Augustinian Youth Encounter (AYE), a global gathering of young people in their late teens to late twenties, who come together every three years to celebrate their faith, their experience as Catholics with an Augustinian ethos, and their diverse cultural experiences.

Thematic Connections

There are several commonalities between Theatre of the Oppressed and Liberation Theology. For the purposes of this chapter, I highlight the concept of "working from the base" and the "preferential option for the poor."

Working from the Base: A basic theme in dialogical pedagogy is that education is not for the oppressed but of the oppressed. That is, the learning and problem-solving process is one in which the lived experience of those who have had little or no voice in the development of existing dominant social and political structures are given the room to articulate their concerns, their wisdom, and their ideas for challenging unjust structures of oppression. The "base" refers to people who are at the bottom of the social structure; those who possess the least social, political, and economic capital and whose existence is a by-product of unjust socio-political structures.

Paulo Freire, working in Brazil in the 1950s, developed an educational philosophy, described in his book *Pedagogy of the Oppressed*, that fostered awareness and the desire to act for change among the social base of society. Boal, also concerned with a popular movement toward thoughtful political action, built on Freire's ideas within a theatrical structure. Both men emphasized dialogue to foster possibilities for eradicating unjust social structures. In Liberation Theology, such dialogue often begins in what is known as the base ecclesial community or BEC.

The structure of the BEC became a model for the nucleic structure of the Worker's Party of Brazil, which, in turn, became the model for Boal's working groups (Branford & Kucinski, 2003, p. 12). The structure and philosophy of the BEC, which had its birth in the Catholic Action Movement of the 1950s, is simple in concept. Local community members, many of whom are at the base of the socio-political structure and are members of the laity of the Catholic Church,[1] gather for the common purpose of prayer, scripture study, and the examination of their social situation. They name problems faced by the community, judge those problems based on reflection about scripture and their lived experiences, and decide as a group how to act to challenge unjust situations.

This is an attempt to glean from scripture wisdom about how to deal with oppression while acknowledging that the historical contexts of Biblical oppressions are quite different from the present. The BECs take seriously the Christian concept of life as a Divine gift and believe that all lives are sacred and must be treated with the respect given to members of the "Body of Christ." From the perspective of Liberation Theology, the term "Body of Christ" is not exclusive—all human beings are created in the image of God.

When one member of the Body suffers, all are affected by that suffering. Working for justice, then, is seen as a Gospel mandate. To respond disingenuously to oppressive situations with a phrase like "It is God's will" is to side with the oppressor, for it implies a satisfaction with the social structure that allows the oppressive situation. Moreover, it implies that if God so desired, the oppressive situation would not exist, thus placing God on the side of the oppressor. Such claims fly in the face of both biblical scholarship and pastoral theology, which demonstrate God's preferential option for the oppressed, and which illustrate the need for human cooperation in the eradication of injustice.[2]

The base ecclesial community relies on Catholic scripture, tradition, and theology to explore possible ethical actions for mobilizing political efforts that benefit the entire society. To take a course of action that in any way dehumanizes others would be antithetical to their identity as members of the "Body of Christ." In other words, they engage in a process of reflection before action in order to find the most humanizing solutions. This methodology, known as "see, judge, act," and described by theologians and brothers Leonardo and Clodovis Boff in their 1987 text *Introducing Liberation Theology*, is central to the method and connects Theatre of the Oppressed with Liberation Theology.

Preferential Option for the Poor: Both Theatre of the Oppressed and Liberation Theology insist upon what theologians term the "Preferential Option for the Poor." The term has been made popular through theological discourse, but it demands an explanation. Liberation theologians do not consider the phrase "the poor" to mean only the materially poor. Rather, they seek to broaden the definition to include others who are denied their full humanity.

> Liberation Theology is about liberation of the oppressed—in their totality as persons, body and soul—and in their totality as a class: the poor, the subjected, the discriminated against. We cannot confine ourselves to the purely socio-economic aspects of oppression ... which would restrict the oppressed to the socio-economically poor. (Boff, 2006, p. 29)

The poor are to been seen "in their totality as persons" who exist in relationship with—and hold a mirror up to—the rest of humanity.

The word "option" in the phrase refers to God's particular relationship with those most neglected and abused. He demands a response from humanity on the behalf of the oppressed. Those who claim a relationship with God must admit their relationship with the poor and come to see them, not as objects of charity, but as members of their (and thus God's) own body who need attention. Like Boal, Liberation theologians stand in solidarity with the oppressed in the battle for basic human rights. There is no neutrality. One either sides with the systems of oppression which are comfortable for some and oppressive to others, or one sides with the suffering and most marginalized members of society and thus must challenge the social structures which perpetuate oppression. To claim neutrality is to opt for the status quo and thus to side with oppressive persons and social structures.

Questions About the Oppressed/Oppressor Binary

Theatre of the Oppressed, born from a highly charged political reality, is inherently Manichean in its outlook and taps into the "smoldering rage" of the powerless oppressed (Bulhan, 1985, p. 141). Both Theatre of the Oppressed and Liberation Theology acknowledge that the story of the oppressed has been neither uttered adequately nor widely understood. Furthermore, both systems understand that the oppressor's point of view has been repeatedly articulated and has frequently been enshrined as the status quo. TO and Liberation Theology rely strongly on the notion that in scenarios of human oppression, both the oppressor(s) and the oppressed can be easily identified. Yet, this tendency to limit the worldview to an oppressed/oppressor binary is in itself an obstacle to what Freire (2003) calls our ontological vocation to become more fully human (p. 44). The reality is that the oppressed and those who oppress them, either through active participation or though acceptance of the status quo, exist. Most Liberation theologians recognize this reality, but point toward an ideal that strives for a dialectic in which each individual is recognized first as being human. I would argue that there also exist oppressed-oppressors: persons who experience oppression because of one aspect of their lives but who also are guilty of dehumanizing others, including their own oppressors, in another. By applying the "see, judge, act" methodology more expertly, the nuances of the oppressed/oppressor dialectic are easier to envision, making it more possible to loosen the stranglehold that the Manichean either/or thinking has on Theatre of the Oppressed practice.

In much current Theatre of the Oppressed practice there exists no methodology that prevents the spect-actor from demonizing, and thus further dehumanizing the oppressor. If, in a Forum production, for example, the spect-actors sanction an intervention that dehumanizes either the oppressor or the oppressed, there is no exterior check within the method itself to either judge the validity of the proposed course of action or the possible dehumanizing effects on the oppressed. The well-trained joker will challenge the efficaciousness of the intervention, but the method itself does not disallow any potential solution, even a violent one. However, in the practical application of Liberation Theology, neither the judgment laid upon the oppression/oppressor nor the actions chosen for addressing the oppression may in any way demonize the oppressor. To do so feeds the Manichean tendency of reversing the power structure, hindering movement toward humanizing both victim and perpetrator. In theological terms, if the oppressor is a human being, then the oppressor is also a dehumanized member of the "Body of Christ." As such, both the wounded nature of the oppressor and the role of the wounded oppressed as a healing agent for the entire body must be recognized.

Theatre of the Oppressed must always and everywhere be a life-affirming strategy for eradicating unjust social structures. TO must also encourage the oppressed to reject a view of the world that focuses on what is lacking rather than on "reciprocal affirmations" of a shared humanity (Bulhan, 1985, p. 140).

The Augustinian Youth Encounter Experiment

In August of 2010, the Augustinian Youth Encounter (AYE)—a gathering of young adults—took place in London, England. The participants, who gather regularly on the local level, come together every three years to celebrate their Augustinian and Catholic connection through prayer, workshops, small group meetings, and leisure activities. They come from Roman Catholic parishes and schools run by Augustinian friars in countries in Europe, North and South America, Asia, Australia, and Africa. All share a common desire to express their faith and work toward a more socially just world. In the autumn of 2009, I was asked to facilitate a Theatre of the Oppressed workshop at the next AYE, and I readily agreed. The workshop was situated within the week-long event, with the theme "I Call You Friends," which was taken from the words of Jesus to his followers.

In preparation for the conference session, I facilitated several short TO workshops with the UK group. After this initial "test-run," an invitation was translated into the appropriate languages and sent to all participating group leaders. AYE participants were asked to read a passage from Chapter 12 of the Book of Revelation, a highly symbolic narrative regarded by many as a prophetic discourse concerning *theeschaton* (or end times). The passage tells an allegorical story about a dangerous encounter between a seven-headed dragon and a woman giving birth to her son. The woman in the story, often considered to be the Virgin Mary, represents Israel. The dragon represents Satan, and the seven heads represent evil governments. The child is the Christ, born to restore justice to the world, despite the attempts of evil persons and powers to destroy the world and its inhabitants. Given the inherently political nature of the text itself, it seemed an appropriate starting place for an exercise about social justice. As a way of "seeing" what they had just read, group members were asked to dynamize it using any artistic method they chose, for example drawing, puppetry, or a human sculpture. It was important that the groups visualize what they had just read and discussed and create a rendering of the dragon in order to better facilitate the next step.

Groups were asked to reflect on their work and discuss the meaning that the passage might have had for the first hearers and the meanings it might hold today. They were asked to name the heads of the dragon in relation to their own socio-political situations, for example the realities of sexism, illegal drug trade, racism, unequal access to education, or homelessness. From there, they were asked to discuss unjust social structures, especially those that affected the individual members of the group or the group as a body. Finally, the local groups were asked to write a report about which oppressions they had identified; which oppressions were prevalent in their locale, even if they did not experience them firsthand; and which personal stories they were comfortable sharing with the global group.

The exercise was borrowed from a brief description of a BEC meeting recorded by Latin American Liberation Theologians Leonardo and Clodovis Boff (1986, p. 16). I chose to use the chapter from the Book of Revelation and to develop the basic exercise in part because it was an effective way for the group Boff describes to talk about social injustices. The exercise I suggested to AYE participants was designed to open them to critical reflection that was theological, socio-political, and artistic. As Boff (2006) wrote concerning the original experience: "Is it critical theology? Yes, it is critical because it is clear and prophetic; critical, not in the academic sense, but really so because it gives an account of causes and puts forward measures for dealing with them" (p. 17).

Having neither the luxury of being able to spend time with all local groups nor any information about their familiarity with TO, I made the decision to create brief, forum-able plays, using a single group of players but based on the information from all the groups. My plan was to work with an Edinburgh Augustinian youth group to create three or four short Forum pieces based on all the responses to the exercise. We would perform the plays at a common Legislative Theatre Session at AYE, and the gathered assembly from around the world would choose which play to forum. This was to begin a process of generating proposals for action by individual AYE groups and their elected Augustinian leadership.

Several issues prevented the project from proceeding as designed. Only three groups replied in writing to the exercise, thus limiting the possibilities for finding a common thread across the groups. The time for working with the Edinburgh group to develop Forum pieces was canceled shortly before AYE because their adult supervisor became unavailable. However, the groups from

Kenya, Poland and the Czech Republic who responded to the exercise identified important issues including: extreme poverty and hunger, unequal access to education, clericalism in the church, religious intolerance in the form of atheism, unequal access to resources, street crime, and HIV/AIDS. To honor their voices and work, I decided, in consultation with AYE organizers, to scale back the experiment to a Theatre of the Oppressed workshop focused on the oppressions identified by the three groups.

The AYE organizers suggested I work with the youth group from the Augustinian parish in Hoxton, who had participated in the initial "test-run" workshop, to develop TO work about these oppressions, which they would then bring to the whole group. These youth, many who are first generation British with African immigrant parents, learned the basics of TO in our two afternoon sessions. They created images of the oppressions from the other groups, as well as of oppressions they face in their own lives. We brought the see/judge/act methodology of our faith into our exploration of the images: we discussed our understandings of the oppressions in the world (see); asked questions brought forth by the images (judge); and set the stage for deciding how to move forward (act). For example, a female participant sculpted an image of peer pressure to engage in sex: a girl seated, head down, with a boy standing over her, unbuckling his belt. The group discussed this image, then added images of gossiping girls and cheering boys adding to the pressure. They gave each character words then discussed their images in relation to the positive and negative influences of family, friends, government, media, and the Church. Then they sculpted their image of the ideal: the young couple alone, hand in hand, looking out at the world. Finally, having seen the oppressive situation for what it was, having judged it as an actual oppression, and having considered what might be, they explored how their faith might guide them in changing the situation.

The group devised a plan for the upcoming three-hour session with the whole AYE assembly. As joker, I would warm up the whole group with quick TO games, then they would present their dynamization of the story of the seven-headed dragon from the pre-conference "test-run" workshop, followed by their images of oppressions. Following this, local groups would meet separately and each would decide upon one oppression that affected them, and create their own image of how their experience related to it. Finally, each group would create an image of the world as it could be. For the rest of AYE and after they returned home, they would work on how to move from the image of oppression to the image of the ideal.

At the AYE gathering, the Hoxton group presented their images to the 250 participants, who then eagerly broke into their national groups and began constructing their own images of oppression. The Hoxton group and I side-coached them, encouraging them to be clear in their images and, if time allowed, to sculpt an image of their ideal world without that oppression. However, an hour into the three-hour event, we were told we had only thirty more minutes for the workshop, due to a scheduling oversight. In the time left, the Czech Republic showed their series of images depicting the effects of Communism on their freedom to express their religion. The Argentineans created images of violence that represented a cultural lack of respect for human life. The Nigerians and the Kenyans, whose delegation was smaller than planned because many of their group members were denied visas, created images of governmental corruption. The Chicago-Tulsa group, from one U.S. region, showed images of unequal access to education and homelessness, and the willful ignorance of the elite to the oppression. Organizers offered us another time slot on the last day to continue the work we had begun, but by then, the momentum of the week was slowing down.

In their written evaluations of the workshop, participants said that even though the workshop was cut short, using TO in the context of theological discourse helped them recognize and critique their participation in oppressive actions and structures while attempting to live as people of faith. The work-shop challenged them to move beyond a reductionist practice of Christian values, to give voice to their own experiences of oppression, and to interrogate both their faith and their socio-political contexts. The combination of Theatre of the Oppressed and Liberation Theology drove home the point that if we call ourselves "friends" with each other and with God, we must see, judge, and act on behalf of and in concert with the oppressed. The use of TO in the context of AYE allowed participants to see the world and its structures for what they are and at the same time call on what they have learned from living their faith. Combining Liberation Theology and TO encouraged participants to acknowledge oppressors as members of the "Body of Christ," albeit "sinful" ones who participate in dehumanizing practices. The workshop highlighted that it is the oppressed themselves, and those who walk in solidarity with them, who can move beyond the either/or of a Manichean binary to see the inherent goodness of all human beings, and, as Paulo Freire advocates, fulfill the necessity to become more fully human (1997, p. xvi). The recognition of this inherent goodness helps us understand the idea of the mystical "Body of Christ," and creates the conditions for the possibility of a more just world.

Concluding Remarks

While the experiment in Theatre of the Oppressed described here retains its Boalian roots, this process of incorporating the methodology of Liberation

Theology with TO transforms traditional practice. First, it encourages the use of faith experience as an integral element in TO. Combining critical theological discourse with TO opens the process to additional possibilities for faith-based ideas and actions for change toward a more equitable world.

Second, the very reason for gathering is transformed. In traditional TO practice, participants come together primarily because of shared experiences of oppression. If the oppression did not exist, neither would the group. Their gathering is predicated on defining themselves as oppressed. While such groups may share common interests, needs, and goals, these are not the main reason for their assembly. The self-identification in such cases reinforces what Franz Fanon and Bulhan refer to as a Manichean Psychology (1985). Manichean psychology traps people in a negative dialectical relationship in which their self-perception becomes bound to their relationship with the oppressor.

A Manichean view is one that divides the world into compartments and people into different species. This division is based not on reciprocal affirmations, but rather on irreconcilable opposites cast into good versus evil, beautiful versus ugly, white versus black, human versus subhuman modes. This duality of opposites is not dialectical and hence not an attempt toward a higher synthesis. Each is defined in terms of its opposite and each derives its identity in opposition to the other (Bulhan, 1985, p.140). Self-identification based upon the negative reality of oppression creates an either/or situation, limiting possibilities for change. One is either an oppressed or an oppressor. Challenging the binary expands the possibilities for the oppressed to understand themselves as human first and victim second. Then, the oppressors can likewise be viewed as human beings first and oppressors second. This may allow more possibility for weakening the power given to oppressors by the formerly agreed upon Manichean power dynamic.

In the case of AYE, while many participants face real oppressions, the group bond is shared faith and a common experience of friendship. Their belief in the "Body of Christ," specifically that if one member suffers, then the entire body suffers, allows for a resonance that can reach across cultures, bind participants together, and allow further exploration of strategies for eliminating oppressive behaviors. AYE has the potential to become a global network of diverse individuals and groups who create change in their Church and in their world. The combination of TO with the see/judge/act methodology of Latin American Liberation Theology makes it possible to more fully comprehend oppressions, engage in continual critical reflection and action on local levels, and return to the international stage to re-examine, critique and continue the process.

Notes

1. The traditional social structure of the Roman Catholic Church is based upon a pyramid, with the Pope, as the accepted Vicar of Christ and head of the Church, at the apex. The bishops are just below him, followed by ordained clergy and the laity. The laity, the largest proportion of the population, forms the base of the Ecclesial structure. The lines of communication, however, tend to be top-down.
2. Liberation Theologians often point towards the Book of Exodus as an Old Testament example of God's preferential option for the poor. Without the cooperation of Moses in the Divine plan, the Hebrew people being oppressed under Egyptian rule would not have experienced their liberation from captivity.

References

Boal, A. (2000). *Theatre of the oppressed* (New ed.) (C.A. & M.O. Leal McBride & E. Fryer, Trans.). London, England: Pluto.

Boff, L., & Boff, C. (1987). *Introducing liberation theology* (P. Burns, Trans.). New York, NY: Orbis.

Branford, S., & Kucinski, B. with Wainwright, H. (2003). *Politics transformed: Lula and the workers' party in Brazil*. London, England: Latin American Bureau.

Bulhan, F. A. (1985). *Franz Fanon and the psychology of the oppressed*. New York, NY: Plenum.

Freire, P., Fraser, J.W., Macedo, D., et al. (1997). Introduction. In P. Freire, J. W. Fraser, D. Macedo, et al. (Eds.), *Mentoring the mentor: A critical dialogue with Paulo Freire* (pp. xi-xix). New York, NY: Peter Lang Publishing.

PART III

Transforming the Joker

CHAPTER ELEVEN

Raphi Soifer

Last-Minute Theatre
Bringing Boal Behind Bars

> *A man is tied up, with his eyes blindfolded, in front of the firing squad. A few seconds more and the officer will shout: "Fire!" Can one make a Forum Theatre scene starting from such givens? Can a spect-actor shout "Stop!" and replace the protagonist to try to find a solution? I think not.*
> —Augusto Boal, Games for Actors and Non-Actors, p. 226

BOAL'S INSISTENCE THAT THE Forum scene must not begin at a moment like the one described above is the problem I have with Forum Theatre. I do not think of the firing squad situation as solvable, but I am not looking for theatre to provide solutions. When I started working with Theatre of the Oppressed, most of the events I wanted to tackle were urgent, violent situations, like the police savagery I experienced during 1999's "Battle of Seattle," or the wave of brutality that overtook Yale University during my junior year of college in response to protests against the Iraq War. In trying to put them on stage, I could not follow Boal's advice to "go back, pick up the story again at an earlier point in time, and find out at what point the oppressed still had a choice of several solutions" (1992, p. 226). I did not feel as though I had that option when I was trying to dodge tear gas and billy clubs in downtown Seattle or when my friends and I were getting spit on or beaten up by our fellow students for staging vigils around campus. In those cases, there was no initial event when I could possibly have sorted things out with my aggressors: the only alternative would have been not to act.

Looking Beyond Solutions

By using theatre to tell these sorts of "impossible" stories, I see the potential to inspire change that goes beyond the immediate problem at hand. The simple action of focusing on oppressed people as protagonists—for example, privileging the points of view of protestors or students threatened with violence—creates a shift in the conventional narratives of an oppressive situation. I was first drawn to Augusto Boal's work because of his reimagining of the actor-audience dynamic. In *Games for Actors and Non-Actors* (1992), Boal writes that the "fundamental principles of TO [are] the intention to transform the spectator into protagonist of the theatrical action, and by this transformation, to try to change society" (p. 224). Though my work does not adhere to many of the structures of Theatre of the Oppressed, it remains closely aligned with Boal's work both in its exploration of spect-actor involvement and in its focus on telling the stories of people who are too often relegated to the roles of spectators in society.

I am especially interested in theatre's capacity to bring disparate protagonists together, helping to define group identities and build community based on shared experiences. By moving away from a focus on solutions, I hope to provoke actors and audience members with questions and experiences that do not culminate or find resolution in a single performance event, but that continue to foment action and solidarity beyond the play's conclusion. Much of my work takes place in prisons, which present unique challenges as well as opportunities for artistic innovation. By immersing myself in prisoners' experiences, learning as much as I can about their living conditions and social codes, I am able to help them create theatre that breaks with traditional narrative forms in order to better reflect their day-to-day reality. This includes diverging from traditional Theatre of the Oppressed practices, especially those pertaining to the joker, the guide figure central to Forum Theatre.

As Mady Schutzman notes in her chapter "Joker Runs Wild," in *A Boal Companion* (2006), jokers in Forum Theatre are "likely to order and direct participants' attention to problem-solving in its most traditional form—as a focused, argumentative, and intellectual challenge to oppression" (p. 134). Though this process can take place in prison, I see greater possibilities for change in engaging the chaotic, visceral reality of life behind bars. Instead of guiding the audience to evaluate "whether or not a spect-actor/protagonist has won," as Boal (1992) suggests (p. 233), I prefer jokering that fragments the theatrical event for both actors and audience, uniting them through shared experience. In this sense, I follow Schutzman's example when she compares Theatre of the Oppressed jokers to the traditional figure of jokers, who

> Instead of being stuck on a resolution of contradictions ... are bent on a playfulness among the irresolute. Consequently, paradox, inconsistency, approximation, ambiguity, and nonsense wreak their divine (and amusing) lessons into the labor of social change. (p. 143)

In *Theatre of the Oppressed* (1995) Boal writes that theatrical choices are inherently political "because all the activities of man are political, and theatre is one of them. Those who try to separate theatre from politics try to lead us into error—and this is a political attitude" (p. ix). Boal's statement is at the heart of my prison work, where I experiment with theatrical forms and conventions in order to highlight the humanity of the prisoners and the complexity of their stories. Although I am attuned to the inherently political content of our theatrical work, I do not consider it to be the totality of the inmates' experience of theatre. Just as dangerous as the idea that art can be apolitical is the idea that it is reducible to easily understood political symbols and solutions.

Signaling Through the Flames

More than thirty years before Boal's experiments with spect-actors and non-traditional approaches to making theatre, the French poet and philosopher Antonin Artaud was advocating a radical "Theatre of Cruelty" that would "abolish the stage and the auditorium and replace them by a single site, without barrier of any kind, which [would] become the theatre of action" (1994, p. 13). I understand this "Theatre of Action" as one that forges an impetus for engagement between actors and audience similar to Boal's. Yet while Boal's approach to theatrical revolution is pragmatic and largely grounded in realism, Artaud's is mystical and based on dreamlike states and dark fantasies. Boal wants to draw the audience in to find solutions to social problems; Artaud wants to terrify them into freeing themselves from established social structures. For Artaud:

> The public will believe in the Theatre's dreams on condition that it take them for true dreams and not for a servile copy of reality; on condition that they allow the public to liberate within itself the magical liberties which it can only recognize when they are imprinted with terror and cruelty. (p. 14)

My interest in Artaud deepened as I began to work closely with Theatre of the Oppressed. Though Boal's vision of an empowered audience inspired me, I later became suspect of Forum Theatre, which often struck me as too theatrically conventional. The Forum scenes I saw usually took place on a proscenium stage and followed a traditional narrative structure, occasionally disrupted by a joker prodding the audience to enter the action of the play. In *Games for Actors and Non-Actors*, Boal defines the joker as being "the wild card, the leader of the game," and entrusts her with guiding the audience's interventions (1992, p. 21). As I participated in Forum Theatre, though, I started to see predictable patterns in the performances—including the spect-actors' interventions—that frustrated me. Frequently the situations presented onstage seemed didactic. And although Boal explicitly states that "jokers personally decide nothing" (p. 232) and that the joker is not "the president of the conference" or "the custodian of truth" (p. 21), I often felt that jokers in the Forums I witnessed were prompting the audience toward specific solutions, lowering the potential for unexpected interactions and audience-driven innovations.

Forum Theatre's approach seemed especially limited as I tried to think about using theatre to take on the situations in which I had personally felt most oppressed. The melee of out-of-control cops who ransacked the streets and assaulted protestors in Seattle, and the shock of thuggish students breaking into Yale dorm rooms to threaten my friends were too confusing, violent, and surreal to make much sense in a naturalistic, linear representation. In thinking about performing scenarios like these, I thought of Artaud's ideal theatre, in which both actors and audience are "like victims burnt at the stake, signaling through the flames" (p. 14). I wanted to address these kinds of terrifying and urgent situations in my theatre work, even though I knew I would not find solutions to the problems they presented.

I came to prison-based theatre unexpectedly, when a college friend and I were interning with a non-governmental organization that suddenly needed volunteers to take over a workshop in Talavera Bruce, the largest women's prison in Rio de Janeiro state. I saw quickly that the prison overflowed with the kinds of situations I wanted to explore: when we prompted the inmates to tell their stories, they shared chaotic memories that often did not have clear through-lines, but that demanded to be put on stage. Instead of trying to explain or simplify the inmates' experience there or in the prisons where I have worked since, my aim is to create theatre that brings its creators and its audience face-to-face with prison's complexities. In order to help prisoners bring their stories to life, to create an environment in which "the spectator is freed from his chains, finally acts, and becomes a protagonist" (Boal, 1985, p. 142), the theatrical language needs to reflect life in prison, with its daily struggles, complex hierarchies, and constant confusion.

Learning the Codes of Prison

Space and time exist very differently in prison. Between the constant influx of new prisoners and the unexpected removal or transfer of veterans to different prisons (or, less frequently, to freedom), the sense of community and social structure in any given cell is always shifting. With these social shifts, the prisoners' physical reality also undergoes drastic changes. In the *carceragem* (jailhouse) where I led a workshop in 2009 in Nova Iguaçu, a city just outside Rio de Janeiro, the population of a twenty-by-twenty foot cell constantly ranged from 35 to as many as 60 prisoners. When it was at its fullest, there was physically not enough room for all of the prisoners to lie down at once. Each night, an unlucky group would have to crouch in the corner.

Time in prison never obeys traditional narrative structures of beginning, middle, and end. Prisoners know not only that they can be transferred, sentenced, or freed virtually at any moment, but also that the use of their present time has varying values. In the *carceragem*, for example, those with coveted custodial jobs have their sentences reduced by three days for every day they spend working; for them, every ten days represent one month. The only common beginning and end that inmates share is that they enter into the prison system, and then some time later, often in the distant future, they depart from it. In other words, the master narrative inside prison is based around coming from or going back to the outside world; the time that the inmates spend inside the prison is disordered and unpredictable.

As a theatre artist working in the prison space, my job is to help prisoners tell their stories by trying to learn as much about their reality as I can, and by looking for common ideas and themes without imposing them. In Nova Iguaçu, the prisoners in the cell I was working with were called the "People of Israel," set apart because they were not linked to any of the three major cartels that control Rio's drug trade. While most prisoners were segregated based on the cartel to which they "belong," the People of Israel were defined for being unaffiliated, for their lack of commonality outside of the prison. In building theatre based on their experiences, what seemed most significant to me was the community that we could construct based on performance, a community of "non-actors" telling their own stories.

My first challenge in prison is always to extend a small degree of expressive freedom to a group of people under extreme physical stress. In Nova Iguaçu, the inmates inevitably showed up hunched and cramped from sleeping on the floor of the overcrowded cell, and those who had not slept the night before skipped the workshop to stay in the cell and catch up on sleep. Boal's games allowed these men a range of physical expression. Games like "Colombian Hypnosis," in which one partner guides another through space using only his hand, often seemed revelatory, as they allowed the prisoners to experiment with movements that their normal living conditions could never permit. Image Theatre exercises, which Boal designed so that participants "don't think with words ... [but rather] with their own images" (1992, p. 3) were also crucial to the prisoners' exploration of the creative potential of their own bodies.

Although I tried to inspire, push, or (frequently) cajole the inmates in Nova Iguaçu toward an expressiveness that was unattainable in their cell, I wanted their day-to-day experiences—including the intense physical discomfort—to serve as the basis for our work. Part of my work in prison, of course, is to communicate strategies that could be useful to the inmates beyond the theatre workshop, and teaching positive self-expression is often the calling card that allows me into the prison in the first place. But I believe that the more important work is helping prisoners represent the hardships of their experiences without succumbing to them.

Furthermore, I do not want the inmates to consider me an all-knowing, all-powerful teacher and director. I do hope to be able to transmit the knowledge that I have to share with them, which frequently involves invoking my authority as a theatre "expert" and—especially—as a non-prisoner. I recognize, however, that the prisoners' stories, experiences, and talents must be the basis of our work together. They are the ones living in a twenty-by-twenty foot cell, and they have developed their own codes—physical, temporal, and social—to survive.

As the prisoners in Nova Iguaçu became more comfortable in the workshop, they also grew rowdier. This meant that they were much more willing to participate in exercises and share their stories, but also that everything tended to happen at once: some would want to repeat a warm-up game while others were eager to begin rehearsing scenes, and another group would break away to discuss a forthcoming soccer game. Fernando (a pseudonym), a short, slight prisoner in his early twenties, had a particularly annoying penchant for foul-mouthed imitations of radio personalities. In the midst of the confusion, he would shout profanity-laced tirades over the din, hitting his throat with his hand to imitate static reception. It seemed to me that each of the prisoners was angling to be the standout, the star actor, or simply to be heard. Since the inmates were accustomed to sharing a cell with dozens of other men, I imagined that making their presence felt at all times would be a necessary strategy for self-preservation. Yet as a workshop leader and joker, I worried about losing control.

Slowly, I learned to welcome the controlled chaos: instead of trying to impose an order on it, I tried to focus it toward the stage. In this chapter, I describe moments from this work, which led, ultimately, to a modified version of a Forum play. I offer only glimpses of the process, but my aim is to provide readers with an understanding of the nature of the workshops and the performance. With only two months from the beginning of the workshop to the performance date, I knew that our group would have to take advantage of our encounters, using our rehearsal process to highlight images, characters, and stories that could be included in our final production. For example, Fernando's "radio voice" became a cue for shifting scenarios onstage. By recognizing the confusion of the prison as a crucial aesthetic element of our work, rather than a hindrance to it, we were able to take interesting moments from games and other workshop activities and transfer them directly into our play. In this sense, recognizing the social shifting and multiplicity of voices as an inherent part of life in the *carceragem* led to one of the defining characteristics of our aesthetic experimentation: namely, the choice to fill the stage with multiple and shifting jokers.

Boal's own view of the joker changed significantly over time. In *Theatre of the Oppressed* (1985), describing the functions of the joker at the Arena Theatre in São Paulo during the 1960s, he writes: "the 'joker's' is a magical reality; he creates it" (p. 182). But later, in *Games for Actors and Non-Actors* (1992), he cautions that in interacting with the audience "jokers must watch out for all 'magic' solutions. They can interrupt the spect-actor/protagonist's action if they consider this action to be magic" (p. 233). He also insists that the joker be both emotionally and physically separate from the audience. "Some jokers," he notes, "are tempted to mix with the audience, to sit with other spect-actors; this can be completely demobilising" (p. 234). After all, Boal intended Theatre of the Oppressed to serve as a "rehearsal of revolution" (1985, p. 155), so the joker's job is to provide a trusted, neutral presence mediating between the onstage action and the urges and intents of the audience.

From conversations with the inmates, I knew that none of them had encountered that sort of trusted, mediating figure during their time on the inside. When the inmates talked about their imprisonment and the people involved in it, their stories were confused events with characters who changed radically or disappeared without explanation. Boal recalls that during his work at the Arena Theatre, "we were much more interested in showing real things (borrowing terms from Brecht) than in revealing how things really are" (1985, p. 167). Similarly, my objective in Nova Iguaçu was not to compartmentalize the prisoners' stories according to the rules of traditional narrative, but rather to bring the audience into the prisoners' world. Our play, which the prisoners named *"Penitenciária 666,"* was an attempt to bring the audience into the bewildering and often frightening experience of daily life in prison.

By settling on constantly shifting jokers guiding the audience, I wanted to give our audience of prison staff and university students a visceral connection to the prisoners' experiences. As in traditional Forum Theatre scenes, the jokers in *"Penitenciária 666"* had the responsibility of drawing the audience into the play. Instead of acting as neutral facilitators hovering above the action, however, they took on the role of agitators, prodding or coercing the public into the performance. These jokers directly and intentionally disobeyed Boal's edict to "avoid all actions which could manipulate or influence the audience" (1985, p. 232). Instead, they offered competing, purposely manipulative influences in an attempt to force the audience into an Artaud-style Theatre of Action.

Schutzman notes that in its origins in the Arena Theatre, Boal's joker was "a trickster of sorts, consciously wielding a strategy of re-articulation to obscure easy answers and to discourage fixed identities" (p. 134). She compares this to the historical concept of the joker, who had "an ability to survive, even evolve, in ruptured landscapes and negative space (the nought)–that liminal space where positions unravel" (p. 143). I recognize that ability in the inmates I work with, and try to honor it by making our theatre reflect their experiences. The result–which I call Last-Minute Theatre, based on prison's constant upheaval– is often intentionally provocative and confusing. "*Penitenciária* 666" was not intended to find solutions to the myriad and complex problems in the prison system. Instead, its goal was to bring audience and actors together–however fleetingly–to "signal through the flames."

Entering "*Penetenciária* 666": An Exercise in Last-Minute Theatre

"*Penitenciária* 666" began in the *carceragem* corridor and opened in classic Forum Theatre mode. Carlos, as the joker, introduced the play to the audience and led them through the "Cross and the Circle,"[1] a time-honored TO game. For our second warm-up game, Carlos asked audience members to find partners and experiment with connecting different body parts: foot-to-foot, pinky-to-pinky, and so on. When he got to elbow-to-elbow, a high-pitched shrieking started at the other end of the corridor, near the entrance to the cellblocks. Carlos continued the game as the noise got louder. Soon, the audience saw that the noise was a siren from the "cop car" made up of four inmates marching toward them, miming semi-automatic weapons and chanting, "You're gonna die. You're gonna die!"

When the "cops" made it to the other end of the corridor, they cut off the warm-up, holding the audience at (invisible) gunpoint while questioning Carlos: "What are you doing here? Put your hands on your head! Lift up your shirt! No, hands on your head! Lift up your shirt!" The lead cop searched him and found a small packet of pot, which led his three colleagues to arrest the whole audience–"Let's go! Let's go! Everybody, hands behind your backs!" The audience was then taken to the "cell" (an empty classroom) where the rest of the scene took place.

The exposure of our joker as totally vulnerable not only put him on an equal level with audience members, but also made him responsible for an oppressive situation in which they were directly implicated (cops in Rio often sweep up anyone found in the general vicinity of a stash of drugs). In a matter of seconds, Carlos' role changed from that of a trusted mentor to a common criminal. Suddenly, he flipped from joker to oppressed protagonist, and the audience's experience was fundamentally altered because of his character's "wrongdoing."

By transforming this fundamental aspect of Forum Theatre, we also altered the audience's relationship to the dramatic action. In a conventional Forum scene, the spect-actors choose when and how to intervene; in "*Penitenciária 666*," they moved from audience to cellmates with virtually no warning, due to circumstances entirely beyond their control, which is how many of the inmates described their arrest and imprisonment. It also briefly transferred the de facto function of joker to the inmates playing the cops, since they became responsible for guiding the audience deeper into the action of the piece.

Once everyone was in the "cell," two different inmates became jokers at the same time, approaching audience members to orient them to prison and give them a crash course on what to expect inside the cell.

BRUNO: On Monday and Friday, when the church visits, the bathroom's closed out of respect. Got it? And midnight is lights out.

FERNANDO: (banging on his throat and shouting in his "radio" voice): You've just arrived in hell! Here, we've got bedbugs and spoiled food!

Although brusque, this introduction was in keeping with a traditional jokering model: the two actors set the tone for the rest of the performance and helped the audience orient to their new surroundings. But the information quickly became contradictory: Bruno wanted the audience to lie down with the others (head-to-foot, on their sides, in order to maximize space), while Fernando said they should spend their first night standing, huddled in the corner. Over the course of only a few minutes, the initial joker, whose role was to gently guide the audience into the world of the play, as in traditional Forum Theatre, was replaced by a number of jokers expressing a cacophony of desperate demands.

When Carlos, the original joker, introduced "*Penitenciária 666*," he told the audience that the events represented in the performance were based on another *carceragem* where many of the men had been held before being transferred to Nova Iguaçu. The conditions there were much worse, he explained: "It's a very different story than what happens here, thank God." From our conversations during rehearsals, however, I knew that much of the performance was based on the prisoners' current conditions, though Carlos and the other actors did not feel able to make any explicit criticisms of their present situation.

After bringing the audience members into the cell and giving them a crash course in prison social norms, the actors continued to treat them as fellow inmates, albeit without drawing them into the action directly. As a result, the audience began to separate themselves physically from the action; while the inmates lay down together in one cramped corner of the performance space, the audience remained on foot around the perimeter of the room. Within the logic of the performance, however, they were still in the cell, and the actors spoke to them as they would to vulnerable new inmates: by giving them orders. As many new inmates do, the audience experienced a loss of agency. Although they took on a passive role, they were not so much spectators as witnesses and observers, sharing the "cell" space with the actors and acknowledged as silent, obedient participants.

The course of the action in *"Penitenciária 666"* introduced the public to the hardships of mundane, everyday events in prison—sleeping or going to the bathroom in an overcrowded cell—and to the violence that such living conditions in the *carceragem* can inspire. When a young inmate ate spoiled food—against the advice of other prisoners —and became sick, his cellmates decided to punish him for his lack of self-control, ultimately beating him to death. As soon as the ritualized killing was finished, a veteran inmate swore everyone else in the "cell" to silence: "Look, nobody saw anything. He killed himself, got it?"

Although the audience's role was passive, their shared status gave them a sort of complicity in the murder, which presented a problem with no possible solution. Here, there was no joker figure to orient them, only a fellow inmate ordering them to shut up: a reminder that in prison, inmates are condemned to inaction.

Ironically, inaction was as close to a solution as *"Penitenciária 666"* presented. When the killing resulted in further crackdown from the guards, the inmates proposed a "hunger strike" to expose the miserable conditions that they suggested were responsible for the murder. After an interlude featuring a parody of sensationalist local news reporting, with one inmate circling the audience and "reporting live by helicopter" on the "rebellion in 666," a guard informed the prisoners that their protest had worked, and that they would be transferred to another *carceragem*. The actors stepped forward to rejoin the audience, and finished the play by reminding their "fellow prisoners" of their common goal. "When I think of freedom," Carlos said, "I think of starting a new life."

Freedom, of course, remained a distant goal both for the characters in *"Penitenciária 666"* and for the actors who represent them, all of whom were bound to spend an undetermined amount of time in the penal system. But we were not being cynical by ending the play with a reminder of the prisoners' hopes for freedom; instead, we hoped to unite actors and audience members in a shared experience that communicated the sensation of imprisonment without either falling into despair or trying to find an "answer" for a situation that renders solutions untenable. Even in liberating the characters in the play, we could not move beyond the structures of the prison system. By bringing the audience into the community of the cell, to "signal through the flames," however briefly, with the inmates, we hoped to create an event that communicated the difficulties, persistence, and fundamental humanity of those who live behind bars.

Boal writes in his autobiography, *Hamlet and the Baker's Son* (2001), that, "metaphorically, the Theatre of the Oppressed was born in prison" (p. 298). He recalls his own time as a political prisoner during Brazil's dictatorship and remembers longing to reach out to the "common" prisoners, "the people I was seeking, piled up on top of each other" (p. 298). During his imprisonment, Boal was struck by the void that prison represented, but also by the possibilities that this liminal space offered. He writes that, "if beyond those walls, social structures exist—structures that we know to be generative of delinquents!—inside the walls, a form of social organisation must be invented." Theatre, he argues, "can be a fit instrument, the proper language for that discourse, that quest for oneself" (p. 297).

In order to build the kind of theatre that brings prisoners together and helps them articulate a quest for themselves, I cannot try to make sense of everything that goes on in the prison. Instead, I have to work with the confusion of the setting, to let the prisoners' stories out in all of their vivid, chaotic reality. Boal argues against addressing these kinds of circumstances—like his man in front of the firing squad—with Forum Theatre, and I agree, inasmuch as I cannot imagine any audience coming up with solutions. But I am adamant not only that these stories deserve to be part of a people's theatre, but also that the process of creation—and the community that stems from it—represents a "rehearsal for revolution," a reclaiming of the protagonists' places in the stories they confront in their lives and represent onstage.

In his final book, *The Aesthetics of the Oppressed* (2006), Boal explicitly addresses the question of how to make theatre in prisons. To work effectively, he writes, participants need to engage the disorientation they find on the inside, creating "an effect of shock and surprise—without an explicit condemnation" (p. 116). By working in prison settings, creating theatre that is bound to happen at the last minute, I hope to use these effects of shock and surprise to create a shared experience between actors and audience. Schutzman writes of an imagined joker who would privilege the artistic imperative over explicit political advocacy. Such a Joker would be a communicator not seeking common ground so much as maximizing possibilities for the articulation (and re-articulation) of uncommon beliefs, working toward a vision of community that thrives on constant reformulation (p. 143).

This re-articulation is at the foundation of what I call Last-Minute Theatre. By telling inmates' "impossible" stories, and creating a theatrical aesthetic derived from their realities, plays like *"Penitenciária 666"* facilitate opportunities for prisoners to show themselves as protagonists amid the chaos of the prison, and to experiment with the transformative possibilities of a new community.

Note

1. In this exercise participants attempt to draw an imaginary cross with their right hand while, at the same time, inscribing an imaginary circle with their left. See *Games for Actors and Non-Actors* (1992), page 50, for a more detailed explanation.

References

Artaud A. (1994). *Theatre and its double* (M.C. Richard, Trans.). New York, NY: Grove Press.

Boal, A. (2006). *The aesthetics of the oppressed*. New York, NY: Routledge.

——. (1992). *Games for actors and non-actors* (A. Jackson, Trans.). New York, NY: Routledge.

——. (2001). *Hamlet and the baker's son: My life in theatre and politics*. (A. Jackson & C. Blaker, Trans.). New York, NY: Routledge.

——. (1985). *Theatre of the oppressed* (C. A. & M. Leal McBride, Trans.). New York, NY: Theatre Communications Group.

Schutzman, M. (2006). Joker runs wild. In M. Schutzman & J. Cohen-Cruz (Eds.), *A Boal companion: Dialogues on theatre and cultural politics* (pp. 133-145). New York, NY: Routledge.

CHAPTER TWELVE

Jiwon Chung

Theatre of the Oppressed as a Martial Art

> *Theatre is a martial art.*
> —Augusto Boal, *Hamlet and the Baker's Son*, p. 314
>
> *Servitude can be broken only through a political practice [that] involves a break with the familiar, the routine ways of seeing, hearing, feeling, understanding things ... so that the organism may become receptive to the potential forms of a nonaggressive, nonexploitative world.*
> —Herbert Marcuse, *An Essay on Liberation*, p. 6

THEATRE OF THE OPPRESSED (TO) is a rich, extraordinarily deep way of transforming oppression in all its manifestations. It includes tools to deal with almost every dimension of oppression: individual/intrapsychic oppression (Rainbow of Desire/Cops-in-the-head), interpersonal oppression and institutional oppression (Forum Theatre and Legislative Theatre), and ideological oppression (Invisible Theatre, Newspaper Theatre, Image Theatre). My TO work with activists in prison reform, anti-racism work, union organizing, immigrant rights, teaching, and social work addresses individual and systemic oppression, true to the philosophy and forms I learned from studying with Augusto Boal. However, Boal often said, "TO deals with oppression, not [physical] aggression.[1] Learn jujitsu or karate, if you would deal with aggression" (1992, p. 254). I understand him to be saying that we can work up to the point of physical aggression, but we cannot work with it directly. Unlike Boal, I do work with situations of physical aggression in my TO work. Though this work is embedded in a broader process of Image and Forum Theatre, this chapter focuses only on my work with moments of violence.

I believe it is important to include physical aggression in TO work because:

- Interpersonal oppression exists on a continuum, from the subtle violence of a gesture or an expression, to verbal aggression, to violent physical assault, rape, torture, or murder. In dealing with oppression, the work of TO seems to be incomplete if certain types of oppression are beyond our capacity to address them.
- In workshops dealing with oppression, physical violence often rears its head. In almost every TO workshop that I have facilitated, there has been

at least one story involving direct physical aggression. The experience of violent oppression is often compounded by shame, self-blame, and silence. TO practitioners therefore run the risk of perpetuating or replicating oppression if we give the message that some experiences are off-limits for exploration.

- Interpersonal physical violence, or the threat of it, is built into institutional violence. For example, the institutional violence of the mortgage/banking system that impoverishes and dispossesses working-class homeowners while enriching financial institutions requires "foot soldiers" to break down doors, physically throw individuals out of houses, and cart furniture and possessions into the street. The threat of that violence maintains the institutional or structural violence.[2]

- Physical aggression frequently occurs, even though we say it is unacceptable. Aggression in heightened situations is instinctual, and I have seen many Forum Theatre performances in which spect-actors intervened with physical aggression. As in real life, these interventions sometimes resulted only in stronger resistance from the oppressor.

- People often feel disempowered by the threat of violence and by their feelings about how they reacted in situations of physical violence. When we learn ways to deal with direct physical violence, we learn the larger lesson that even situations that seem unsolvable (and therefore un-forumable) can be challenged, resisted, and ultimately transformed.

In my work, I take Boal's statement about theatre being a martial art not as a metaphor but as an actual prescription for exploration. I use the martial arts and TO together to actively explore physical aggression and violence in oppressive situations. I believe TO can simulate the reality of physically oppressive situations, while teaching spontaneity, courage, and creative transformation of the violence. TO as a martial art can then reveal essential truths about power relationships as it allows both aesthetic transformation and practical problem solving.

Why TO, Not Just Martial Arts?

Why not simply teach a martial arts class? I believe TO is needed because traditional martial arts tend to be hierarchical and often replicate oppression in terms of seniority, gender, size, and ability/ableness. Martial arts classes usually operate on the model of the expert who has secret advanced knowledge that students must learn before they can defend themselves. This is the "banking model" of education in which an expert deposits knowledge into passive receptors, and it tends to be disempowering instead of empowering (Freire, 1970).

Many traditional martial arts classes and self-defense classes are inefficient and sometimes ineffective ways of learning to transform aggression. Tradition may trap people in one set of actions (for example, only kicking or punching), or it may teach an unrealistic, stylized or limited set of responses to a potential infinity of aggressive acts. Like language learners who go to a country where the language is actually spoken, people who train in martial arts are often stunned when they realize that life does not conform to textbook examples or models and that they are incapable of defending themselves in real situations.

Through its problem-posing approach, the Forum Theatre process, in particular, allows people to practice ways to deal with oppression and physical aggression through exploration and experimentation. This generates a spontaneous, creative mindset that can be applied in any aggressive situation. In Forum we can use all the elements of theatre to create a situation in which the protagonist experiences physical and emotional states close to what she would experience in a violent situation. This makes it more likely that she will be able to access what she learned when she is in real danger. Experiencing agency under duress, in the presence of allies, is effective and empowering.

The Process of TO as a Martial Art

In my TO work I use Boal's entire arsenal of exercises, as well as exercises from other movement and martial arts approaches. I believe Boal's demechanization, the process of dishabituation of the usual habits of perception, movement and thought, is often under-emphasized in TO work. I focus on demechanization throughout the entire process of developing Forum plays, as well as in the initial exercises. Demechanization serves as a somatic (physical) preparation for containing and channeling the powerful energy that may arise in the TO process. Understanding how we are mechanized gives us awareness of how we limit and oppress our own bodies (usually as attempts to protect ourselves). This moment-to-moment awareness becomes a skill that, with practice, we can apply in every moment of life. Demechanization of perception leads to an expansion and acuity of awareness that allows us to notice aggressive tendencies and energies sooner. We can apply this awareness to prevent some situations from becoming violent, and to intervene more effectively when violence does erupt against us. Demechanization of movement patterns allows spontaneity in our thinking and in our responses to external situations. It can transform the startle reflex, allowing us to act without fear, or to move beyond paralysis to action, even when fear is present.

Expanding Awareness

I use the following exercises to develop kinesthetic awareness as a teleceptor, a sense that extends awareness beyond the boundaries of the self.[3] This is a perceptual skill we all have, and it is basic to the arsenal of TO as a martial art, as it cultivates the ability to sense the opponent's body in space and to anticipate his movements.

Blind Sculpt Variation:[4] In pairs, facing each other, one person creates an image with her body. Her partner, with eyes closed, gently and respectfully touches her body with her hands to sense her position. The partner then recreates the image with her own body. Both people open their eyes and compare their images. After they have exchanged roles, I, as joker, introduce a variation. Once again, the first person creates an image with his body, while the partner has his eyes closed. This time the partner with closed eyes places his hands out in front of himself and shuffles forward until he makes contact with his partner. As soon as he touches his partner, he stops. Next he touches his partner only two times, in two places. He then backs away and recreates the whole image. After each partner has done this, they repeat the process, recreating the image after touching only once. Usually the participants are surprised at how accurate their images are.

Complete the Image: I also use a variation of the TO Complete the Image exercise to explore conflict from an internal, kinesthetic perspective and to build energetic and somatic awareness. As in Boal's classic Complete the Image game, two partners begin by making an image of shaking hands. One person steps away and then comes back in to "complete" the image with a different body position, creating a new relationship, and freezes. The other person then steps out and steps back in to create another image. They continue this process, experimenting with various relationships, exploring many somatic/sculptural possibilities of interaction.[5]

Next, the pairs continue the image-making, now always maintaining some point of physical contact. I suggest that each person focus his awareness on the point of contact, and then increase his awareness of the rest of his partner's body. As participants continue making images, I often give prompts, asking them to make images that show, for example, support, seduction, domination, and oppression. After this, the pairs repeat the process, but instead of starting with the image of handshaking, they begin with an image in which one person is physically overpowering the other. They continue as before, stepping in and out to make a series of images, now exploring ways in which a person can overpower another.

The next step is a shift to one partner as protagonist and one as antagonist. Instead of releasing each other, the antagonist continues with the intention to oppress her partner. The protagonist slowly moves to a count of eight to try to neutralize the oppression. They repeat this many times. As joker I guide the participants to focus on their breathing and to observe the kinesthetic sensations that indicate force, angles, and leverage. As the exercise progresses, I guide the antagonist to escalate her oppression and the amount of force she uses (from a scale of one to ten). The protagonist continues to explore responses to the oppression. If the energy escalates too fast, or if individuals seem to be struggling, panicking or using excessive force, I dial down the steps and resume at a lower intensity. Once participants are comfortable with the level of stress, they dial it up again.

When participants use common movements like a choke hold, a hair pull, a pin, or a lock, I may ask the pair to explore that specific movement to look for ways to neutralize the oppression in that moment. They work to notice moments of advantage, disadvantage and opportunity, as well as any lapses in awareness by either partner. They focus on expanding their kinesthetic awareness to sense where the other person is in space, where his balance and contact with the floor is, and ultimately, what his intentions are. In this exercise participants explore how physical power manifests, and what it looks and feels like. As pairs repeat this exercise over and over, it becomes a dance of transformation, akin to Tai Chi or Aikido: the sensuous transformation of combat into dance, the gentle melding of other into self and self into other.

Sticky Hands/Push Hands: This is a classical exercise from Tai Chi Chuan that trains proprioception (awareness of the relative position of parts of the body) and spontaneity. It also introduces participants to the experience of being powerful without exerting large amounts of force or trying to dominate their partner. It is the physical practice of "power with" rather than "power over." In this exercise partners place one wrist gently against the other person's wrist. One person moves her arms, and the other person follows, passively, maintaining constant contact at the wrists. As joker, I guide participants to notice when they, as followers, absent-mindedly take on control, or when as leaders, they give up control. They focus on how they lead, how they follow, and how they react when wills collide. Next, they expand their awareness to include all of their own bodies, and then their partners' bodies as well, including their contact with the floor. With practice, people can sense not just the motion, but the texture and direction of the energy and intention that precedes the motion.

Next they each try to unbalance the other person, pressing the other person, using only the amount of force it would take to lift a dime. Again, I guide participants to notice what happens when they feel imbalanced, and how to accommodate or transform the situation by pressing into the ground. After this, they move to actual physical blows, in very slow motion, using the same quality of attention and energy. Through these exercises participants become more and more aware of the other person's energy, movement, and intention, as well as their own. This builds the capacity to be more conscious and to respond spontaneously in any moment, without stopping to think.

Preparation to Forum Violent Oppression

Preventing Re-traumatization. The process of working with moments of violence can be highly charged, so it is vital that protagonists, antagonists, and audience are not re-traumatized. Though Forum theatre is traditionally performed for general audiences, I only forum scenes of aggression with participants who have done preparatory exercises together in a workshop. The sensitivity of the joker and the support of the group greatly influence the depth-level the protagonist is willing to explore, as well as the degree to which she can safely relive and potentially transform heightened and terrifying moments. During all phases of the process I believe it is vital for the joker to:

- Check in with the protagonist frequently, making sure she feels she can handle the emotions and that she wants to continue. Check in frequently with all participants, and change, stop, or verbally process as needed.
- Guide participants to work with still images and slow motion: still images reflect the frozen nature of the violent incident; slow motion reflects the suspended, expanded sense of the event. Both are ways of working in small increments, and allow the action to be safer, more easily controlled and contained, and easier to understand and ultimately transform.
- Allow the protagonist to create distance from the event if he needs to by choosing a "double" (i.e., another person) to stand in for him in the scene.[6] Often protagonists will witness their scene first, then step back in as protagonist.
- Use Image Theatre to create images of what could have been different: this seeds the possibility of change.
- Give the protagonist directorial control over the creation of the scene: allow her to stop the images, play them backwards and forwards, in slow motion, or to change them at will.

Developing the Forum Scenes. I follow Boal's progression for developing Forum: participants share stories of oppression, create and show images of those oppressions, and then form small groups based on commonalities in their images and/or stories. In these groups they create conventional Forum

Theatre scenes, each showing the anti-model, leading to the point of crisis. Eventually we fully forum the scenes, with workshop participants as audience/spect-actors. However, during the process of creating scenes, protagonists have the option of including moments of physical aggression, either as one or more frozen images or in stylized slow motion. Depending on the story, the depiction may involve one key action, or a chain of several aggressive actions. Here is the summary of a scene from Jean, a participant from a workshop in the Bay Area in California:

Jean is returning home from shopping, carrying a bag of groceries. As she opens the door to the lobby of her apartment, a man follows her inside. She looks nervous but continues down the corridor. When he continues to follow her, she turns around to ask him if he wants something. He suddenly attacks her, pushing her back into the wall. She screams and he begins choking her. Neighbors come out into the lobby. The assailant runs off, leaving Jean sobbing.

Because Jean had decided to work with this moment, we did not yet move to foruming the scene. Instead, Jean sculpted the body of the participant playing her assailant and then placed herself in the image in relationship to him. She created a frozen image of herself pinned against the wall, with his hands choking her. During this process, I watched carefully and checked in with her frequently to make sure she was not overwhelmed or re-triggered. She then picked someone to replace her in this image, and made final adjustments in the image. Next, she and the man playing her assailant acted out the attack in slow motion, ending with the final image of choking. Again, she stepped out and picked a second double to stand in for her, as she fine-tuned the sequence.

We used still images and slow motion to reflect the frozen nature of the incident for the protagonist, as well as her suspended, expanded sense of the event. This made it safer for the protagonist, allowing her more control and helping to prevent re-traumatization. Then, everyone in the group found a partner, and very gently the pairs reconstructed Jean's first image of being choked. This is the Boal's "embryon," the essentialized representation of a moment used to develop Forum Theatre scenes (1992). Each protagonist looked for a way to escape. Each attacker offered only enough resistance to challenge her partner. I asked that during this process the participants actively extend their kinesthetic sense into the other person's body, sensing her whole body, including the feet. This awareness prevents the body from contracting into the startle reflex and stiffening or freezing. In turn, it allows the protagonist to sense the other person's energy, so she can take appropriate action to co-opt the forces directed at her. Next the pairs dynamized the images in slow motion: one person moved in slow motion toward the other person, hands up, as if to choke his partner. This made it easier for the protagonist to find a way to transform the aggression. After the pairs had tried a few different responses in slow motion, they were ready to create the Forum Play.

Playing the Forum Scenes

Because Jean wanted to forum the moment of violence within her larger scene, the actors from her original scene presented it to the group again. The protagonist (the double for Jean) and the antagonist depicted the action up to the moment when Jean turns around to ask the attacker if he wants something. At this point, I gave the cue for the movement to turn into slow motion, until she is being choked and pinned; then the actors froze. As joker, I reminded the workshop participants that they had already practiced a series of interventions in this moment of the scene with their partners. We replayed the scene, and as in conventional Forum Theatre, I invited participants to stop the scene at any time, replace the protagonist, and replay the scene with a different intervention. However, the interventions were all in slow motion, and the antagonist also improvised responses to the interventions in slow motion.   Because we were dealing with a moment of physical violence, I emphasized that whether interventions succeeded or not was secondary to the courage and solidarity spect-actors demonstrated by entering the scene and trying an intervention. I said, "Every action you take is a contribution to the process of our collective learning and problem-solving. We discover what works by eliminating what doesn't, and we can only do that by experimenting. Each attempt brings us closer. Finally, if you 'fail,' you reaffirm the difficulty that the protagonist faced: that she was not weak, but that this situation was truly oppressive, and that is why we have to work together to try to find ways to overcome it."

The actors started the scene again and several individuals tried interventions, one at a time, in slow motion: One individual replaced the protagonist and tried to pry the attacker's fingers off her neck in the chokehold. She was not successful and both actors escalated force. I asked them to slow down, breathe, and to look for a way to work together to explore and learn. I coached the protagonist to position her body for maximum leverage. She used the large muscles of her back, torso, and arms to twist the attacker's weaker fingers against his wrist, disabling him long enough to break out of the chokehold.

After this intervention, I asked the group if we could derive any lessons about how to respond from this intervention. They were not sure, so I asked everyone to pair up and to explore it kinesthetically. After the pair word, one participant pointed out, "If a person is stronger than you, usually you can find a part of his body (a joint) that is weaker than the force you are applying at that moment. In this case, the fingers of the assailant were weaker than my arms, and if I use the strength of my legs, I am even more powerful." Another person stated: "If I use brute force, they will sense it and react. But if I am subtle in my actions, they don't know what I'm doing. It's like I'm picking their pockets!"

In another intervention, the protagonist placed her hands together, creating a wedge shape with her fingers and arms. She moved very slowly first, then jerked her hands upward between the assailant's arms, breaking the hold. I asked the group if this intervention could be successful in a real situation. Most people said they were not sure if they could make it work, so again they worked in pairs, trying it several times. In the discussion afterward, one person noted that not panicking and expanding her energy into the other person made it possible for him to take action. Another participant mentioned that the simple movement of shifting his weight backwards slightly was enough to unbalance the attacker and weaken his hold. We tried many more interventions and discussed each.

Discussion and Insights

At the end of the Forum process, the group discussed general conclusions we can draw about what responses might be effective in violent situations. The following comments were shared by spect-actors after Jean's Forum scene was performed: "The simple fact of not freezing, not going into immobility allowed me to feel empowered, regardless of the outcome." Another person pointed out that sensing the other person's body gave her confidence to take a counter action: "It's like a poker game where you get to read their cards before they put them down." Others in the group agreed, and said that they were now more aware of signals of aggression from others, and thought they would be able to anticipate aggression and react sooner. "I could feel his energy start to attack me before his body did. When I sensed that, I felt like I was looking several moves ahead in this scary chess game. I felt I could avoid it or shut it down before it got too dangerous." Someone else shared his insight that when a person is attacking they're so focused on what they're trying to do that they don't see what else is going on. I agreed and offered the thought that at the heart of oppression and violence is always blindness, a blindness that we can use to reverse the situation.

A Final Step in the Forum

After the discussion, I asked Jean if she wanted to replay the scene again, now that she had practiced several of the spect-actor's interventions in the pair work. She did, so she replayed the scene in slow motion several times, trying many of the spect-actors' tactics to break the attacker's chokehold, first in slow motion, and then with increasing speed and vigor. After several attempts, flushed and trembling, she successfully broke away from her assailant. She looked at the group and as she caught her breath: "I don't know if I can always defeat an attack, but now my mind feels powerful. I can focus, I can try something, react. Before, I was a hysterical cloud of mush. It's interesting, something I never realized before ... if you take a microscope to the violence, like we did, you realize that it is full of moments of weakness and transformation, like a video screen being refreshed all the time. If you stop being paralyzed by fear, and subconsciously acquiescing to their aggression, then you can see that the wizard behind the curtain is really not so powerful. I think what I've just realized is that within every moment of aggression, there are spaces and moments of freedom and choice." She paused then continued, "Through this process, I feel I have a host of angels in my head and at my side. Each one of you is a guardian angel that could be there in my moment of need." We all looked at her, humbled and empowered by her words.

Conclusion

TO as a martial art is true to Augusto Boal's practice, but it emphasizes expanding kinesthetic and proprioceptive exploration to encompass intention and energy. My work emphasizes demechanization and integrates exercises from the martial arts, which allows spect-actors to explore situations of physical conflict through Image and Forum Theatre. With practice, participants gain awareness and insight they can apply every moment. TO as a martial art affirms that coercion, control, and domination are ultimately self-defeating. It is an experience of how genuine power comes from connection to the earth, to our minds and bodies, and to each other. When we are able to reach toward each other in solidarity, we are able to "liberate ourselves and our oppressors" (Freire, 1970, p. 44).

Notes

1.   Boal uses the term "aggression" to refer to physical violence, in comparison to "oppression" (1992, p. 254). I use the term in the same way, interchangeably with the term "physical violence." The term violence, unqualified, can refer to structural or metaphorical violence.

2.   This structural violence also manifests horizontally, as when the homeless rob and assault each other.

3.   Phenomenological philosopher Elizabeth Benhke uses the term "interkinesthetic affectivity" to refer to this mode of perception (2008). The somatic discipline Eutony uses the term "contact" for inclusive kinesthesia, and "transport" when this awareness involves

a weight bearing component (Alexander, 1981). The Chinese martial arts have the term "Ting Jing," or "Listening Power." Trigant Burrow uses the term "cotention" to refer to this general idea of inclusive awareness, especially as a means of defusing conflict (1964, p. 71). I use the terms telekinesthesia and teleception to emphasize that the proprioceptive/kinesthetic sense can be expanded at a distance and through inanimate objects (such as a prosthetic limb, a weapon, a tool, or a vehicle).

4. The original exercise, as described in *Games for Actors and Non-Actors* (1992) is "Swedish Multiple Sculpture" (p. 120).

5. See *Games for Actors and Non-Actors* (1992), page 139, for a description of this exercise.

6. The protagonist should participate in the scene only if s/he feels ready.

References

Alexander, G. (1981). *Eutony: The holistic discovery of the total person.* New York, NY: Felix Morrow.

Boal, A. (1979). *Theatre of the oppressed.* New York, NY: Communications Group Books.

—. (1992). *Games for actors and non-actors.* New York, NY: Routledge.

—. (2001). *Hamlet and the baker's son.* New York, NY: Routledge.

—. (2006). *Aesthetics of the oppressed.* New York, NY: Routledge.

Behnke, E.A. (2008). Interkinaesthetic affectivity: A phenomenological approach. *Continental Philosophy Review,* 41(2): 143-161.

Burrow, T. (1964). *Preconscious foundations of human experience.* New York, NY: Basic Books.

Freire, P. (1970). *Pedagogy of the oppressed.* New York, NY: Continuum Books.

Hudgins, K. (2002). *Experiential treatment for PTSD: The therapeutic spiral model.* New York, NY: Springer.

Marcuse, H. (1969). *An essay on liberation.* Boston, MA: Beacon Press.

CHAPTER THIRTEEN

Hector Aristizábal & Diane Lefer

The Wounded Joker

IN 1982 I WAS a Theatre artist and psychology student committed to social justice when I was falsely accused of being a member of the guerilla movement, then arrested and tortured by the Colombian military. Several years later, my younger brother was abducted by a right-wing death squad, tortured, and killed also because of his alleged involvement with the guerrillas. My identity is not defined by the experience of being tortured or of facing the horror of my brother's brutal murder, but these were pivotal moments in my life, leaving deep wounds—wounds I now refuse to see as incapacitating. For years, though, these events left me with a raging desire for revenge. I engaged in a constant internal struggle as I worked my way back to a commitment to nonviolent activism, back to being a man who loves beauty, who wants to create, not to destroy. This chapter tells the story of the evolution of *Nightwind*, a play I developed as part of my pathway to healing, in collaboration with my frequent writing partner Diane Lefer.

Nightwind

Seven years after my release from military custody, faced with ongoing death threats, I left Colombia. In exile in the United States, I initially continued the acting career that had been central to my life, but I also began to speak out against U.S. military support for the criminal regime in my homeland. While I spoke often about what was done to my brother, I revealed no details about the torture I myself had endured—until photographs emerged from the American military prison at Abu Ghraib in 2004.

Soon after those images were published, Michael Nutkiewicz, then the executive director of the Program for Torture Victims, a nonprofit organization based in Los Angeles providing free medical and psychological care to survivors, asked me to participate in a program recognizing the United Nations International Day in Support of Victims of Torture. He suggested that instead of making a speech, I improvise scenes from my own experience. For years I had resisted doing this. I feared that working with autobiographical material would be merely self-indulgent, but given what had emerged as post-

9/11 American policy, I felt it was my responsibility to present the reality of torture from a personal perspective. The audience response to my improvised performance was of a different emotional quality than when I simply spoke about torture. Though they seemed shocked by the graphic description of my experience and its similarities to the Abu Ghraib images, they also seemed inspired by the courage it took to depict such images. It was incredibly healing to be able to share with others what had been a personal nightmare; I felt the power of ritual as the creation of a container that can hold the elements essential for transformation. I later asked playwright Diane Lefer, Theatre director B.J. Dodge, and musician Enzo Fina to help me develop the performance that became *Nightwind*.

The play opens with me covered by a black piece of cloth, as I create a series of abstract images with my body, sound, and a few props. Most audiences interpret the images as the Statue of Liberty and the attack on the Twin Towers, followed by what may be my own birth or the birth of terrorist rage. The action of the play becomes more personal and specific as I re-create the blows and beatings, the fear, the electric shocks, and the times I was waterboarded, brought to the point of drowning. As I portray a variety of characters, I am able to play myself as the protagonist as well as my own antagonist, the interrogator who tortured me. I embody my brother's mutilated corpse as I enact his autopsy. In the final sequence of the performance, my consuming desire for violent revenge is interrupted by my young son who shows me the poster he is drawing: "Peace Now." The play ends with me inviting my small children to attend a peace demonstration, dancing with drums and stilts. I conclude, "We must keep dancing to kill the terrorist within." *Nightwind* is designed to travel and so the playing area is almost bare. This minimalist aesthetic is grounded in the principles of "Poor Theatre," as expressed by vanguard Polish Theatre director Jerzy Grotowski (1968) in which the traditional audience/stage configuration becomes unnecessary, technical requirements are limited, and performances can take place anywhere while easily adapting to each new environment (p. 19). Grotowski's ideas took deep root in Latin America, given the literal poverty of most Theatre companies there. As I perform *Nightwind*, audience members must make repeated perceptual leaps as I use a simple length of black silk to represent a rifle, straps of a backpack, my mother's shawl, a blindfold, handcuffs, helicopter rotors and more. A balloon is a pregnant belly and a soccer ball and, upon bursting, offers the sound of a rifle shot. These instant transformations reinforce the idea that images, like life's ordeals, can transform themselves and shift meaning. The play's theatrical language is based largely in these images and in the physicality of movement rather than words. As Steinman (1995) has suggested, "... movement seems to be a particularly potent force in unlocking memory's vivid detail" (p. 71), and indeed, the more I perform *Nightwind*, the more I remember, yet these memories no longer evoke the visceral feeling of violation. What happened in 1982 is carved in every part of my physical body, but when I remember through *Nightwind*, I also re-member—or put my members and memory back together in a different way. By taking control of situations over which in life I had little or no control and by turning the trauma into art, I have found an extraordinary sense of release. As I reenact pivotal scenes, I am able to bypass verbal rationalization and, instead, use aesthetic language to create a symbolization of my experience. It is now offered to others as a model and as a springboard to reflect and to imagine what could be done not only about torture but also other horrors and traumas activated for the spectators. As my personal experience becomes political, it reminds us of the power of art to be a place for the healing of the community, just as therapy provides healing for the individual. Thoughts need to be fully expressed in order to be fully thought; thoughts swimming in the mind alone are not fully thought. In my work I seek to counteract the Cartesian mind-body split, what Lawrence and Shapin (1998) have described as the "persistent feature of learned culture," (p. 4) that knowledge is something "disembodied," that it must be pure and separate from the physical body in order to be true (p. 1). As Boal (1985) noted, images have "the extraordinary capacity for making thought visible" (p. 137). In fact, even when we speak of the most abstract concepts, our thoughts need to be expressed—pressed out—by the muscles of the body. And so, in performance, thoughts rise with the pulsing of my blood. I call this "blood-thinking." Through spontaneous movement and the visual impressions of my images, my body summons the psyche so that healing can take place. I work with what Kubie (1953) has termed the "gut" component of memory (p. 439) and I trigger the circuitry of what Boal (2006) called "aesthetic neurons" which "process, jointly, ideas and emotions, memories and imagination, senses and abstractions" (p. 26). According to Boal, while only some people are given the title of artist, every human being is, substantively, an artist: "For the Aesthetics of the Oppressed, the most important thing is the Aesthetic Process ... [which] allows the subjects to exercise themselves in activities which are usually denied them, thus expanding their expressive and perceptive possibilities" (p. 18).

The Wounded Joker in Practice

As I perform *Nightwind* I have been able to address my own needs as an artist as well as a human rights activist. At first I took the play to Theatres and to conferences and seminars on the subject of torture and U.S. policy. Audience members were anxious to participate in post-play discussions, but they rarely moved beyond intellectual discourse about politics and theory. People offered opinions about the books and magazine articles they had read and what they had learned from the news. These were well-intentioned responses, but I believed they were defensive, a way to hold emotions and any genuinely personal reaction at bay. What else could they make of their witnessing? What could they do with it? I wanted to invite them to leave their seats in the audience and become spect-actors by actively responding to what they had seen. I wondered what would happen if I substituted TO exercises for the standard post-performance talkback session. When I began to follow performances with TO-inspired workshops, I found myself exploring a different approach to the role of TO Joker. Instead of maintaining a neutral position, I tell a personal story and intentionally show my own pain. Then I invite the spectators to reflect with me and with each other. I do not ask them to replace the characters in the play and try different alternatives to the plight of the protagonist. After all what can a person do when confronting a torturer? The experience renders one helpless in the moment of life-threatening violation, which is the essence of trauma; the only thing left to do is to heal by feeling what was too overwhelming to feel at that moment and to imagine what could be done to stop it from happening in the future. Through the use of Image Theatre, I invite spectators to become spect-actors as they explore their immediate reactions to the issue of torture. Then collectively we engage in creating images of how we can address this horror. In this way, I follow Boal's lead, inviting people to create images of what reality can be instead of staying trapped in what is. Most of us tend to feel paralyzed when faced with atrocities. The pain is so intense that we do not know how to respond. When an atrocity like human torture is explored in the ritual space of Theatre framed by my experience as a survivor, spectators seem encouraged to explore their own fears and pain, as if the courage I demonstrate to tell my story serves as an invitation to explore their own courage. As a social justice activist I am using Theatre and my understanding of healing to help inspire activism in others.

Jokering the Post-Performance Workshop

When the 35-minute performance ends, people think their participation is over. In fact, it is just beginning. German Theatre artist and Marxist theorist Bertolt Brecht (1977) suggested that empathy and identification with a protagonist prevent spectators from breaking out of their entranced passivity (p. 101), but I proceed on the understanding that empathy reaches both consciousness and conscience and could awaken the desire to act for change. Empathy can therefore be a first step toward engendering reflection and action. When people watch *Nightwind* and are moved by my pain, an emotional door opens, encouraging them to join me in the aesthetic space and enter the action. Instead of inviting them to intervene in the play and replace the protagonist as in Forum Theatre, I seek their active involvement as we energize blood-thinking, and I invite them to respond to what they have witnessed in a visceral way. Instead of exploring possibilities for action primarily through words, we first use our bodies to create symbolic representations of action. If we are in a Theatre, I invite everyone to join me on the stage. If we are in an academic setting or conference room, we push back any chairs, desks, or tables to clear an open space. If some people prefer not to participate, I encourage them, but no one is coerced to stay and play.

While I vary my approach according to the allotted time and the particular needs of a group, the workshops have certain common elements. We begin with a ten-minute dynamic meditation. Many participants feel paralyzed after witnessing scenes of torture, but as we engage in chaotic breathing, the vigorous inhalations and exhalations of breath involve the entire body, releasing some of the pain and tension while accessing the unconscious. We shake our bodies in an energizing way I have learned from Kundalini yoga and then enter what I call "divine madness" as I invite everyone to move and scream out whatever thoughts and emotions may want to emerge. I ask people to freeze their movements and become aware of energy in their bodies and their initial reactions to the performance. I then play African-inspired rhythms on the *djembe* drum. The warm-up exercise lessens self-consciousness and inhibitions so almost everyone accepts my invitation to dance and in this way we begin to create a community.

As the audience engages in this dynamic meditation, many find themselves screaming out loud, some access their tears, some express outrage, and others connect to disbelief. We go through the influx of diverse emotions in ten minutes and end up dancing. With our bodies more fully present, we start to process the play through Image Theatre. I invite audience members to use their entire body to create an image to express their immediate, spontaneous, visceral reaction to the play. Most bodies constrict; most people look down, but in the same room, other reactions emerge: a person aiming a weapon, a person praying, a person hiding her eyes. People look at each other and see responses that might not ever have occurred to them. The images contradict and yet co-exist because in this process we can hold opposing ideas in the same space. While one person's initial reaction is of a sorrowful prayer, next to him is someone in a fist-fighting posture; another person crunches in horror as his companion aims a rifle at an invisible enemy. Boal (1985) wrote, "... we are used to expressing everything through words, leaving the enormous expressive capabilities of the body in an underdeveloped state" (p. 130) and yet as soon as those creative capabilities are tapped, we often speak most powerfully without words. In Image Theatre, Boal has offered an embodied way to create dialogue not only with each other but within ourselves.

"Shake it out," I say and we all shake our bodies. "Another response to the play!" There's no right answer. The images give access to the capacities to react to different social conditions--including the contradictory ones--that exist inside each of us. I keep the pace fast, making it impossible for people to get stuck in a single position. We discover a range of possibilities and witness the variety of potential reactions now embodied on stage. For example, when a person who opposes violence feels the impulse to take up a weapon or make a fist, he or she might feel paralyzed or overwhelmed by the feeling and will simply freeze in place. The desire to get rid of or repress the response is that strong, but the constant shifting and transforming of the bodies generates a feeling of freedom, a realization that each one of us has agency, that many responses are possible. Once at a QUIT conference (the Quaker Initiative to End Torture) a woman found herself portraying a torturer in a tableau created as a group reaction to the play. Afterwards she commented how embarrassed she felt about her own spontaneous choice. Then she added when asked to transform the tableau: "I was both able to recognize the feeling of anger in me and transform it into something closer to my practice as a nonviolent person." Spect-actors find themselves creating both individual and group images in response to the issue of torture that was depicted in front of them and then create what I call the antidote: images of how they would like to respond to torture. Their bodies now embody images of expansion, liberation, witnessing, agency, telling others, militancy, protest, healing, and solidarity. This ability to imagine action is the necessary seed for individuals and communities to become active in social justice issues, or at least, more humane in their relationship to themselves and others, which is my great hope.

As Auslander (1994) wrote, "The Boalian body never comes to rest in a neutral state; rather, the point is for the spect-actor to be able to move from one mask to another while retaining a critical distance from all masks" (p. 131). And so as we spontaneously move from one image or mask--meaning how we act or present ourselves in the creating of an image with our bodies--to another, we see that no matter how intense, instinctive, and visceral reactions may be, we are not defined by these reactions. They do not reveal our essential selves. We can try our responses on like masks and whatever the response may be, it can be transformed.

I like to use the common Theatre game of The Machine which begins with one person standing alone and making a rhythmic gesture. She or he is then joined by another person with his or her own gesture and then another and another. As spect-actors spontaneously create a group image, they lose individual control of what is being created while still participating. We leave the abstract machine behind and I ask the group to create The Machine of Torture. Certain images recur with predictable regularity. Once we have a machine we problematize it by asking questions to the machine of torture:" What is the role of the citizen?" People want to answer with words. "No," I say. "Don't tell me. Show me." Almost invariably, people create images which show that they see themselves as not engaged or responsible. I ask: "What is the role of the religious community? Of the university? Of the media?" Over the years I have seen a myriad of images of people refusing to look at the issue, or busy lost in consumerism, watching TV, using drugs, overeating. Images of people isolated or alienated with consumption, as victims of the social institutions: army, government officials, media lies, complicit silence, medical and psychological participation in torture, and the Patriot Act have consistently emerged after the performance. I don't have to present a lecture about society's complicity. When invisible complicity becomes visible, we have an opportunity to reflect self-critically on the way in which we have been involved in torture and have responsibility for its continued existence.

Using dynamization techniques I invite people to add sound, then movement to the Machine of Torture, and then I invite the spect-actors to transform the machine into the machine of what they would like to do about torture. Then, as I tap people on the shoulder inviting them to speak, we finally add words improvisationally. I ask, "Why are you here?" And answers come.

"I'm here to say no more."

"I'm here as a witness to document and stop this atrocity."

"I am here writing letters to the editor."

"I will write to Congress."

"I am here to offer healing."

"I will organize an event at my church."

"I am here to fight against oppression."

"I am praying for those who are suffering."

"I will attend the next protest at the School of the Americas in Fort Benning, Georgia."

When I ask the group to create the antidote to torture, what is remarkable and telling is that over and over again, people tend to create closed circles. They often join hands and sing a social justice anthem such as "We Shall Overcome," "We Are the World," or "Kumbaya." When I invite the group to look at the tendencies expressed by their choice of image, we notice the circle faces inward, protecting itself, as if suggesting that solidarity exists only among people who are already part of the circle. Moments of awareness like this might help people recognize the ingrained societal patterns that can become like prisons that silence us from asserting our citizenship and our unique capacities for expression and creativity. People start looking outwards—a transformation in outlook that applies to many community issues, not only torture. This realization and change occurs without verbal discourse. It is a lived experience.

It is at this point that I begin to move the focus to the more immediate concerns and direct experience of the spect-actors, because the work with torture is a potential model to address other issues of concern to the particular community. "I'm new here," I say. "Can you show me The Machine of this place?" In colleges and universities, spect-actors offer images of football and other sports, images of heavy drinking and vomiting, images of sex. "So where is the learning?" I ask. After shrieks of laughter, students usually respond with images of zombie-like instructors, students staring at computer screens, chain-smoking, or tearing out their hair. After spect-actors have a chance to comment on the stress they experience and the lack of joy and often the lack of true learning, I invite them to create the antidote. Suddenly we see images of professors and students talking, making eye contact, others reaching out to the surrounding communities. It is as if the processing of the play has quickly opened an imaginative space in which people can hold their own situations up to view and feel the freedom to explore alternatives. Now that spect-actors have had a taste of the expressive power of blood-thinking, I ask what else they would like to see. All sorts of Machines appear, for example, the Machine of Domestic Violence, of Date Rape, of Street Gangs. Whatever is important to members of the group appears in the form of a Machine and offers opportunities for reflection as we transform Machines of hurt and pain into images of what we want to see instead.

Conclusion

My exploration of torture and the wound it gave me have now become a conscious and intentional element in the TO workshops I offer following performances of *Nightwind*. Theatre has its origins in ritual and one of the functions of ritual has always been to weave wounded or troubled individuals back into the fabric of their communities, at the same time offering healing to the community itself. When I perform, the audience, by bearing witness, ends the isolation I felt in the torture chamber. The stage becomes a ritual space and the people watching help me to carry the pain I carried for so long alone. By sharing my story and then allowing myself to appear as a Wounded Joker, not holding myself apart and separate, I am part of the community that is spontaneously created at each event. Spect-actors, by bearing witness, turn my memories of the torture chamber into a space where I am safely held. In return and through the process, I am able to create an aesthetic space in which they feel less constraint about allowing their own free flow of emotion. We are able to recognize the community's complicity in torture as well as the community's power to confront the practice. As the workshop changes focus, I revert to the traditional Joker's neutral stance as we explore issues specific to the group. I do not tell spect-actors what action to take or what to do with their own situations and emotions. If I do help power the engines of change, it is by awakening the imagination. It is by offering spect-actors, through the spontaneous creation of their own images, access to what they already possess: desire in the soul, knowledge in the blood, energy in the body, fire in the mind.

References

Auslander, P. (1994). Boal, Blau, Brecht: The body. In M. Schutzman & J. Cohen-Cruz (Eds.), *Playing Boal: Theatre, therapy, activism*. New York, NY: Routledge.

Boal, A. (2006). *The aesthetics of the oppressed* (A. Jackson, Trans.). New York, NY: Routledge.

——. (1995). *The rainbow of desire: The Boal method of theatre and therapy* (A. Jackson, Trans.). New York, NY: Routledge.

——. (1985). *Theatre of the oppressed* (C. & M. McBride, Trans.). New York, NY: Theatre Communications Group.

Brecht, B. (1977). *The messingkauf dialogues* (J. Willet, Trans.). London, England: Eyre Methuen Ltd. (originally published in German under title *Dialoge aus dem messingkauf*, Suhrkamp Verlag Frankfurt am Main, 1963).

Grotowski, J. (1968). *Towards a poor theatre* (T.K. Wiewiorowski, Trans.). New York, NY: Touchstone/Simon & Schuster.

Kubie, L.S. (1953). Some implications for psychoanalysis of modern concepts of the organization of the brain. *The Psychoanalytic Quarterly, 22*(35), 439-440.

Lawrence, C. & Shapin, S. (1998). *Science incarnate: Historical embodiments of natural knowledge*. Chicago, IL: University of Chicago Press.

Steinman, L. (1995). *The knowing body: The artist as storyteller in contemporary performance*. Berkeley, CA: North Atlanta Books.

CHAPTER FOURTEEN

Chen Alon *

Non-Violent Struggle as Reconciliation Combatants for Peace
Palestinian and Israeli Polarized Theatre of the Oppressed

PAULO FREIRE SAID, "THE minute you freeze history or ideas, you also eclipse the possibility of creativity and undermine the possibility of the development of a political project" (1997, p. 311). The conflict between Israelis and Palestinians often seems frozen, but it has been going on long enough for both sides to know that reality is never static. Even though we seem to be in a no-win situation, we know that history is dynamic and flexible. This is true of theatre as well, and we know human imagination makes flexibility and transformation possible, and we know that hope results from it.

From Uni-national to Bi-national Struggle Against the Israeli Occupation

This chapter tells the story of the Tel Aviv/Tul-Karem Activist Theatre Group (TA/TK), a wing of Combatants for Peace (CFP). CFP is a non-violent movement of Palestinian and Israeli ex-combatants that uses Theatre of the Oppressed to struggle against the Israeli occupation of Palestinian territories and to work for dialogue and reconciliation. In 2002 when I was called to reserve duty as an officer in the Israeli army (Israeli Defense Force, or IDF), I refused to serve in the occupied territory and was incarcerated for a month. I came to the conclusion that I could not serve in the occupied territory based on what I had seen and done as an Israeli army officer, as well as because of the army's actions in the West Bank and Gaza. It was not only a moral or political issue. I realized that I was a part of the problem. I was personally responsible for horrible acts. I had guarded almost every Israeli settlement, had been in every refugee camp, and at every roadblock. It was I who had invaded

---

* With thanks to Ellie Friedland for helping me tell this story by offering wisdom, patience, and sensitivity during the editing process. Her contributions to the work went beyond revision, and I am grateful for the true dialogue and for the mutual learning.

Palestinian houses in the middle of the night, it was I who had humiliated adults and intimidated children. I had to report this to my conscience.

At the time I was in the army reserve I was also acting in the well-established Be'er Sheva Repertory Theatre. Often I would perform in a play, take off my costume, put on my reservist uniform and go to the front in Gaza, an hour away, and arrest people at checkpoints. My refusal to serve in the occupied territory led me to also refuse to participate in art that seemed to perpetuate the status quo. Acting in a repertory company felt like doing cultural reserve duty, and I wanted to find a way to use my love, and need, for theatre for a new path. I needed to stop living a split existence.

I was active in the Courage to Refuse movement for three years, working to bring the message to Israelis that the occupation is destructive to the state of Israel. In 2004, some of us in Courage to Refuse heard that there was a similar group of Palestinian ex-combatants, most of whom were from the Fatah group, who were refusing to participate in violence.[1] We realized that both sides must take responsibility for stopping the violence and that we must do it together. Some of us from Courage to Refuse joined some of the Palestinians from their group to co-found Combatants for Peace as a movement of Palestinians and Israelis who have taken an active part in violence: Israelis as soldiers and Palestinians as part of the armed struggle for Palestinian freedom. After brandishing weapons for so many years, we decided to put down our guns and struggle together non-violently to bring an end to the occupation and to achieve peace.

Combatants for Peace operates in five regional groups to end the Israeli occupation, halt Israeli settlement in the West Bank, and establish a Palestinian state with its capital in East Jerusalem, alongside the State of Israel. We work to:

- Raise the consciousness of the public in Israel and Palestine regarding the hope and suffering of the other side and to create partners in dialogue.
- Educate toward reconciliation and non-violent struggle in the Israeli and Palestinian societies.
- Create political pressure on both governments to stop the violence, end the occupation, and resume a constructive dialogue.

In 2007 Nour Al-Din Shehadda and I founded the Tel Aviv/Tul-Karem Activist Theatre group (TA/TK) as the Theatre of the Oppressed sub-group of CFP. Nour is a Palestinian ex-combatant who was jailed twice for participating in armed struggle. He is the same age as I am, and soon after we met we realized that we had confronted each other in violent combat. By then, he, like me, had already experienced a transformation to non-violent activism. Nour emphasizes that though he is against violent resistance, this does not mean that he thinks the Palestinians have no right to resist the Israeli occupation. Just as Nour and other Palestinians are clear that they are resisting the occupation, I, and the other Israelis in CFP and in our TO group, are clear that we are not joining or supporting the Palestinian struggle. This is my struggle as an Israeli. I cannot and must not give up my identity as an Israeli and a Jew, with all the history that comes with it, as I act against the occupation.

Theatre of the Oppressed as Non-violent Struggle

I knew when we began TA/TK that I wanted to use Theatre of the Oppressed as our method for strategizing and for taking action, and I felt the need to extend Boal's TO to fit our context. The fifteen Israeli and fifteen Palestinian members of TA/TK spent the first year together exploring how to use and adapt TO methods to fulfill our needs. As Boal often said in workshops, Theatre of the Oppressed is born as a consequence of a need. We used TO techniques to define our needs, and agreed that the purpose of TA/TK is:

- To work for reconciliation and active dialogue between Israelis and Palestinians. Much so-called "dialogue" between Palestinians and Israelis serves to normalize the occupation. As one of the Palestinian members of the group said in our first meeting, "We can't have a dialogue while your boot is on our necks." (This kind of dialogue is called *tatbia* in Arabic.) We are interested in active dialogue that is part of activism against the occupation. For example, we hold "house meetings," following the model of the South African Truth and Reconciliation Committees in which we visit Palestinians or Israelis in their homes, and together we tell our personal stories of transformation from violence to non-violence. This creates trust and healing, and at the same time allows people to take mutual responsibility for the violence.
- To use Theatre of the Oppressed as the way to understand each other and work together, and to strategize our non-violent actions. All of our internal work in TA/TK employs TO techniques, and some of our public action is TO-based. Our actions sometimes require civil disobedience, and include rallies, marches, demonstrations, and Forum Theatre performances for mixed groups of Palestinians and Israelis (our use of theatre actually makes it possible for us to meet in places in which we would otherwise be forbidden by Israeli laws and regulations in the West Bank to gather Israelis and Palestinians together).
- To use theatre to bridge language barriers, since most Israelis and Palestinians do not share a language. We always work with translators, mostly

for processing and reflecting, as most of the work is communicated by action and movement.

Playing Polarities

We knew when we began TA/TK that, as Israelis and Palestinians working
together, we would each bring our memories of violence and oppression. For
example, from my duties as an Israeli soldier I am familiar with checkpoints,
arrests, curfews, entry permits, home invasions, searches, eavesdropping,
expropriations of land, tree clearing, fences, and more. I have images of
innocent victims from both sides. I think of Smadar, the sister of my Israeli
friend Alik~a co-founder of CFP~who was murdered in Jerusalem in a suicide
attack on September 4, 1999. I think of Abir, the daughter of my Palestinian
friend Basam, a co-founder of CFP, who was shot by an Israeli soldier in her
schoolyard in Anata in the east of Jerusalem on January 16, 2007. Abir was
ten years old when she died, the same age my daughter Tamar is now. Everyone in our group has memories and images like this, and we have been taught
to blame each other.

In TA/TK our experiences, many of them traumatic, are the fuel that allows us to dream the utopian dream of an end to the occupation and peace,
independence, and justice for both sides. In Boal's words, "The role of utopias
is not to be reached; it is to stimulate us to try harder and go further. To be
able to dream is already a dream come true" (1992, p. 10). Every time we meet
we must begin with the reality of our polarization. Our process is modeled on
the structure of the Truth and Reconciliation Committees in South Africa,
and we are inspired by Desmond Tutu's statement: "To forgive is not just to
be altruistic. It is the best form of self-interest. What dehumanizes you
inexorably dehumanizes me. Forgiveness gives people resilience, enabling them
to survive and emerge still human despite all efforts to dehumanize them"
(1999, p. 3).

Every time Palestinians and Israelis gather together our mutual struggle is
for humanization itself. When we meet we share at least one story from each
side about past violent experiences, allowing us to take mutual responsibility
for our own stories. This part of our work is personally and collectively
therapeutic, and it is our way of building an activist alliance. Like Augusto
Boal (1995), we agree with Che Guevera's statement that solidarity means
running the same risks (p. 3), but when we began, we had to find out how to
do that without abandoning our different and directly oppositional identities.

One early experience exemplifies this complexity, and led to what I call
the Polarized Model of Theatre of the Oppressed. This transformative moment for me, and for others, took place in one of the theatre workshops I led

for the members of the TA/TK group. Before the workshop I had asked each person to bring five different photos from her/his personal album. I explained that "personal album" was purposely vague so each person could define it for him- or herself, and so that it would generate questions and discussion when we met. Everyone brought photos and shared them. Sima, a Palestinian co-founder of TA/TK, had been imprisoned in Israel and her husband, brother, and cousin had been killed by the Israeli army. She brought photographs of her beloved relatives, who in the pictures wore khaki coats and Kuffyas, and held M-16s. I looked at the photos and the first sensation in my body was fear. Next came anger, and then the mix of strong emotions that comes when any Israeli looks at photographs of "terrorists." Plus, I knew from talking with Sima that some of her relatives in the photos had killed innocent people.

My friend Oren, another co-founder of TA/TK and formerly an officer in the paratroopers' elite unit of the Israeli army, also showed his photos. One was of his friends from the elite unit, in which some of the men were standing, some were kneeling. They wore khaki coats and held M-16s. I looked at these photos and opposite reactions rose up in me: I thought, "What a great group—the salt of the earth." I felt security, togetherness, belonging, familiarity. Later in the workshop I realized that I had forgotten that Oren had told me that they too had killed innocent people. And then I stopped. I looked at Sima, Shiffa, Nour, Iyyad, and all our Palestinians partners, and was pulled away from my point of view. "Is it possible that when they see the images in Oren's photos they feel the same way we feel when we look at Sima's photos?" Impossible. These are wonderful young men in Oren's photos. These are our friends who volunteered to protect our country. Yes, and in her photos are Sima's friends and relatives from the refugee camp Tul-Karem, who put themselves at risk in the armed struggle against the oppression and the Israeli occupation.

We all walked around looking at our photos in silence, yet we felt the intensity of the moment. We looked at each other, and that courage to look directly at each other—with the acknowledgment that who we are now is also who we were in the past—is at the heart of our TO group. Next we used Image Theatre to show our responses to the photos. First we made silent, static images, and then images with sound and words. We stayed in our polarized groups as we showed each other our images, a line of Israelis facing a line of Palestinians. Image Theatre allowed us to bridge the impossible polarization between us, and after this non-verbal dialogue, we added words, then sentences to the images. Then we were ready to discuss and reflect. As joker, I asked everyone to reflect on what touched us, what resonated, and how we could identify with the "other."

TA/TK's theatrical work and activism are grounded in the collective intimacy we develop through experiences like this, which I call "polarized intimacy" because it is based on traumatic experiences and memories, seemingly from opposite sides of the trauma, but, in fact, it is based on shared experiences and memories of a common pain. It is different from typical notions of intimacy, which is usually perceived to be based on tenderness. In TA/TK we attempt to touch our sense of loss, together with those who caused the losses, and examine the violence that we initiated against each other, in order to build joint memory that makes it possible to create a new alliance for a shared future. This is possible only if we acknowledge our polarization and our pain, as well as the needs and ambitions of each side. The Polarized Model of Theatre of the Oppressed is based on the acknowledgment that we will not turn away from the society we come from, yet we invite those who oppose us to join us in a search away

Figure 1: *The scene–Palestinian grandfather and his two grandchildren stopped by the soldier at the checkpoint. Photo by Einat Gutman (CFP).*

from "us and them" to our shared pain, and toward shared justice.

Israeli and Palestinian "Cops–in-the-Head"

We have learned that to be able to work together, we need to meet separately to keep contact with our identities and our different needs, so between every bi-national session of TA/TK we spend some time meeting uni-nationally. In these uni-national meetings we focus on issues and obstacles we face in our own societies because of our activism, and we reflect on the difficulties in our recent sessions with the "other" group. We try to identify our own blind spots and how they were created. We then rejoin both groups, and build our next activities, decisions, and actions on what we have done separately.

Recently in our joint sessions we used Image Theatre and Forum Theatre to figure out how to deal with opposition from those in our own societies to our activism against roadblocks and "apartheid roads" (roads for Jews only) in the West Bank. One Palestinian member was told by his boss that if he traveled with our theatre group he would be fired from his job. He shared this with the whole group and this led to stories from both sides about the increased pressures we are facing in our societies for "serving" the "other" side of the conflict. We divided into groups of four—two Palestinians and two Israelis in each group—to make images and scenes of the different pressures we face. Each person shared a story with the small group, then the groups created images for each story. Each group chose one story and used the images to create a scene.

We reconvened as a whole group, showed the scenes, and decided to Forum two scenes. One Israeli woman's scene was about her father's voice in her head as she planned a demonstration with her Palestinian TA/TK colleagues. Her father's "cop-in-the-head" voice was played by an Israeli, standing on a chair behind her talking to her non-stop: "How can you believe them? They are your enemies! They are all the same; they want to throw us into the sea. The problem isn't the occupation; the problem is that they don't want us here, period. You're naïve! They are exploiting your naivety for their cause!"

Right after the performance, I, as joker, asked if that could happen in a Palestinian family too. When the Palestinians said, "Yes," we forumed the scene in two phases: first we improvised the "mirror scene," with the cop-in-the-head of a Palestinian member of the group. In this scene the Palestinian mother's comments were similar to those of the Israeli father: "How can you work with them while they are occupying us? They are not truthful; they don't really want peace because they don't want to return the land they took from us. They are all soldiers; they took our land in '48, but it was not enough for them so they took more in '67." We then created a new scene that included the cops-in-the-head of both protagonists. Israelis and Palestinians replaced the protagonist first from their own side, and then from the other side. When we use theatre in this way, to reflect both sides of the polarization, we are able to understand the obstacles both sides face. Only then can we strategize the specific actions that we need to take together.

Polarized Forum Theatre and the Role of the Joker

Polarized Forum Theatre is specifically designed for mixed groups who have extreme conflicts. It allows spect-actors to replace the antagonist as well as the protagonist. It invites everyone to play the "other" and to confront each other's questions and dilemmas. This creates meaningful dialogue in which each side is respected and fully heard. In discussions I had with Boal, I was surprised that he accepted Polarized Forum, including inviting spect-actors to replace the antagonist as well as the protagonist. In an interview with Peter

Duffy in *Youth and Theatre of the Oppressed* (2010), Boal said in response to a question about work with the "oppressors":

> ... like here, in Brazil, there is a group for men who have beaten their wives or part-ners, and they make an association to try and understand why they did that. So, they are the oppressors, but they make forum theatre to try and look at their situation and to ask, What would you have done? And they are, all of them, oppressors. The only one who is not an oppressor was one of my assistants who works with me here, and the oppressors, they play the situation out and the other men who are also oppressors or have been oppressors of their wives or partners, they replace the oppressed and try to analyze what happened to them that makes this monstrosity that is to beat a woman whom you supposedly love. So this I believe is perfect to work with oppressors of that kind who are willing to change. But, the example from Israel, the example from this group of men, and other examples like in prisons--sometimes you work with prisoners, sometimes you work with guards--the guards are the oppressors, but by playing prisoners they understand the situation, they humanize the relationship, and that I think is okay. (p. 261)

In the Polarized Model we do not "give equal time" to the voice of the oppressor. We always acknowledge the oppressive power structure of the occupation, but we also acknowledge the layers of oppression experienced by both sides. For example, we presented a Forum play in which an elderly Palestinian man, just released from the hospital, and his grandchildren are forbidden by Israeli soldiers to pass a check point to get to their home. The old man is the primary protagonist, but a Palestinian spect-actor replaced the grandson. He immediately became violent, pushing and striking out at the soldiers (played by Israeli and Palestinian actors). I, as joker, stopped the intervention at that point to talk with the audience of Palestinians and Israelis about how such violence immediately creates polarization, and that the intervention made this real, in this moment. We all agreed that part of the creativity of using theatre as a non-violent weapon is to learn how to represent violence as a "rehearsal for transformation," rather than allowing it to become real violence.[2]

Immediately after this, an Israeli woman, who was visibly upset by the first spect-actor's intervention, came on stage. She also replaced the grandson, but she dropped to her knees and begged the soldiers, almost crying, "Please, please let us pass." The Palestinians in the audience laughed at this interven-tion. Next, another Israeli woman from the audience replaced the Israeli soldier. She threw away her weapon and tried to convince her commander to do the same. The Israeli officer in the scene, played by a Palestinian, vehe-mently refused to allow the old man to pass through the checkpoint, "in order to safeguard the country's security." I stopped the scene and asked: "Did these interventions solve the old man's problem?"

"No," said the Palestinian who had played the violent grandson. "I didn't solve a thing, but I restored my pride."

The Israeli answered the same question, saying, "No, but it was important for me to demonstrate that violence is not an option no matter what."

The Polarized Forum Model is based on these principles: (1) the Forum is performed for audiences of Israelis and Palestinians together, by Israeli and Palestinian actors. Our plays show the oppression of Palestinians by Israelis under the occupation; we never deny that. But spect-actors may replace characters other than the protagonist. This allows us to ask what those on both sides of the conflict can do to create transformation. (2) Our Polarized Forum Theatre is based on true personal stories, including Israelis' stories. For instance, the Forum scene described above is the true story of an Israeli soldier. Though he was oppressing the Palestinian grandfather, he was oppressed by his officer. The soldier may be replaced by spect-actors, but his very presence, and the presence of all the Israelis in this situation, is a demonstration of the oppression of the Palestinians and acknowledgment that the oppressed protagonist in the scene is the old man who is not allowed to pass through the checkpoint. (3) Palestinians and Israelis know the complexities of our conflict. Creating opportunities for both sides to be in the shoes of "the other" strengthens our new activist alliance.

I have questioned my role as joker in Polarized Forum: is it possible for Palestinians and Israelis to have a true dialogue, to ask the necessary questions, when I, an Israeli, am in the role of joker? James Thompson (2003), who did TO workshops in Sri Lanka during violent conflict, emphasizes that the joker in such situations is not neutral or objective:

> It is stating the obvious to say that any workshop facilitator in a conflict situation is not some neutral arbiter between the participants and the issues at stake. I do not simply pose problems or questions. The facilitator has the power to direct the focus of the inquiry for the audience. (p. 185)

Thompson says that he was not neutral—he wanted the conflict to end, but without either side being defeated. He wanted to help both sides see the truth of each other's stories.

This is how I see my role as joker as well. The questions I asked the audience during the roadblock scene were not neutral, and I did not accept facile magic solutions. I made it clear that I want the conflict to end, and that I wanted the Forum to demonstrate that the conflict originates, at least partially, in each side's insistence that there is one true story. Boal often said in his workshops that a joker has to be a difficultator, not a facilitator. In TO all narratives have to be challenged; this is especially true for polarized TO work.

Figure 2: *Real Israeli officer (wearing beret) interrupts the scene to arrest Munir, the actor playing an Israeli officer soldier (in cap and sunglasses). Chen (far right), the joker, intervenes to prevent the arrest. Photo by Einat Gutman (CFP).*

Polarized Theatre of the Oppressed: Strategies and Tactics

There are few places now (in 2010) where Israelis and Palestinians are allowed to gather together, so trespassing is a strategy we often use in our public actions. This choice is ethical, activist, and aesthetic. Boal often said that TO asks us to trespass, to break the barriers between the stage and the audience, between the dominant and the dominated, in order to remove the borders of oppression defined by the oppressors. We decided to present our Forum Theatre piece about the grandfather at the road block at an actual road block outside the village of Shuffa, close to the Israeli settlement Avnei-Heffetz, in the occupied territories. In this performance the soldier, a medic, was played by the Israeli, a member of TA/TK, who had told the original story. He is in conflict with his commanding officer, a medical doctor, who was played by a Palestinian actor. The old man was played by an Israeli actor, and the two grandchildren were played by a Palestinian and an Israeli.

As is typical, we translated everything, and we had cross-language actors. For example, when the Israeli soldier asks his commander a question (in Hebrew), the officer, who is played by a Palestinian actor, repeats the question in Arabic and answers in Arabic. The soldier repeats the answer in Hebrew, and so on. Similarly, for the spect-actor's interventions, the actor repeats the spect-actor's words in his/her language and answers in the other language.

We performed the play with an audience of fifty Palestinians and forty Israelis, at a real checkpoint, with Israeli soldiers all around. At the point when the Palestinians are arriving at the checkpoint, the soldier appeals to his commanding officer, "We must follow our medical ethics here. We can tell this man is telling the truth, we can see that he has just had an operation and is very weak." But the officer continues to say the man cannot pass. The soldier tries to argue, but the play ends with the commanding officer insisting that the soldier has to tell the Palestinian grandfather that he cannot pass and cannot go home.

In this performance, when we reached the moment when the Palestinians arrived at the checkpoint, a real Israeli officer and some of his soldiers rushed into the stage area and started to arrest the Palestinian actor who was playing the Israeli officer. He said he was arresting him for "contempt of the Israeli Defense Force (IDF) uniform." As joker, I responded as if this was a sincere spect-actor intervention. I stepped in and said, "Stop, stop! What's the problem officer? This is only theatre; this is not a real situation or a real soldier. Why are you arresting our actor, Munir? He is just playing his role, like the other actor who is also playing a soldier. Is it just because Munir is Palestinian and Eyal is Israeli? They are both playing the same type of role in the play!"

He repeated, "I won't let you show contempt for the IDF uniform!" Ridiculously enough, the officer interrupting the scene was the same rank as Munir's fictitious officer in the play. A real colonel was arresting a make-believe colonel on the same "stage." Our Palestinian translator Iyyad simultaneously translated all that was happening into Arabic, and the hundred people watching, Palestinians and Israelis, were laughing out loud. Munir's six-year-old child was in the audience, and he broke into tears. I offered a solution to placate the officer: I asked both the Israeli and Palestinian actors to take off their uniforms. I held up the two jackets and showed them to the audience, saying, "This is the power of theatre. The soldiers' power is of course much greater, and we will do what they tell us to do. But we have the power of imagination. We can continue our play with Eyal and Munir playing Israeli soldiers without their uniforms. As you watch the play, please remember two things: first, I will hold up the shirts for you, so the uniforms are still represented, but not actually on Munir's Palestinian body and Eyal's Israeli body. They both represent the same thing, but if you forget, look at the shirts. If that doesn't help, look at the soldiers, the road open only for Jews, and the Jewish settlement behind us."

Then I realized that a soldier was filming us, as surveillance. I said to the audience, "But the power of our imagination goes beyond these two actors/soldiers and their shirts. We can imagine the end of the occupation; we can imagine Israelis and Palestinians living in peace. These soldiers can't, they still can't. But I believe that one day they will be able to imagine this, one day they will join us. We all have to believe in that." When it was over I realized we were all on the edge, in new territory. This was not Forum Theatre, not jokering as I know it. It was something else entirely. I understand now that there is no way to do "conventional" Forum Theatre when the actors and spect-actors are in real danger, when there is no safe space for mutual learning, for true interaction between the play and the spect-actors.

I do not know how to name or categorize this event and the role I played in the presentation yet. But it represents a reality that we can participate in, reflect on and ask questions about. Most importantly, we must consider how to take action to change it. This is a strange moment for all Israelis and Palestinians, for all of humanity, a moment of hope and hopelessness. As Boal wrote:

> Let us hope that one day—please, not too far in the future—we'll be able to convince or force our governments, our leaders, to do the same; to ask their audiences–us–what they should do, so as to make this world a place to live and be happy in—yes, it is possible—rather than just a vast market in which we sell our goods and our souls. Let's hope. Let's work for it! (1992, p. 246)

Notes

1. "Ex-combatants" for Palestinians means that they have fought in armed resistance and served time in Israeli jails. In Israel they are called "terrorists" and in Palestine they are called "freedom fighters" or "political prisoners."
2. This is a paraphrase of Boal's original statement "Perhaps the theatre is not revolutionary in itself; but have no doubt, it is a rehearsal of revolution!" (1985, p. 155).

References

Boal, A. (1985). *Theatre of the oppressed* (C.A. and M.L. McBride, Trans.). New York, NY: Theatre Communications Group.

—. (1995). *The rainbow of desire: The Boal method of theatre and therapy* (A. Jackson, Trans.). New York, NY: Routledge.

—. (1992). *Games for actors and non-actors* (A. Jackson, Trans.). New York, NY: Routledge.

—. (2006). *Aesthetics of the oppressed* (A. Jackson, Trans.). London, England: Routledge.

Duffy, P. (2010). The human art: An interview on Theatre of the Oppressed and youth with Augusto Boal. In P. Duffy & E. Vettraino (Eds.), *Youth and theatre of the oppressed* (pp. 251-262). New York, NY: Palgrave Macmillan.

Freire, P. (1997). A response. In P. Freire, J. W. Fraser, D. Macedo, et al. (Eds.), *Mentoring the mentor: A critical dialogue with Paulo Freire* (pp. 303-329). New York, NY: Peter Lang Publishing.

Thompson, J. (2003). *Applied theatre: Bewilderment and beyond.* New York, NY: Peter Lang Publishing.

Tutu, D. (1999). *No future without forgiveness.* New York, NY: Doubleday.

CHAPTER FIFTEEN

Toby Emert & Ellie Friedland

Considering the Future of Theatre of the Oppressed
An Interview with Julian Boal

TOBY: I WANT TO ask you about your story. How were you drawn to this work that your father began?

Julian: There was not a clear starting point for me because I saw many performances throughout my life, and that sparked the interest. When I was in my mid-twenties, I took a master's degree in history in France. I became interested in what was happening in Brazilian theatre in the 1960s. Most mainstream theatre was European in concept—in the plays, the actors even spoke with Portuguese or Italian accents. The director might be Polish. On the political theatre side, Brazilian theatre saw itself as serving the role of enlightening the audience. They were seeing the audience as inferior, as in need of being enlightened. Theatre of the Oppressed considers that people already have a sense of liberation, so I thought that Theatre of the Oppressed was more interesting. Also, I met Jana Sanskriti, the movement in India. It was those two things that made me really willing. Jana Sanskriti is a group that involves more than 20,000 persons in Theatre of the Oppressed throughout India. The performances are amazing, and the political lines they defend are really interesting.

Toby: Does TO feel like your life's work? Obviously it's part of the work your father did for his whole life, but do you feel like that's the case for you as well?

Julian: I think yes ... very likely. I really enjoy the work, I enjoy being a teacher, I enjoy being a joker, I enjoy being part of groups, I enjoy meeting people. I have made connections that give me friends around the world. I'm seeing opportunities, I'm seeing possibilities that I am willing to grab, and I would like to evolve the work. So, yes ... you can never say never. You can never say always ... but, yes.

Ellie: What do you know about how the work of Paulo Freire and the work of your father happened at the same time? I read Freire's *Pedagogy of the Oppressed* at the same time that I read your father's book, *Theatre of the Oppressed,* so I learned about them simultaneously. Not inside an academic program—none of my academic programs addressed either of them. But for me, because I read both of the books at the same time, they have always been connected. And I think that's true for many people in the United States.

Toby: That's true for me as well. I learned about both Freire and Boal at the same time.

Julian: I think that there is still a story to be written about this. It would show the parallels and the differences between them and the connections between their concepts, experiences and stories. My father even said in one of his books "my last father Paulo Freire." Those are very strong words to say.

Some things Pedagogy of the Oppressed and Theatre of the Oppressed have in common are ideas about the banking system of education, the idea of the world as a transformative process, not a thing that is transformed—there is not an identity that is being transformed; it is the transformation itself that is the identity. There is this very beautiful sentence from Freire that I do not know how to translate exactly: "The world is not. The world is just being." Also the idea that the facilitator is not away from the process, bringing things to the people, he is part of the process and is liberated by the process. This idea is often lost in TO if we jokers don't consider ourselves oppressed, but see ourselves as bringing things to the oppressed. We are oppressed.

So how do we define oppression? I heard a woman in India working with Jana Sanskriti say, "I am not oppressed by domestic violence because I deserve to be hit." In Switzerland, people in the workshop told me they felt oppressed by the beggars. They may be aggressed, but not oppressed. If you think oppression is whatever people believe is oppression, you would work against the Swiss beggars. Self-definition of oppression is not a good criterion.

Oppression is a matter of relationships between social groups that bring benefit to one group, but not the other—one has and one has not. We are not bad or good, oppressed or oppressor. In France, I am in the social group of men; men earn 25% more than women, so, for instance, let's say that I am in a relationship with a woman who earns less than I do. I am a nice guy, so I will pay for things more than she does. I would say I didn't decide to receive 25 % more, and I am using my power in a nicer, more enlightened way—I am using the power society gave me. Our relationship is not equal, and I am perpetuating the idea that the woman should only expect that she will have a nice man with more power ... like a slave should have a nice master. But the question needs to be why this is this way and how can we change the social structure so there is more equality. We each belong to many social groups; in some we are oppressed, in others we are oppressors.

Some of the power relationships between groups are not visible. If aliens from outer space put cameras in the street and watched for a long time, they would understand that cars go when the traffic light is green and stop when it's red. Pedestrians move when the cars stop, etc. The aliens might believe that streetlights have lots of power. They won't be able to know who made the rules, who put the street lights there, who will fine you if you don't follow the rules. They won't see that it's those who have power who set the rules for the streetlights, so we need to understand that systems of oppressions are more than bad actions done by single individuals. Similarly, we can only end oppression collectively, as movements. We can't stress only the individual level, although this is what often happens.

For example, in France there are groups working with women to give them makeovers so they can succeed in job interviews. This is saying there is not a problem of unemployment, there is a problem of excessive ugliness in women applying for jobs. I saw a Forum Theatre performance in which the boy offered to buy the girl coffee. She says no, but he insists and she accepts. The next day the same thing happens with beer, and on the third day he offers sex. She says no, he insists, and he rapes her. The point of the play was that it was her fault she was raped because she had been giving him mixed messages before that day. Another Forum play was about domestic violence and had a scene with a woman and a man about to hit her. The spect-actors kept replacing the woman just before she was hit, which gave the message that there was a right way of talking to her husband. She should be different in order to not be beaten; she should know how to handle her husband. This is a serious mistake in Forum. A core idea of Freire is showing the people there is always the possibility of emancipation. Also the idea of starting from where the people are, which, by the way, is also a Leninist idea, not only Paulo Freire's. In the book *The State and the Revolution*, Lenin said that the idea of taking over the state is not to replace those ruling the state but to deconstruct the structure of the state and that the state should relate to the citizen so there would not be a dichotomy between state and citizen. This is like Freire's idea of the vanishing teacher—the teacher needs to gradually disappear. This is like my father's idea that we are all actors, the stage is not for specific special people.

Two things Freire and Boal do not have in common: my father was not a Christian, and Freire was influenced by Christianity. And Freire's idea of *conscientização*—is about thought, and includes the idea of a goal. In TO, demechanization is an embodied process without a precise endpoint. Maybe for Freire there is a God, so maybe there is a truth. The connection between them, I think, is never made in any other place in the world as much as it is in the U.S. Maybe I'm having this impression because my entrance door has been in the U.S. most of the time, but I don't hear so much about this connection in other countries. Maybe it's even more in the U.S. than in Brazil. It was actually in the U.S. that they presented at the same table, no? And this was the only place—at the 1996 PTO Conference in Omaha. So I think the U.S. is where this idea of the connection between Freire and TO is strongest. The U.S. may also be where the work of Freire is most institutional-ized in the bad sense, and this is true of the work of my father too. Pedagogy of the Oppressed is about changing education, not only changing the content of the education. Changing education has to mean changing the whole system of education. Breaking the passivity of the spectator-educator is equivalent to breaking the passivity of the spectator-citizen. Therefore the idea of changing this passivity, breaking this muteness is connected with the idea of breaking the muteness of the citizenship. The U.S, I think, is the place that is the least politicized. The work of Freire is no longer a radical critique of the education system. It's becoming a way to fit into the system. For the Theatre of the Oppressed it is the same. People are using the interactive techniques and not taking the part of Theatre of the Oppressed that is a critique of theatre and of society. TO and PO become one of many alternative approaches, and that is not what they are. There is a tendency toward de-fanging the work, but not entirely so. There is a ghost haunting Freirian institutions and now also TO groups. This brings meaningful and fruitful tensions.

Toby: Freire suggests that education should change radically. Is one of the tenets of Theatre of the Oppressed that theatre should change?

Julian: Yes, but it's not only that education should change. Education should change in order to change the society, and Theatre should change in order to change the society. I have the impression that here in the U.S. and other places, it is one of many trends. It's another way of educating but not a way to criticize and change the system. I think the banking system is, how do you say it, automatic. Automatic, and taken as a metaphor. When Freire talked about the "banking system," maybe he was saying something about capitalism. The banking system of education is in a system in which the banking approach is the very core of the society. So changing the banking system of education is changing the banking system of life itself. In the first book that my father ever wrote, when it was not even *Theatre of the Oppressed* yet, technically it was *Latin American Popular Theatre*, he says something like, the elite say that there is no such thing as popular Theatre and there should not be such a thing as popular Theatre. And then my father says a beautiful thing. He says that we want popular Theatre ... I'm making a rough translation ... we want popular

Theatre, but we don't want only popular Theatre, we want the education to be popular, we want the banks to be popular, we want the beach to be popular, we want universities to be popular. In other words, we want life itself to become popular. So it's always an articulation of transforming the theatre in order to radically transform the society. These ideas of a radical transformation have been lost in many places, but here in the U.S. I think that Pedagogy of the Oppressed and Theatre of the Oppressed are not perceived with the explosive content they can bring. They are seen as one more trend, another way of doing it.

Toby: When I was beginning to learn about Freire's and Boal's work, I already knew a lot about education and about theatre. I had been trained as a teacher and as an actor and director, so these ideas were essentially add-ons. They seemed to be additional ways to think about work I was already doing—at least that's how I viewed the ideas when I was first being introduced to them.

Ellie: This is actually what my chapter in this book focuses on: I am integrating TO into my teaching, and therefore I have to ask if I am perpetuating the system. I'm working with people who are going to go out into the world as teachers. The reason that I'm working with them is so that they change education, but we're doing it all within the educational system. I've always grappled with the fact that I've made the choice to be in the higher education system, preparing people to go into our educational system as it exists. But that's because I believe in bottom up change, that the change has to come from the people with the least power, which in our educational system is the teacher—only students have less power than teachers. So I intend to create subversion, because I don't believe the revolution is going to happen. My students and I quietly subvert the system, but we are working within it. And I constantly have the internal dilemma: Am I making TO just a technique? And can I change the system while I'm part of the system?

Julian: There is no place that is outside of the system, so we can only work within the system. Maybe the big lesson we have in all of this is that there are contradictions within each system. All of the characters have, let's call it, their good side and bad side. And it's precisely their good sides that make their bad sides work, and it's their bad sides that make their good sides work. So we have to try to amplify this contradiction. For instance, schools are the places where the future workers learn the techniques and the ideologies that will make their exploitation possible. At the same time, schools are the place where society dreams itself by asking what are the values that should be common to all of us? What should we all have access to? How can we help children become better adults than we are? So this is a contradiction that we need to amplify. But at the same time, I think that if you are a social worker or a teacher or whatever, and you do only your work, then you are not doing anything political. Like when a social worker says, "I work so much, I do so many things, I help the people so much. How can you tell me I'm not doing anything political?" Political is not to do what your role is intended to do. For instance, it is not political for a social worker to distribute subsidies to the people. What is political is to question why there are problems that cause people to need subsidies. So the political way of doing it is to question.

Toby: So, Julian, Freire's work and your father's work were introduced several decades ago in Brazil. Do you believe the work changed the education system, did it change the theatre, and did that by extension change the culture?

Julian: Well, it depends on what you call change. Brazil is a very strange country. I would say some change happened and more is coming. So the thing is ... that for Paulo Freire's work and for my father's work, there are many people who are using the ideas when they choose to. I can point to some things that were good, like the first law to protect witnesses that came in Rio as a result of my father's Legislative Theatre; then it became a state law, then it became federal law. So that was a major change that was very good. Many who are in the ministries of government in Brazil were educated in Freirian education. The Landless Movement began to do TO something like ten or twelve years ago in a training with my father and the Center for Theatre of the Oppressed (CTO), Rio. He was very dearly attached to this movement, so he spent a lot of time with this nucleus. Then it multiplied, and now in Brazil, it's not even possible to count the numbers of TO workshops that are given or TO groups that are inside the Landless Movement. We will say hundreds of hundreds. Very sincerely, they cannot count them because everything is far apart. Many people from the first nucleus became national leaders, so people said TO must be empowering for the people. More people became powerful within the Landless Movement and they spread TO within the movement. So maybe it is too early to speak about the change from Freire and Boal in Brazil. I can sort of quote Mao, who when he was asked about what change happened thanks to the French Revolution, he stroked his chin and said, "Maybe it is too soon to know the change the French Revolution brought us."

Toby: This brings us to the question of what's next for TO. Because in that story, the one you just told, your father was the impetus for the growth, so one of that group's earliest interactions was with your father and CTO Rio and that interaction expanded into something else. But now that your father is no longer the foremost TO practitioner in the world, what happens next?

Julian: I don't know, but I think that we should not fear that much. Very likely there will be new bridges that are going to be built between different movements, in a rather organic manner. I'm hoping that Pedagogy and Theatre of the Oppressed is one of the organizations that can provide a space for those bridges to be built. You have something that many people don't have: money and a political orientation. PTO brings together political activists from the U.S. and around the world. The meetings between community organizations and academics that happen at PTO are extraordinary—you are a link between school as an institution and school or education as a dream, and between theatre as an institution and theatre as a dream.

PTO can offer the work a lot of visibility; PTO has a role to play, this is true. But there will be other places like PTO. I hope that there will be a place for international meetings; I think there should be publications. I think there will be breaks; there will be people that will not talk to other people that will found new schools that will be, I don't know, the "Fourth International of the Boalists"; that will very likely happen.

Toby: And does that seem acceptable, like that's the natural progression?

Julian: As we were saying yesterday, I'm not a restaurant: when I'm providing a workshop, I don't want everybody to be happy, you know, I'm OK if everybody's not happy. I'm doing a lot of workshops expecting to meet people who will become allies, to promote a certain vision of Theatre of the Oppressed. That's what I'm doing mainly in Europe. There is a guy in Croatia who's a very good friend of mine, and he invites many people that are friends of mine to his festival in Croatia; in Barcelona, it's the same. So there are places like this in which people are getting together in order to make TO projects. But I'm no longer willing to be in places where there are people who work for corporations. Why should we waste our time? We are not stronger with those people. If people don't see a system of oppression in the corporation they don't see systems of oppression in society. They are bullets that we are shooting at our feet.

But it is good to express where we don't agree in order to be clear to make meetings among allies—so we can have a meeting of those who do not want to work with corporations and those who want to work in corporations can meet too … it is constructive to meet, but it is not constructive to meet just to fight.

My father created TO as a tool for struggle but now the world of TO has become a battlefield—there are conceptions of the work that are completely different. The social workers, community organizers, artists are not expendable—we need to try to reach these people and find those who have the same questions we have. There will not be perfect agreement.

Ellie: That sounds like the controversies, for example, that always exist at PTO. There are approaches that are based in TO, but have changed it substantially. Within the group of us who regularly go to the PTO conference, there's a lot of discussion about this reality. My sense is that it's part of what's going to happen, that people will continue to use different bits of the work and take bits of it in different directions.

Julian: I don't want to defend TO as a set of techniques. I defend TO as retaking possession of the aesthetical means, as a way of retaking the means of production. Quoting my father, taking over the stage equates with taking over life, in general. If taking over the stage is not articulated as a process that leads to taking control of life in general, there is no reason to do it.

I defend the idea of criticizing not only the content but the relationships between actor and audience, stage director and actors, teachers and students, U.S. president and citizens—to change the institution of the U.S. president. So those things I will defend. I will defend the idea that the capacity of the emancipated is already inside all of us, it's not something that you bring to someone. I will defend the idea of the equality of intelligence that is inside TO. I will defend the idea that is inside of TO that every relationship is socially constructed. I will defend many things that are inside TO: the oppressed/oppressor system and relationship, dialectical relationships. These things I will defend, but not as a set of techniques. It's not using the games or techniques.

I know that my father learned games from others, and it was not the games that were important but the purpose he articulated for the games. So it's not the exercises themselves, it's the orientation that you give to it that is most important. It's important not to make Theatre of the Oppressed another interactive method. The political orientation of Theatre of the Oppressed must not be forgotten. Barbara Santos from CTO said that you can animate a children's party by using *Games for Actors and Non-Actors*, but that is not Theatre of the Oppressed.

Ellie: I was thinking about how the games have seeped into all drama education, certainly in the U.S. People who study drama in any context here know many of the games and don't know that they are TO games.

Julian: I have no problem with people who take games and use them in another context—that's fine. I have a problem when people take them and say it is about oppression and it's not—for example, Forum Theatre that shows that a woman raped is responsible for getting raped. In a Forum performance about domestic violence I saw, when the spect-actors intervened, one woman hid the cell phone that was the cause of the conflict and another talked nice to the man to try to soothe him. The message was that there is a way to talk to the husband so he doesn't hit her. Because there was no dialogue about the intervention, it placed the responsibility for the violence on the woman, which is exactly what the abuser does. This is not Forum Theatre. I have problems with people using Forum Theatre in ways that blame the individual for the oppression she experiences in the guise of finding solutions.

Toby: Another reality, of course, is that we are really privileged because we get sit in this room and talk with you about these things and we've also had the opportunity to work with your father more than once. If I had just read the books, I don't know that I could have interpreted it at all the way that I've been able to as a result of getting the opportunity to sit and talk to you and to take workshops with your father.

Ellie: And now there are going to be many people getting it through us and our interpretation of the ideas.

Julian: Some TO practitioners around the world must be thinking, since my father's death, who's going to be the next king of TO? Which is very sad because I never thought of my father as a king and certainly not of TO as a kingdom. So, this question who's going to be the next guy doesn't interest me at all. If someone comes up to me believing that I am more trained or more smart or more close to my father because of my DNA, this guy is a stupid guy, you know? I'm sorry, but to think DNA means something—it's a racist belief.

That being said, there are also questions now. My father created a system that is very open and dialectical. Many people are using his work all over the world, which is a very good thing. So there is great latitude and there are many stretchings, really big stretchings, but some are stretching it so much I think it is no longer Theatre of the Oppressed. I think it is role-playing when it becomes only about how to react in certain situations, like what to do when your husband tells you he has HIV or what to do when your boyfriend is stopped by the police because he's gay, not addressing patriarchy or homo-phobia in the play—dealing only with the consequences, but not with the systems that construct those oppressions.

Toby: Can there be Forum plays that are not Theatre of the Oppressed?

Julian: Yes definitely. The best example is this association I heard about that exists here in the U.S.; I don't know where. They teach how to react if you are a Black guy and you are stopped by the police in your car. So: hands on the wheel to be visible, slow movements if you are going to get your papers, always talk in a soft tone, and things like this, which may work great. Their idea is to help people avoid getting shot. But this is not Theatre of the Oppressed, according to me, because they don't ask why any Black person, or any person at all, should be afraid when they are stopped by the police! So I think that many Forum Theatre performances are only on the "hands on the wheel" level; they never reach the questioning of why should we be afraid.

Toby: This really brings out the importance of the dialogue—that the play has an intention of creating a dialogue.

Julian: Well, actually it's going to depend on how you define dialogue. For me dialogue only exists when there is an equality of power. Therefore, an exchange of words between the police and a citizen is not a dialogue. That's not a real dialogue for me.

Toby: So, let me play this out for you Julian and see if it makes sense. I was doing a workshop with teachers and ...

Julian: You are not going to ask me if it was good or not are you?

Toby: No, I'm just going to ask you to think this through with me. The teachers were talking about issues for the Forum pieces they were going to create, and they decided to do a piece on a teacher who had witnessed two girls kissing in her high school hallway. Her reaction was to tell them to stop immediately and go to class. They decided they would develop this scene. But what became important in the work, I think, was not that they made the scene, but that they had a conversation about that moment and what it meant and what might be possible responses to it.

Ellie: This let them have a conversation about why that is happening in the school. Why would the teacher respond differently than if there was a boy and a girl kissing?

Toby: That's what I mean: in that case, it was the dialogue that developed out of the piece that became the most potent part of the workshop.

Julian: I think that a good Theatre of the Oppressed session allows the oppressed to create a kind of tribunal in which they are going to bring the whole society as the guilty, well not the guilty, but the one that has to be in front of the oppressed, the one that is being analyzed. And not the other way around. I don't know how it is here, but in France we have professional groups that go to schools to perform Forum Theatre and then they leave. So, what happens is that, for instance, the performers go with the agenda that has been set by the ministry of education: "stop smoking," maybe. Thirty-year-old actors stage a little performance for children about smoking; so, therefore, the story does not originate with the oppressed, nor does it allow the audience to look at the role of society in perpetuating smoking; it does the opposite. The people at the top are defining the issue and they are saying that inside these four walls we can solve the problem. So instead of expanding, they are reducing.

Toby: Let's talk about the role of the joker.

Julian: Jean Luc Goddard said that if objectivity is to give equal time in your movie to the perspective of the Jews and the perspective of the Nazis, then he is against objectivity. So being a joker is not "OK, we have a person here who hates Jews, and we have a person here who is a Jew, so it's good for us to hear both opinions." This is not what being a joker is about, because opinions are linked to power and oppression. Like being in favor of patriarchy, in favor of domestic violence, in favor of homophobia or allowing homophobia or hate crimes to be presented as acceptable opinions. Being a joker is not about allowing people to express how racist, how homophobic, how sexist they are. This would be a very individualistic perspective, that every time the individual speaks, it's good, because the individual doesn't get to speak enough. Well, I think the individual is speaking too much. Nowadays we believe that our inner voice is something absolutely amazing that we should completely trust. But according to me, our inner voice speaks like Fox News. So if we only acknowledge individual expression, we would only, most of the time, be acknowledging how society works right now.

So the tricky part is that as a joker you have to both take the point of view of the oppressed on the stage and defend the oppressed in the audience (in the best case scenario, we take their point of view and defend them because we are one of them). It isn't about giving everyone a chance to express him- or herself. There are individuals who are racist—it helps hate crimes if we give equal time to racists to express their ideas, simply because we are striving for equality. This just reinforces oppression and the status quo. So, as a joker you cannot honor the voice of the oppressor as much as the one bringing the voice of the oppressed into the room. But you need to be careful. Otherwise you will become, as my father and Paulo Freire would say, a banking educator. If you are completely shutting down the audience, you will be a banking system educator; if you accept everything without a critical attitude and dialogue, then you will just reinforce society as it is. I think you have to negotiate between those two poles.

If a young woman says she had an abortion and she is not a criminal and another says abortion is a crime, that first woman is putting herself at risk. The joker has to take the point of the view of the oppressed, defend the oppressed, and not shut down those in the audience who are expressing different views. But you cannot let another voice shut down the voices of the oppressed—an example is that in a school if you let kids say homophobic things, this will hurt those who are gay and give credibility to the voice of oppression.

Ellie: What do you do when "spect-actors" come up with solutions that you personally as a joker disagree with?

Julian: You have to send it back to the audience as a problem. In one of the Forum Theatre performances at PTO in Omaha in 2009, a woman raised her hand in order to replace the boss, the boss being the antagonist who was hiring undocumented workers. I asked her if she thought that the actor was performing the role of the boss in a way that conformed to reality. She and the audience said, "Yes, most of them behave like this." I asked her, "Why would you like to come on stage with an intervention? Is it to make a better boss, and then wouldn't that be something that doesn't really exist in reality?" She admitted that, yes, that was her intent, and she realized that replacing the boss would be "magic." That boss doesn't exist in reality. What we should remember is that to be oppressed is a social position, not a political strategy. Among the oppressed, there will be many political strategies. Look at the differences between Martin Luther King, Malcolm X, Stokely Carmichael, and so many others. And some oppressed will even ignore their oppression, give answers to it that will make it worse or will not believe in the possibility of putting an end to it. You, as a TO facilitator, you are also an oppressed. You are not above anyone, nor are you outside the society you want to change. So you will have to make choices, with no guarantee at all of having the truth, and some of those choices will make you confront, at least in the initial moment, others who are oppressed.

Ellie: Would you let spect-actors play out any interventions, or would you talk about them before they come on stage?

Julian: Most of the time I don't ask anything before they come on the stage, and after the intervention, I encourage the audience to react, judge, and analyze. Most of the time the audience will go in a direction that is realistic and interesting. I just asked that woman because she was asking to replace the boss instead of the protagonist. Most of the time I let the people do whatever they want. I remember, here in the U.S., in North Carolina, someone wanted to replace the U.S. military and I allowed it. I was thinking in my little head, "Now I'm going to demonstrate it's not possible to have a U.S. military that's pacifist," and then the woman came on stage and played a pacifist U.S. military. She was representing the U.S. army in general, and then I turned to the audience and I asked, "Can you see that it is a contradiction in terms?" In their responses people in the audience were saying, "No, no, no, this is real, this can happen because some U.S. generals wrote a letter against the way the

Iraq war was conducted." I don't know if I said this then, but if I didn't, I should have said, "How many medals do they get for pacifism? They were not against the war, they were against how this war was being done."

Toby: I think what is most important is what happens after the scene when the audience gets to have the conversation—it's the dialogue that is so important.

Julian: For me, too, actually, for me that's the most important thing. My main default as a joker is that I don't allow the stage to exist that much. I'm more focused on the debate within the audience—the collective debate—than the theatrical conventions.

Ellie: Is there anything that you haven't said that you'd like to say?

Julian: Maybe that Theatre of the Oppressed does something important through the stage. We want to create a certain world in which all of us will be actors. We want to create a certain world in which we are not bound by identities. We want to create a world in which individuals will be able to express themselves in front of the collective, in which every single aspect of our reality will be able to be criticized, discussed, and changed. A world in which agency will not encounter any boundaries. We need to be not only TO performers, but also a TO movement. Something Sanjoy Ganguly, the founder of Jana Sanskriti, said, which I think is very beautiful, is "Our work starts when our theatre is done." TO can be an important moment to recognize oppression, to empower ourselves, to develop our strength, to share some intimacy with others who feel the same oppressions. But what's most important is the next day, what we do about it.

GLOSSARY

Banking System of Education: Freire's analogy for the traditional model of education in which the "expert" teacher deposits information into passive students who receive and later return the information in the form of rote responses to tests and questions from the instructor.

Cop-in-the-Head Exercises: Boal's term from his Rainbow of Desire techniques for games that address internalized oppressions. Boal suggested that we often stop ourselves from taking action in the face of oppressions because fears and negative messages from others (the "cops" in our heads) have been internalized.

Conscientização **(conscientization):** Freire's Portuguese term for the development of critical consciousness, which allows us to question our historical and socio-political situation in order to take action toward developing a truly democratic society.

Demechanization: Boal's system of inventive movements and games designed to alleviate our mechanized physical, emotional, and mental tendencies, developed through repetition/habituation over time, releasing us to think and act more creatively.

Dynamization: Boal's term for the activation of human images sculpted by spect-actors by adding sound, movement, and lines of dialogue.

Image Theatre: Boal's series of wordless exercises in which participants use the human body as a tool to represent feelings and ideas, often about a specific concept or theme. Through "sculpting" others or their own bodies, participants develop images of a situation or oppression. The images become the impetus for reflection and dialogue.

Joker: Boal's term for the master of ceremonies for a TO performance. The joker guides the audience through the TO event, assisting, coaxing, questioning, explaining, and exploring. The joker is an adaptable figure, open to the widest possible range of spect-actor interpretations, solutions, and imaginative interventions.

Magical Solutions: Solutions offered by spect-actors that are unrealistic, too ideal, or too facile; they misrepresent the complexities of the oppressive situation depicted in the scene.

Oppressor/Oppressed: A reference by both Freire and Boal to the hierarchical social and political systemic structures that affect human interactions. Oppressors are those who hold power over the oppressed, whether they recognize their oppressive power or not. Power is, in fact, maintained, specifically by denying equity to others, thus oppressing them.

Pedagogy and Theatre of the Oppressed (PTO): A not-for-profit organization with the following mission: "To challenge oppressive systems by promoting critical thinking and social justice." PTO organizes an annual conference focused on the work of liberatory educators, activists, artists, and community organizers.

Praxis: Freire's concept of informed action. Freire speaks of praxis as the pairing of critical reflection and intentional action; transformation of oppressive circumstances requires thoughtful analysis of the circumstances coupled with action that responds to the analysis.

Rainbow of Desire: Boal's body of theatrical "psychotherapeutic" exercises that examine individual, internalized oppressions that influence the ways in which we view and interact with each other and the culture at large.

Simultaneous Dramaturgy: Boal's early approach to Forum Theatre in which, during the play, the actors stop the action and ask the audience for suggested solutions to the situation depicted. The audience voices ideas that the actors then play out on stage.

Spect-actor: Boal's term for TO audience members who choose to participate in the action of the Forum scene.

CONTRIBUTORS

CHEN ALON is a Ph.D. candidate in the Theatre Department at Tel-Aviv University, where he is a facilitator/lecturer in "Activist-Therapeutic Theatre." As a Major (reserve) he co-founded "Courage to Refuse," a movement of officers and combatant soldiers who refuse to serve in the occupied Palestinian territories, an action for which he was imprisoned for a month. Alon is co-founder of "Combatants for Peace," a movement of Palestinian and Israeli ex-combatants who abandoned the way of violence. Currently Alon, with Combatants for Peace, is developing a new model of Polarized Theatre of the Oppressed, working with Israeli and Palestinian youth, other mixed audiences of Palestinians and Israelis, as well as in state prisons and drug addiction/homeless rehabilitation centers. Chen Alon has facilitated TO workshops in Los Angeles, Minnesota, Omaha (USA), Paris, Marseilles, Nice (France), Pula (Croatia), Basque Country, Barcelona (Spain), Belfast, Enniskillen, and Donegal (Northern Ireland).

HECTOR ARISTIZÁBAL was born and raised in Medellín, Colombia, where his commitment to human rights work led to his arrest and torture and eventual exile in the US. He holds an M.A. degree in Psychology from Antioquia University in Medellín and a second master's as a Marriage & Family Therapist from Pacific Oaks College in Pasadena, California. As the founder and creative director of the nonprofit organization ImaginAction, Hector works as an independent consultant for organizations throughout the U.S., Canada, and the world. He offers his unique blend of techniques combining Theatre of the Oppressed and Council Circle to communities dealing with difficult challenges, including in conflict zones such as Afghanistan, Israel/Palestine, and Northern Ireland. He has worked extensively with at-risk and incarcerated youth, immigrant families, people affected by HIV/AIDS, and in hospice programs. As an actor, he has performed on stage and screen, and has toured the world with his autobiographical play, *Nightwind*. The *Blessing Next to the Wound: A Story of Art, Activism, and Transformation* (Lantern Books, 2010), coauthored with Diane Lefer, covers his tumultuous life and his multifaceted work. Hector helped found the Center for Theatre of the Oppressed/Applied Theatre Arts, Los Angeles which, beginning in 2001, brought Augusto Boal to Los Angeles for several years running to teach and to inspire. He has served on the national board of PTO (Pedagogy and Theatre of the Oppressed).

BRENT BLAIR is the Founding Director of the Applied Theatre Arts program and of the new Master of Arts in Applied Theatre Arts at the University of Southern California. He holds an M.A. in Counseling Psychology and is currently completing his Ph.D. in Depth Psychology with an emphasis on Liberation Arts and Community Engagement. A Fulbright fellow with a focus on indigenous community-based Theatre in Eastern Nigeria, he trained as a voice teacher with Kristin Linklater in the late 1980s and has taught directing, acting, voice and/or applied theatre arts courses at numerous colleges and universities across the United States and around the world. He worked and trained with Boal since 1996, and is the co-founder of the former Center for Theatre of the Oppressed and Applied Theatre Arts, Los Angeles (2001–2005) which hosted Boal four times. He is currently working on a book about Liberation Arts and Community Engagement (LACE).

JULIAN BOAL lives in Paris and Rio de Janeiro and has worked as an independent workshop facilitator of Theatre of the Oppressed for many years. In addition to his own work as a TO trainer, he collaborated extensively with his father, Augusto Boal, and has presented numerous workshops throughout the world, including France, Brazil, Switzerland, Bosnia, Italy, Spain, and the United States. He also works in India with the famed theatre company Jana Sanskriti, and was the initiator of that troupe's annual tour to Europe. For the past several years he has co-facilitated annual workshops for the Theatre of the Oppressed Laboratory (TOPLAB) at the Brecht Forum in New York. He is the artistic director of the *Groupe du Théâtre de l'Opprimé* (GTO) in Paris and is one of the forces behind the International Theatre of the Oppressed Organization (ITO). He is the author of *Images of a Popular Theatre*, as well as many articles, and is the translator of the French edition of Augusto Boal's *The Rainbow of Desire* and the editor of the new French edition of *Games for Actors and Non-Actors*.

JIWON CHUNG is a professional actor and director, and a pioneering theorist in the integration of somatics, political theatre, and the martial arts. He is a teaching fellow at the Institute for the Critical Study of Society, adjunct professor at the Starr King School at the Graduate Theological Union, and the founder and artistic director of Kairos Theatre Ensemble, a theatre company dedicated to challenging structural and systemic oppression. He has worked intensively in the areas of conflict resolution, environmental justice, racism, war trauma, and issues of systemic structural violence and large-scale historical atrocities, and has used theatre in presentations on Palestine/Israel, Rwanda, Iraq, the Holocaust, Hiroshima, and with survivors in New Orleans after Katrina. He has also worked locally on the building of wrap-around health care systems for low-income immigrant communities. His approach to individual, interpersonal, and institutional change is informed by his experiences as a veteran and three decades of Vipassana meditation.

TOBY EMERT is a theatre artist and professional educator who has worked with hundreds of pre-service and in-service teachers across the United States on methods to combine literacy instruction and the arts. He holds a B.A. in English and Theatre Education from Longwood College, an M.Ed. in Educational Administration from the College of William and Mary, an M.A. in English from the University of Tennessee, and a Ph.D. in Education from the University of Virginia. He is an associate professor in the Department of Education at Agnes Scott College near Atlanta, Georgia, and he also teaches drama-based education courses, including Drama for Community Leadership, through the Creative Arts in Learning graduate program at Lesley University in Cambridge, Massachusetts. His research agenda includes explorations of the connections between deep learning and artistic expression particularly how theatre-based structures can be adapted for any classroom content. He served on the Board of Directors for Pedagogy and Theatre of the Oppressed for six years and was president of the organization in 2008-09.

JENNIFER L. FREITAG is a doctoral student in the Department of Speech Communication at Southern Illinois University. Her research interests include performance studies, critical communication pedagogy, feminist rhetorical criticism, and gender/sexuality studies. She is a former member and interim director of SAVE (Students Against a Violent Environment) Forum Actors at the University of Northern Iowa as well as the founder of The Current, a peer theatre troupe dedicated to gender violence prevention, at the University of Central Missouri. In 2010, Freitag was awarded the Thomas J. Pace Teaching Award by the Department of Speech Communication at Southern Illinois University. Her published work has focused on intersections of feminism and spirituality through her ethnodrama, "Bible Beater/Bra Burner." Most recently, she co-authored "Forum Theatre for Bystanders: A New Model for Violence Prevention" with Karen S. Mitchell, a forthcoming article in *Violence Against Women*.

ELLIE FRIEDLAND has been an activist teacher educator, writer and performer for more than 25 years, specializing in teaching for social justice, and integrating drama, Theatre of the Oppressed, and movement into early childhood education and teacher education and professional development. She is Associate Professor of Early Childhood Education at Wheelock College in Boston, where her research and publications focus on teaching anti-bias early education, especially LGBT inclusive practice, in the U.S. and Guatemala, culturally competent teaching and learning, and teaching through drama. She holds a B.S. in Human Development and Family Studies/Nursery-Kindergarten Education from Cornell University, an M.S. in Human Behavior and Development from Drexel University, and a Ph.D. in Education and the Arts from The Union Institute in Ohio. She leads workshops for teens and adults in Theatre of the Oppressed for the Wheelock Family Theatre, nationally renowned for its long history of inclusive, community-based theatre. She served on the Board of Pedagogy and Theatre of the Oppressed for seven years and was president of the organization from 2005–2007.

AUBREY A. HUBER is a Ph.D. student at the Southern Illinois University in Carbondale, Illinois where she currently teaches courses in public speaking, pedagogy, and performance. Her research interests include communication pedagogy, performance, and cultural studies, in which she seeks to subvert traditional pedagogical narratives and centralize voices on the margin. Working at the intersection of research and pedagogy, Huber views pedagogical inquiry as a mode for research, having practical and theoretical implications for her classroom and her scholarship. Her teaching and research both focus on the body as a medium for learning, as well as a site for the practice of social justice. She is a former member of the University of Northern Iowa's SAVE (Students Against a Violent Environment) Forum Actors. She is also the 2009 recipient of the Thomas Pace Teaching Award at Southern Illinois University.

SONJA ARSHAM KUFTINEC is Associate Professor of Theatre at the University of Minnesota and a graduate of Stanford University's Ph.D. program in drama. She has published widely on community-based theatre including *Staging America: Cornerstone and Community-Based Theatre* (2003), which received honorable mention for the Barnard Hewitt Award in theatre history. From 1995-2007 she developed collaborative theatre projects with youth in the Balkans and Middle East. Her co-production "Where Does the Postman Go When All the Street Names Change?" won an ensemble prize at the 1997 Youth Theatre Festival in Mostar. From 2000-2005 Professor Kuftinec worked with youth from the Middle East and Balkans as a facilitator for Seeds of Peace. In her newest book, *Theatre, Facilitation and Nation Formation in the Balkans and Middle East* (Palgrave, 2009), she explores how Augusto Boal's Theatre of the Oppressed work has been adapted within a conflict context.

DIANE LEFER's ongoing collaboration with Hector Aristizábal encompasses works for the stage and the printed page, including their book *The Blessing Next to the Wound* (Lantern Books, 2010) as well as social action workshops using the techniques of Theatre of the Oppressed. She has taught creative writing and theatre to gang members, emotionally troubled youth, teenage activists, senior citizens, and for 23 years mentored graduate students at Vermont College of Fine Arts. Her plays have been produced in New York, Chicago, Los Angeles, and other cities. Her fiction, which has been widely published and anthologized, often addresses issues of social concern, as in her most recent short-story collection, *California Transit* (Sarabande Books, 2007), awarded the Mary McCarthy Prize.

DANIELLE DICK MCGEOUGH is doctoral candidate in performance studies at Louisiana State University, where she teaches courses in performance studies and gender communication. She actively participates in and directs shows in the Hopkins Black Box Theatre at LSU. As an M.A. student at the University of Northern Iowa, she was an active member of SAVE Forum Actors as an actor, joker, and a presenter at Pedagogy and Theatre of the Oppressed conferences. Her research interests include adolescent sexuality and desire, toilets, and family storytelling. McGeough's interests are diverse but all consider how people experience their bodies and how bodies are implicated in various social and cultural practices.

KAREN S. MITCHELL (Ph.D. Louisiana State University) is a professor of communication studies at the University of Northern Iowa where she teaches courses in performance studies and critical communication pedagogy. She is the Artistic Director of UNI Interpreters Theatre and the founding director of SAVE (Students Against a Violent Environment) Forum Actors. Her work with SAVE was originally part of a major grant to combat gender violence on campus, awarded to the UNI Women's Studies program by the Department of Justice in 2000. In addition to SAVE, Dr. Mitchell also mentored TO peer theatre troupes at the University of Central Missouri, Iowa State University, and the University of Iowa. Her directorial work at UNI Interpreters Theatre includes stage adaptations of novels ("Extra-Curricular: A Novel of Rape on Campus by Anne Hasselbrack"), investigations of popular cultural phenomenon ("Barbie Undone"), and hybrid works such as her ethnography of romance readers ("The Rainbow Season: Romancing the Romance"). Dr. Mitchell is the 2009 recipient of the College of Humanities and Fine Arts Faculty Excellence Award and received the Iowa Regents Award for Faculty Excellence in 2004. She is a former president of the organization Pedagogy and Theatre of the Oppressed and is an active member in the Performance Studies division of the National Communication Association. Most recently, she coauthored "Forum Theatre for Bystanders: A New Model for Violence Prevention" with Jennifer L. Freitag, a forthcoming article in *Violence Against Women*.

DOUG PATERSON earned his M.A. and Ph.D. degrees from Cornell University and is Professor of Theatre at the University of Nebraska at Omaha. While he has published on numerous topics, his passion remains theatre and social change. He is co-founder of three theatres including the Dakota Theatre Caravan in South Dakota, the Circle Theatre in Omaha, and an Omaha group dedicated to the theatrical methods developed by Brazilian director Augusto Boal and his Theatre of the Oppressed. To date Doug has offered over 200 Theatre of the Oppressed workshops and presentations in Omaha, across the U.S., and around the world. International sites include Rio de Janeiro, Brazil, Israel, Iraq, Liberia, Australia, India, Palestine, and Croatia. Doug began the Pedagogy and Theatre of the Oppressed (PTO) series of international Conferences in 1995, now in its seventeenth year. He continues to work actively to promote the work of Augusto Boal and Paulo Freire and is a peace and social justice activist in the Great Plains.

RICHARD J. PIATT is a theatre practitioner and professor, currently teaching at Merrimack College in Andover, Massachusetts. He holds a B.A. in English with a concentration in Theatre from Lafayette College, an M.A. in Theatre from Villanova University and an M.Div. from the Washington Theological Union. Currently, he is finishing his Ph.D. dissertation, entitled "The Art of Liberation: Theatre of the Oppressed and Latin American Liberation Theology in Dialogue," at Goldsmiths, University of London. His published work includes a chapter entitled, "There Are No Good Torturers: Theatre of the Oppressed and the Problem of Evil" in *Mis/Representing Evil: Evil in an Interdisciplinary Key*.

MICHAEL ROHD, a creator/writer/director/facilitator, is the founding artistic director of Sojourn Theatre, a national theatre ensemble based in Portland, Oregon, which was a recipient of the Animating Democracy Exemplar Award in 2005. He is on the faculty at Northwestern University's Theatre Department in the School of Communications, the founder of Hope Is Vital, and author of the book *Theatre for Community, Conflict & Dialogue*, published by Heinemann Press in 1998. He has given master classes and conducted residencies in university, community, and theatre contexts internationally, and has been awarded grants and support from the National Endowment for the Arts, Theatre Communications Group, The Multi Arts Partnership Fund from Creative Capital, the Doris Duke Foundation, and family foundations and arts councils around the nation.

ALEXANDER SANTIAGO-JIRAU is a theatre artist, advocate, and educator who has worked extensively with youth and fellow arts educators using theatre as a tool for social change. Alex holds a B.S. in Urban and Regional Studies from Cornell University and an M.A. in Educational Theatre from New York University. He is Associate Director for the Career Development Program at The Center for Arts Education in New York City, where he counsels youth pursuing arts careers and leads professional development workshops for teachers, counselors, and youth development professionals. Alex is co-founder with S. Leigh Thompson of The Forum Project (www.theforumproject.org), a Theatre of the Oppressed training and facilitation organization. His research explores how theatrical work with queer youth—particularly through Theatre of the Oppressed techniques—may play a role in healthy adolescent development, impact political participation, and create spaces for community dialogue and education. Alex is also an adjunct instructor in the Program in Educational Theatre at New York University. He served on the Board of Directors for Pedagogy and Theatre of the Oppressed for four years and was president of the organization in 2009-10.

RAPHI SOIFER is an American performer, writer, and theatre educator based in Brazil. A former student at Augusto Boal's Centre for the Theatre of the Oppressed (CTO) in Rio de Janeiro, he has created performances in community groups, schools, and prisons throughout the United States and Brazil. He lives in Rio de Janeiro, where he develops street and prison-based performance projects. He holds a B.A. in Theatre Studies and Anthropology from Yale University and currently is pursuing a master's degree in the Science of Art at the Universidade Federal Fluminense.

S. LEIGH THOMPSON is a social justice artist, community organizer, and educator and has spent the last decade working for the queer movement and for trans rights. Leigh has a B.A. in Theatre with an emphasis in directing from the University of Nebraska at Omaha and an M.A. from New York University focusing on utilizing Theatre of the Oppressed for political and social change. In 2008 Leigh co-founded The Forum Project (www.theforumproject.org) with Alex Santiago-Jirau, a Theatre of the Oppressed training and facilitation organization. Leigh has worked for several social justice organizations and currently works at GLSEN, the Gay, Lesbian and Straight Education Network, as a national community organizer. He has worked with many different communities, including refugees, survivors of sexual violence, people with disabilities, and is currently dedicated to working with and for queer youth and transgender and gender-nonconforming people. He is also a freelance consultant, speaker, and facilitator on queer and social justice issues.

JENNY WANASEK (B.F.A., University of Wisconsin, Milwaukee) is co-founder of the Center for Applied Theatre which specializes in Theatre of the Oppressed techniques and new play development. She has trained with Augusto Boal, Healing Our Nation (Beyond Racism and Ally Building), and Dell'Arte Theatre. She has facilitated workshops and production projects with groups as diverse as PEARLS for Teen Girls, the Private Industry Council, Growing Food and Justice Initiative, the University of Alaska, Arts @ Large, and HIRE. She has distinguished herself as both director and actor with the Milwaukee Repertory Theatre, Milwaukee Chamber Theatre, Next Act, Renaissance Theatreworks, and First Stage among others. Jenny has been teaching acting and applied theatre techniques at University of Wisconsin, Milwaukee since 1999, and was the recipient of Excellence in Teaching Awards in 2007 and 2010.

MARK WEINBERG (M.F.A., Ph.D., University of Minnesota) is co-founder of The Center for Applied Theatre. He has over 35 years of university teaching experience in theatre and communication skills. He began his study of TO with Augusto Boal in 1992 and has conducted workshops and training sessions for educators, administrators, students, business leaders, and community organizations in the U.S., Australia, and Canada. He has published and lectured widely on theatre and social activism and chronicled the development of collective theatre in his book *Challenging the Hierarchy: Collective Theatre in the United States* (Greenwood Press, 1992) and recently finished his first Forum Theatre piece that combines live and videotaped performances. He has taught Applied Theatre techniques at the University of Wisconsin, Milwaukee and Theatre History at Marquette University.

MARC WEINBLATT is Founder and Director of the Mandala Center for Change based in Port Townsend, Washington. Marc has been a professional educator, theatre artist, activist, and workshop facilitator since 1980 having extensive experience with both adults and youth. Formerly Co-artistic Director of the Seattle Public Theatre, Marc is an internationally recognized leader in the use of Augusto Boal's groundbreaking Theatre of the Oppressed (TO) to stimulate community dialogue and social change. He has worked with diverse communities ranging from police to homeless youth, grassroots organizers and laborers to University deans. Internationally, Marc has worked with theatre activists in Canada, refugees in Azerbaijan, community workers in South Africa, slum families in India, actors in the Republic of Congo, and victims of war, among others, in Afghanistan. Marc was recently named "Cultural Envoy" by the U.S. State Department for his work in the Congo in spring 2010. Marc regularly facilitates T.O. based diversity/anti-oppression workshops in a wide variety of contexts across the U.S. with a commitment to bringing a deep sense of spirit and humanity into social justice work. He also directs the multi-generational (teens to elders) Poetic Justice Theatre Ensemble which incorporates TO and Playback Theatre techniques to generate community dialogue on burning social issues. One of Augusto Boal's "multipliers," since the early 1990s Marc has trained thousands of people in the use of Theatre of the Oppressed techniques through his classes and annual week-long intensive trainings.

INDEX

Studies in the Postmodern Theory of Education

General Editor
Shirley R. Steinberg

Counterpoints publishes the most compelling and imaginative books being written in education today. Grounded on the theoretical advances in criticalism, feminism, and postmodernism in the last two decades of the twentieth century, Counterpoints engages the meaning of these innovations in various forms of educational expression. Committed to the proposition that theoretical literature should be accessible to a variety of audiences, the series insists that its authors avoid esoteric and jargonistic languages that transform educational scholarship into an elite discourse for the initiated. Scholarly work matters only to the degree it affects consciousness and practice at multiple sites. Counterpoints' editorial policy is based on these principles and the ability of scholars to break new ground, to open new conversations, to go where educators have never gone before.

For additional information about this series or for the submission of manuscripts, please contact:

> Shirley R. Steinberg
> c/o Peter Lang Publishing, Inc.
> 29 Broadway, 18th floor
> New York, New York 10006

To order other books in this series, please contact our Customer Service Department:

> (800) 770-LANG (within the U.S.)
> (212) 647-7706 (outside the U.S.)
> (212) 647-7707 FAX

Or browse online by series:
> www.peterlang.com